Methods of Research on Human Development and Families

For Emory (TNG)
For Frank, Alex and Miles (SND)

Methods of Research on Human Development and Families

Theodore N. Greenstein

North Carolina State University

Shannon N. Davis

George Mason University

Los Angeles | London | New Delhi
Singapore | Washington DC | Melbourne

FOR INFORMATION:

SAGE Publications, Inc.
2455 Teller Road
Thousand Oaks, California 91320
E-mail: order@sagepub.com

SAGE Publications Ltd.
1 Oliver's Yard
55 City Road
London EC1Y 1SP
United Kingdom

SAGE Publications India Pvt. Ltd.
B 1/I 1 Mohan Cooperative Industrial Area
Mathura Road, New Delhi 110 044
India

SAGE Publications Asia-Pacific Pte. Ltd.
18 Cross Street #10-10/11/12
China Square Central
Singapore 048423

Printed in the United States of America

Library of Congress Cataloging-in-Publication Data

Names: Greenstein, Theodore N., author. | Davis, Shannon N., author.

Title: Methods of research on human development and families / Theodore N. Greenstein, Shannon N. Davis.

Description: Los Angeles : SAGE, 2019. | Includes bibliographical references and index.

Identifiers: LCCN 2018058530 | ISBN 9781506386065 (pbk. : alk. paper)

Subjects: LCSH: Families—Research—Methodology. | Economic development—Research—Methodology.

Classification: LCC HQ10 .G727 2019 | DDC 306.85072—dc23 LC record available at https://lccn.loc.gov/2018058530

This book is printed on acid-free paper.

Acquisitions Editor: Joshua Perigo
Editorial Assistant: Noelle Cumberbatch
Production Editor: Jyothi Sriram
Copy Editor: Diane DiMura
Typesetter: C&M Digitals (P) Ltd.
Proofreader: Alison Syring
Indexer: May Hasso
Cover Designer: Dally Verghese
Marketing Manager: Zina Craft

19 20 21 22 23 10 9 8 7 6 5 4 3 2 1

Detailed Contents

Preface

I first taught research methods 40 years ago. Each time I taught the course, I became increasingly convinced that the approach I was taking was all wrong. I was trying to teach people how to *do* research—to give them a metaphorical toolbox of technical skills so that they could someday design and conduct their own research. Although I knew that few of my students would actually do research, I continued to teach the course the same way for years.

When SAGE asked me to write this text, I realized that I had an opportunity to correct this mistake. *Methods of Research on Human Development and Families* reflects our philosophy that what most people want (and need) to learn about research methods is not how to *do* research but how to *read* research. Few of you will become active researchers, but all of you will need to know how to read and interpret research reports. Whether you work in a commercial organization, a government agency, or some not-for-profit group involved with families and children, you must be able to critically examine reports of research relevant to your work. Becoming a critical consumer of research reports is important even if you don't find employment in a family- or human development-related field because our daily lives are increasingly filled with research findings. Newspapers, the Internet, television, and magazines routinely report results of opinion polls, evaluations of social programs, and other research. Without some understanding of research methods, it's impossible to be an active and knowledgeable 21st-century citizen. *Methods of Research on Human Development and Families* will help you to acquire this understanding.

—*Ted Greenstein*

The first course I taught as a graduate student was a social research methods course. And like Ted Greenstein, I quickly came to realize that I wanted the students in all my classes, but especially in my research methods courses, to become critical consumers of social research. It is our hope that this book will prepare students across disciplines who want to know more about families and human development to be able to critically read and potentially produce scholarship on these key aspects of our social lives.

—*Shannon Davis*

The Goal of This Text

The goal of this text is *not* to teach you to be a researcher. No single book or course can do that. Instead, this text is aimed at helping you become an intelligent and critical *consumer* of research on families. To that end, the text will introduce you to how research on families is conducted and how to read journal articles and books reporting such research. The focus will be on interpreting and understanding research techniques commonly used in research on families rather than on the mechanics of actually doing the research.

By the time that you finish this text, you should be competent to read and evaluate published reports of research on families and children. This is a valuable skill, because we are inundated with reports of research findings every day. Whether you plan to be a practitioner, a teacher, or an administrator, some knowledge of research methods will be essential to your career success. Some of you may even be inspired to seek out additional training so that you can become a producer of social research yourself.

To the Student

This text has several features to aid in the learning process. Key terms and concepts are boldface when they first appear in the text; all the boldface terms appear and are defined in the Glossary. The lists at the end of each chapter present additional or more advanced treatments of the issues discussed in the text. Exercises designed to enhance your skills appear in the Study Questions sections. Even if your instructor doesn't require you to do these exercises, you may find that they help you to prepare for exams.

To the Instructor

We've never encountered a text that completely fulfills our needs in teaching a course, and *Methods of Research on Human Development and Families* is no exception. We expect that you will want to supplement the text with an assortment of journal articles and research monographs (and possibly newspaper and magazine articles) reporting relevant research. We have presented many examples in the text. If time permits, you may want to assign the original articles to your students.

You may wish to create a set of readings organized around research strategy: one article using sample survey methods, another using an experimental design, and so forth. Or you might assign different research monographs to a number of student teams for classroom critique. One valuable extended exercise is to find a newspaper or magazine article reporting some family-related study, then assign both that article and the original research report for reading and comparison by the students. Students will be amazed at the discrepancies between the actual research and how it is reported in the popular press! Throughout your course, we hope you will emphasize that simply because a piece of research is published—even if it's in a major journal—doesn't mean the study is perfect. On the contrary, encourage your students to critically analyze what they read.

Organization of This Text

The sequencing of chapters in *Methods of Research on Human Development and Families* closely follows the usual flow of the research process. Chapter 1 begins with a discussion on the nature of research and some relevant issues in the philosophy of science. Chapter 2 introduces the important issue of research ethics. Chapter 3 presents the crucial concept *variable* and the various theoretical roles that variables can occupy in family research. Chapter 4 shows an analysis of the structure of a typical research article in a professional journal and provides an introduction to literature searches. Chapter 5 provides an overview of sampling procedures. In Chapter 6, the key issues of measurement and operationalization are introduced. Creating and finding scales and indices is the topic of Chapter 7. Chapters 8 and 9 outline the basics of quantitative and qualitative research strategies, whereas Chapter 10 introduces the idea of mixed methodologies. Chapter 11 covers the increasingly important topic of locating and using secondary data sets. Chapter 12 serves as a brief introduction to descriptive and inferential statistical techniques. Chapter 13 covers some of the analytic techniques specific to studying dyads (couples) and families. Evaluating applied family programs is discussed in Chapter 14. Finally, political issues in family research are presented in Chapter 15.

However, we encourage instructors to rearrange the chapters as they see fit. For example, some will want to cover ethical issues (Chapter 2) later in the course. You may want to change the order of presentation of quantitative methods (Chapter 7) and qualitative methods (Chapter 8).

Acknowledgments

I owe a great debt to the instructors who introduced me to social research methods. Bill Crano sparked my interest in social research when I was an undergraduate at Michigan State University. Michael Allen, Duane Alwin, Howard Bahr, Charlie Bowerman, Lew Carter, Lee Freese, Vik Gecas, Gary Lee, and especially Louis Gray shaped my thinking about methods as a graduate student at Washington State University.

North Carolina State University provided a research leave to work on the first draft of the manuscript during its early stages. SAGE Series Editors Dave Klein of Notre Dame and Bert Adams of Wisconsin made extensive comments and suggestions on earlier drafts throughout the writing process. I would also like to thank the many anonymous individuals who were so generous with their feedback. Any errors, of course, are our own.

—*Ted Greenstein*

My passion for teaching social research methods is a direct result of having been taught by instructors who were also passionate about teaching social research methods: Marcia Ghidina and Bill Haas at the University of North Carolina–Asheville, and Cathy Zimmer and Don Tomaskovic-Devey at North Carolina State University. Ted Greenstein has shaped not only the way I teach and write about social research methods but also the way I do social research. I am so grateful to have the opportunity to be a co-author with him on this text.

—*Shannon Davis*

We also wish to thank Fatima Nayani and Katriina Juntunen, undergraduate research assistants supported by the George Mason University Office of Student Scholarship, Creative Activities and Research and Avery Walter, graduate assistant supported by the Department of Sociology and Anthropology at North Carolina State University.

Reviewers to acknowledge:

Anna Ayala, East Los Angeles College

Dorothy Berglund, Mississippi University for Women

Chiyoung Cha, Ewha Womans University

Tapo Chimbganda, Leeds Trinity University

Toya Conston, University of Houston

Kathleen Corpus, Shepherd University

Maeve Dempsey, Institute of Technology Carlow

Katharine Didericksen, East Carolina University

Janean Dilworth-Bart, University of Wisconsin-Madison

Anne Fletcher, University of North Carolina at Greensboro

Sharon Friend, University of the West of England

Rowena Hill, Nottingham Trent University

Nichole Huff, North Carolina State University

Lauren Jacobson, Pennsylvania State University

Natalie Knesek, Tarleton State University

Mee-Gaik Lim, Capella University

Nancy McElwain, University of Illinois

Christine McGeorge, North Dakota State University

Carol McGowan Dundalk, Institute of Technology

Deanne Perez-Granados, California State University, Monterey Bay

Cydne Perrt, Shepherd University

Kamala Radamdos, Syracuse University

Jacqueline Rippy, Tarleton State University

Nicolette Roman, University of the Western Cape

Juhhyun Shin, Ewha Womans University

Doris Sikora, Western Kentucky University

Hiromi Taniguchi, University of Louisville

Yuying Tsong, California State University - Fullerton

Bridget Walsh, University of Nevada-Reno

Dana Weiser, Texas Tech University

Herb Wong, John F Kennedy University

Pearl Wong, Pfeiffer University

Katharine Zeiders, University of Missouri

About the Authors

Theodore N. Greenstein is professor of sociology at North Carolina State University. His research interests include work and the family, the division of household labor, and maternal employment.

Shannon N. Davis is professor of sociology at George Mason University. She studies the division of household labor and gender ideologies, as well as undergraduate researchers and their mentors.

Why Do Research on Families and Children?

To many people, doing research on families and children seems a waste of time. After all, we all have families, don't we? We know about families through our own experiences. Most surveys simply confirm what we already know, right? So why bother to do social research on families and children?

To really understand why we do social research, we have to recognize that curiosity is one of the most basic of human drives. Some biologists believe that the human brain is hardwired to solve challenges and answer questions. It's probably this drive that led the human species from learning to light fires to landing on the moon within a few hundred generations. Humans seem to have an innate need to know why things happen the way they do. Albert Einstein reportedly said, "God does not play dice with the universe," meaning that we don't like to believe that events simply happen. We need or want to believe that events happen for reasons. Much human activity is centered on discovering these reasons, a major manifestation of which is the search for personal understanding—the need to know why things happen.

When we find ourselves in an ambiguous or unfamiliar setting, we often feel a need to impose some kind of structure to help us make sense of it. Answering the *why* question helps to impose that structure. We have an innate need to understand: why family sizes are declining, why some husbands abuse their wives, why children from certain types of families are more likely to use drugs, why some intimate relationships fail.

Humans have developed two systems—religion and science—to help them answer the *why* question. These two take very different approaches to knowledge. For religion, faith is the key. The true believer accepts religious teachings despite a lack of concrete, objective evidence. Faith allows us to accept as fact that Moses really did bring the Ten Commandments down from Mount Sinai, that Jesus really did rise from the dead, that Mohammed really was God's prophet.

Science, however, asks us to take little on faith. Science attempts to answer the why question by constructing and testing theories. The key test for any theory is whether it is supported by concrete, observable, replicable evidence.

We take the latter approach in this text. How does science help us to understand the world around us? Specifically, how can scientific research methods help us to understand families? Let us begin by discussing the stages of social research.

What Are the Stages of Social Research?

Exploration

A basic purpose of social and behavioral research is to find out what, exactly, is going on in society. At some point in any research study, we know little about the phenomenon in which we're interested, and we begin our **exploration**. Because we obviously need to start our research somewhere, we begin by casting a wide net in our search for explanations. We start out with a few ideas about what the phenomenon is or how it works. Perhaps we are curious about what factors are correlated with the birth rate or whether the age at first marriage is increasing or decreasing; or we may need to find out what types of therapies work best for children from abusive households. We often won't have any specific ideas about what key issues we need to study. At this stage in the research process, library research is essential. Before beginning any research project, we need to find out what research has already been done on the topic and what is known (and, more important, what is unknown) about the phenomenon in question. Most of Chapter 3 is devoted to the methods of searching the literature.

Once we have a handle on the existing literature, we might begin our investigation by simple, unscientific observation—watching people going about their daily lives. These preliminary observations are often purely qualitative and interpretive in nature, but from them, we can begin to define the problem. What are the key processes and concepts that need to be understood? What aspects of behavior are important? What are the characteristics of the setting or the situation under study? What factor or factors seems to be related to the outcome?

Another way we might begin our research is to ask, in an unstructured way, a small number of people about their behavior. Let's say that we want to study how new parents make decisions about employment plans. We might begin by identifying a few couples—most likely friends or acquaintances—and talking to them informally about their own experiences. Did the couples have a plan for employment before their children arrived, or did they wait until after their children were born to decide who was going to work? What kinds of problems did they encounter in making these decisions? What factors did they consider to decide how much each parent would work outside the home? These discussions can sensitize us to issues we hadn't considered originally. Although this procedure won't produce the most representative sampling of responses, it should help sensitize us to the nature of the problem.

Description

Once we have established some parameters for our research, the next step typically is to formulate a **description** of the characteristics of some group of people or families. For example, the Census Bureau tells us that the average U.S. family size is 3.14 persons (U.S. Census Bureau, 2017). In 2016 (Raley, Sweeney, & Wondra, 2015), the U.S. teen birth rate fell to a historic low of 22.3 births per 1,000 women ages 15 to 19 (Centers for Disease Control and Prevention, 2017). In 2015, about 683,000 children in the United States were victims of abuse or neglect (U.S. Department of Health & Human Services, 2017). These descriptions, although informative, do not tell us *why* the differences or patterns exist; they merely assert the existence of the differences or patterns.

In this stage, we are concerned with identifying and labeling phenomena. A good parallel in the natural sciences is the taxonomic classification system of all living organisms into phyla, genera, species, and so forth. The classification system doesn't tell us anything about *why* living things fall into certain categories; it merely gives a useful structure in which to classify our specimens. Knowing that the house cat is a member of the genus *Felis* and the species *catus* doesn't tell us anything about why a cat is different from, say, a horse or a frog.

Another important process in this stage is that of **conceptualization**, which involves defining our terms at both the theoretical (abstract) and empirical (concrete) levels. Chapter 6 addresses the issues of conceptualization and measurement.

Explanation

Explanation is specifically concerned with answering the *why* question. Why do families headed by Asian Americans differ from those headed by Hispanics? Why do educational outcomes for children of employed mothers differ from those whose mothers are full-time housewives? Why are working-class parents more likely to use physical punishment than middle-class parents? Why does the division of household labor within families change over time? Here, we go beyond classification and description to explain the phenomena that we have observed.

This process is often the most complex because meaningful explanations of social and behavioral phenomena require explicit and formal models that show why, of necessity, certain conditions bring about, or are associated with, particular outcomes. We call such a model a **theory**. A theory is a set of logically related statements that claims to explain why, given certain conditions, a specific outcome occurs. Once a theory is confirmed—when it has been shown to accurately account for the phenomena it's supposed to explain—we can then take the theory and use it to predict future outcomes and even to design **interventions** that use the theory's arguments to modify the world around us in a systematic way.

The explanation stage is really about theory construction and testing, a topic that is well beyond the scope of this text. Chafetz (1978) and Reynolds (1971) each present good introductory treatments of the topic.

Prediction

Although the idea of **prediction** seems pretty straightforward, it's important to distinguish between predictions, which are based on theory, and *forecasts* or *prophecies*. When the leading investment experts tell us what the stock market is going to do over the next year, they are not typically basing their projections on some body of theory. Although they may be basing their forecast on current and past conditions, we must remember that the past does not predict the future. Teenage marriages aren't more likely to fail simply because they have been more likely to fail in the past. When we observe a particular pattern or relationship among variables repeatedly over time and across populations, it's likely that some real underlying cause produces the observed outcome or effect. There are sound theoretical reasons why teenage marriages have a higher likelihood of divorce, and a good theory should be able to tell us what those reasons are and even under what conditions teenage marriages might be as stable as other marriages.

To predict outcomes, we must know why they happen, which requires theoretical explanation. If we know why certain outcomes occur—that is, if we understand the underlying processes that lead to the outcome in question—we should be able to predict when the outcome will occur and when it will not.

Similarly, just noting that children from single-parent households have lower academic achievement than do other children is not, in and of itself, an explanation of *why* children from single-parent households do not perform as well in school. It may be that the real causal factor may be something that is related both to family structure and to academic achievement (for example, household income). Or the apparent association between family structure and academic achievement may be an anomalous pattern specific only to a particular set of data. The observed association may even be a methodological artifact resulting from flaws in the sampling, data collection, or measurement processes. Without theories to organize our thinking, any speculation about the underlying causes of specific family phenomena is just guesswork.

Interventions

Kurt Lewin said, "There is nothing so practical as a good theory" (Lewin, 1951, p. 169). If one is truly concerned with changing society, good theory is a necessity. Armed with a good theory, we can design and implement interventions designed to change the world around us. If we really understand why an outcome occurs, we have the knowledge (but not necessarily the resources or technology) to change that outcome. One reason why so many social programs—including those involving children and families—don't seem to work is that they aren't usually based on sound, theoretical knowledge of the process involved. If we have a good theory— one that tells why, of necessity, certain outcomes have to occur given certain conditions—then we should have the knowledge necessary to design effective interventions.

Let's consider a concrete example. A theory that might explain the likelihood of a child becoming delinquent depends in part on the amount of time parents spend with that child. If this theory is correct—that is, if the theory is confirmed with empirical evidence—programs that lead parents to be more involved with their children should result in reduced delinquency rates.

Evaluation

Once new programs and policies are in place, it's useful to know whether they really work. Do laws that require jail terms for wife abusers really reduce marital violence? Do stricter divorce laws reduce the rate of divorce? Do subsidies to support additional training of child-care providers improve the quality of child-care? Even though a theory may have strong confirming evidence to support it, sometimes our social programs—even those based on good theory—don't work. Maybe we didn't implement the program correctly, or maybe the theory is too specific and doesn't work in all situations. In any case, before allocating scarce resources, we need to know whether specific programs work. **Evaluation** of programs and policies tells us whether they are producing the desired types of outcomes or achieving established goals.

In the case of the delinquency project mentioned earlier, we would want to design a careful evaluation of the program's effects. Ideally, this evaluation would be built right into the program itself and not just conducted after the fact. A careful evaluation tells us whether the program really does increase parents' involvement with their children and whether this involvement really does result in decreased rates of delinquent behavior. Chapter 11 focuses on methods of evaluating social programs.

How Is Research on Families and Children Different?

Although the fundamentals of research on families are similar to those of the more general methodologies found in sociology, political science, psychology, and anthropology, important differences exist. For additional discussion of these points, see Gelles (1978) or Larzelere and Klein (1987). The five major differences between research on families in particular and social and behavioral research in general are the following:

1. Families are systems of individuals.

2. Defining the family is problematic.

3. Family members occupy multiple roles and statuses simultaneously.

4. Much family behavior is private and hidden.

5. We all have preconceptions about families and family life.

Families Are Systems of Individuals

Perhaps the most important difference between research on families and most other research lies in the primary focus of family research: families. In most behavioral and social-science research, the focus is on the individual. If we follow an individual over time, despite marriages, divorces, and job changes, we are still only dealing with a single, identifiable individual. In family research, however, our focus is usually on a *group*—a family—whose composition and characteristics change over time.

Consider a life-course study of a particular married couple. They probably form a family by marrying when both the wife and her husband are in their 20s. Within a few years, they may have children. The couple might divorce at some point, creating two residential groups where there had been only one. Following the divorce, one or both of the spouses might remarry and have children with a new spouse, creating a blended family or stepfamily. One spouse might pass away, leaving a widow or widower. Over time, the children mature and leave home, often to start their own families.

You can see the problem that studying this family presents to a researcher. The composition of the family is constantly changing, sometimes growing, sometimes shrinking. New members enter through the process of birth or marriage and then leave through death or divorce. How can we answer a question as simple as the size of this family when the size is changing over time?

A second problem created by the fact that the family is a system or group of individuals is the **unit of analysis**. Are we focusing on individuals or groups? Is our concern with the marital dyad, the nuclear family, or even the extended family? If we want to measure an individual's social class, then we typically look at the person's occupation, education, or income. On the other hand, how do we measure the social class of a family? Is it the husband's characteristics? Or is it the wife's? Do we somehow combine data for both spouses? What about household income for children of divorced parents? Do we count only the custodial parent's characteristics, or do we figure in the noncustodial parent's characteristics as well? Even if we decide to limit our analysis to couples (rather than families), we're still not off the hook. Maguire (1999) and Sayer and Klute (2005) present some of the methodological and analytic approaches to handling dyads (couples) as the unit of analysis. We will return to the issue of unit of analysis in more detail in Chapter 2.

Defining Family

A fundamental problem in studying families is that we lack a generally agreed-upon definition of what exactly a family is. The U.S. Census Bureau defines a *family* as a group of two or more people (one of whom is the householder) related by birth, marriage, or adoption and residing together.

This definition is unsatisfactory, however, because it excludes many groups that might reasonably be considered families. Are cohabiting couples families? What about gay and lesbian couples? Do foster parents and the children for whom they are responsible constitute families? What about groups living in a communal setting where child-care is shared among unrelated adults? Under the U.S. Census Bureau's definition, some groups are considered families even though many observers might disagree. For example, should we define two elderly siblings who live together as a family? Are childless married couples families?

A 2003 national survey found that although nearly all respondents would define a married couple with children as a family, almost 80% also considered an unmarried heterosexual couple living together and raising children a family; over half defined two gay men or two lesbian women with children as families as well (Powell, Bolzendahl, Geist, & Steelman, 2010). Evidently, there are many possible definitions of family. This uncertainty about what constitutes a family causes major problems for researchers. Without a generally agreed-upon definition of family, how can researchers know who to study or exclude from their research? Gubrium and Holstein (1990) have discussed these issues in some detail.

Multiple Statuses and Multiple Roles

Gelles pointed out, "Families are made up of individuals occupying multiple statuses and enacting multiple roles" (1978, p. 408). Each member of a family is simultaneously a potential parent, sibling, employee, spouse, and son or daughter. When collecting data about a family member, be sensitive to responses that may depend on which roles and statuses an individual is occupying at the time of the interview. Interviewing adults in the presence of their children, for example, might produce vastly different results than we might obtain by interviewing the same adults in the presence of their own parents.

Backstage Behavior

Another problem in studying families is the fact that much of what goes on in families is what is known as *backstage behavior* (hidden from public view). Important behaviors such as child abuse, domestic violence, and child rearing are not generally visible to persons outside the family. Until recently, for example, the rate of domestic violence was widely believed to be relatively low. As better research produced higher quality data, social scientists realized that because incidents of domestic violence are often known only to members of the family and perhaps close friends, rates of such behavior can be grossly underestimated.

There is another problem related to this backstage behavior. "Families develop private, idiosyncratic norms and meanings about their own activities" (Larzelere & Klein, 1987, p. 135). Each family has its own patterns of, and rules for, behavior. Often, these are the result of years (or even generations) of living together. Think about your own family: Aren't there unwritten rules about who sits where at the dinner table or a pecking order for seats in the family car? Often, these rules are not shared with the outside world, and a researcher studying the family may not be privy to these secrets.

Families even have ways of restructuring the way they view themselves to fit these rules and expectations. In *The Second Shift*, Hochschild and Machung (1989) talk about "family myths" that are "versions of reality that obscure a family truth in order to manage a family tension" (p. 19). One couple explained that they "shared" the housework by dividing the house into an upstairs and a downstairs. The wife was responsible for all the tasks associated with the upstairs, which included the kitchen, living areas, bedrooms, and bathrooms. The husband's downstairs responsibilities covered the garage and activities such as auto maintenance, yard work, and general household repairs.

In response to the interviewer's questioning, both husband and wife presented this housework "sharing" as an equitable solution to the division of household labor, even though an outside observer might think the arrangement was anything but fair or equitable. The public image that a family chooses to present to the outside world can be different from the private, internal image.

Preconceptions About the Family

Another problem that interferes with our ability to study families is that everyone is familiar with families; we all have ideas about what are right, good, or appropriate family behaviors and structures. If you study invertebrate zoology, you are unlikely to have strong beliefs about worms and insects; when you sit down to study French philosophy, you probably don't have strong feelings one way or another about Voltaire or Descartes. That's not the case with the issues that family researchers study, however. We all have attitudes and beliefs about topics such as premarital sex, abortion, same-sex marriage, extramarital affairs, day care, corporal punishment, the employment of mothers of young children, and the allocation of household chores. It's difficult for us to study such phenomena without our own beliefs intruding into the analysis.

These preconceptions take at least three forms. First, our own backgrounds may *bias* us in favor of or against certain forms of family behavior. People whose own mothers were employed outside the home, for example, are more likely to approve of the employment of mothers of young children. Members of certain religious groups are more prone to oppose legalized abortion than are members of other groups. Political conservatives are more apt to emphasize the importance of the husband's dominance of the marriage relationship than are political liberals.

Second, our own experiences can serve as limits to what we know or understand. Most middle-class people have little contact with welfare recipients, for example, so they may not have much sympathy for, or understanding of, people who use and need the social welfare system. Christians in this country have relatively little firsthand experience with religious discrimination and may not be sensitive to the messages they send to non-Christians when they conduct religious pageants in public settings.

A third factor that leads to preconceptions about the family has to do with *ethnocentrism,* which is the belief that the ideas and practices of our own ethnicity, gender, or social class are somehow *the best* or *right.* Sociologists remind us that we need to be aware of the multiple and intersecting effects of race, social class, and gender. Most of the family phenomena we study differ by race—compare the family structures of white and African American families, for example. And family behavior varies by social class; one of the best known empirical generalizations in the study of child rearing is that the use of corporal punishment is highest among working-class families and lowest among upper class families. We must also recognize that the family is a highly gendered environment. Much of what goes on in families varies by gender: who does which tasks around the house, who cares for the children, who is the primary breadwinner, what are the educational and career expectations for the children, and so forth.

When we study families, we cannot simply ignore these preconceptions. We need to be aware that our own beliefs may affect the topics we choose to study and the methods we use to study those topics. As difficult as it is, we need to take care to design our studies so that our biases don't influence the results or our interpretations of those results.

The Benefits of Well-Conducted Research

By this point, you have probably reached the conclusion that doing quality research on children and families is not an easy task. You're right; it's a lot of work to design and execute a research project that will yield solid, meaningful findings. And we are bombarded daily by the results of poor research. Do you really trust the results of a telephone opinion poll in which respondents have to pay 99 cents to give their opinions or a survey of likely voters run by the candidate's own campaign organization?

So, why is it important to do good research?

First, as we suggested in the beginning of this chapter, the familiarity of the family often makes it difficult to explain general family processes and theories to the lay public. When we talk about our research on families to groups outside the university, the audiences often react with, "Sure, I knew that." However, the fact that a particular research finding "makes sense" or is "obvious" does not make it any less important.

A second problem is that what seems obvious at first glance often isn't so obvious after all. A popular media device is to make fun of researchers who study behaviors and relationships that are obvious to everybody. However, that which is obvious is not always true. For example, it's "obvious" that older Americans are more likely to be victims of violent crime than are younger people, right? Older people are more vulnerable and easier targets for thieves. Yet exactly the opposite is true: Americans older than the age of 65 years are approximately one sixth as likely to be victims of violent crime as is the general population (U.S. Census Bureau, 2010).

Another "obvious" relationship is the effect of cohabitation experience on marital stability. It makes sense that those who have lived together before marriage should have a lower chance of divorce; presumably, cohabitants learn relationship skills that they can use to improve the quality of their marriages. However, this does not seem to be the case. Research suggests that (a) women who cohabited with their husbands before marriage were approximately 50% more likely than noncohabitants to have their marriages disrupted, and (b) those who cohabited with someone other than their eventual husbands were more than twice as likely to experience separation or divorce as those who didn't cohabit (Bumpass, Martin, & Sweet, 1991).

Complicating these issues is that some aspects of family life such as births, divorces, and marriages are easy to observe and measure, but others including child abuse, marital happiness, and family dynamics are difficult to measure in any objective way. Sometimes, we like to think of the study of the family as a *hard science* because it's so much harder to do research on marriages, families, and children than it is to study electrons, microbes, or chemical reactions.

One crucial reason we need quality research on families and children is rooted in our motivation for choosing to study them. If you're like us, one of the reasons you're interested in studying families and children is because you'd like to bring about change. You might see neglected children and hope to place them in homes where they will get lots of love and attention. Or you might want to help unhappy married couples communicate with and respect each other. Perhaps you want to help abusive husbands deal constructively with their anger (or maybe you just want to lock them up and throw away the key). To accomplish these goals, you need the best, most objective information available—the kind of information you'll get from quality research.

STUDY QUESTIONS

1. Find and briefly describe examples of published research on families or children at each of the six stages of social research (exploration, description, explanation, prediction, intervention, and evaluation).

2. List as many of the roles and/or statuses that you occupy in life as you can. Give an example of one of these roles or statuses (e.g., *employee* or *student*) that conflicts with a family-related role or status (e.g., *spouse* or *parent*). How do you deal with or resolve this conflict?

3. Ask three friends or acquaintances to define *family*. Discuss the similarities and differences between their definitions. Give examples of groups that would be considered *families* under one or two of the definitions but not the other(s). How might these definitions affect the way you would do research on families?

4. Choose some aspect of families that interests you (e.g., child well-being, intimate partner violence, marital stability, fathers' involvement with children), and give three examples of how a researcher's preconceptions or personal opinions might affect the way that research is done on that topic.

5. From your own family, give an example of a *family myth*—something that is generally accepted to be real or true even though some or all of your family members know that it isn't. Why do you think your family has created this family myth? What purpose does it serve? What are the benefits of accepting the myth and not challenging it?

6. Even though most people think older Americans are more likely to be victims of crime than younger people, research shows that this is untrue. Find a published study on a family- or child-related topic that reports a finding that is contrary to the conventional wisdom. Why do you think that people accept this conventional *wisdom*?

The Ethics of Research on Families and Children

L ike our counterparts in the natural sciences, social scientists believe that the key value underlying all scientific activity is that the chief goal of science is the discovery of new knowledge (Sjoberg & Nett, 1968). However, social scientists (unlike their counterparts in the natural sciences) recognize that the subjects of their research are sentient beings with lives of their own. As a result, sometimes social scientists are forced to choose between the value of scientific knowledge and the value of the welfare of their subjects. This creates an ethical dilemma for us. In this chapter, we center our discussion on two areas where ethical dilemmas rise: how we treat our participants and how we perform our science.

The Rights of Participants in Research on Families and Children

Although a physicist studying subatomic particles need not worry about harming a neutron and a microbiologist doesn't have to consider a protozoan's feelings, the rights of human research participants should be of paramount concern to social scientists. In the United States, the issue of protection of rights of human research participants is administered by the Department of Health and Human Services (DHHS). The regulations are laid out in what is known as Title 45, Protection of Human Subjects (45 CFR Part 46). The National Institutes of Health's (NIH) Office for Human Research Protections has an extensive website listing recommendations and specific regulations at www.hhs.gov/ohrp; the site even has a series of videos to orient researchers to the special ethical and safety issues associated with research involving human subjects. The rights of participants in social research may be defined in five broad areas: minimization of risk or harm, informed consent, anonymity and confidentiality, right to knowledge of the findings, and right to remedial services.

Risk or Harm to Research Participants

One of the most important ethical cornerstones of scientific research is that no harm come to the research participants. Usually when we think of "harm" or "risk" we're thinking of physical harm, and it's true that most research on humans in general and children in particular is unlikely to pose a threat of physical harm to the participants. But there can be other kinds of harm, as well: providing false feedback about results from personality inventories, for example. One could imagine a study where children were told that their responses to a personality test indicated that they were pathological liars, or adolescents might be told that their sexual orientation didn't match that which they presented to the world. In such cases, there could be serious psychological harm done.

Informed Consent

The cornerstone of ethical research on human subjects lies in the principle of **informed consent**. In general, DHHS regulations prohibit research on human subjects without the legally effective, informed consent of the subject or the subject's legally authorized representative. The regulations require that each potential research participant be provided with the following:

- A list of possible risks or discomforts
- A description of possible benefits
- A statement concerning confidentiality
- Information about who to contact concerning the study

- A statement that participation is voluntary and that the individual will suffer no adverse consequences either for declining to participate or for withdrawing at any point during the study

Children and others who are deemed unable to fully comprehend the research process (such as someone diagnosed with dementia) cannot provide informed consent. Therefore, any study using children or someone with diminished mental capacity must receive informed consent from a legal guardian and then secure assent from the participant (the child or other individual to be studied).

Anonymity and Confidentiality

Compared to the potential for harmful effects on subjects of work by our colleagues in the biomedical fields, there is rarely the possibility of physical harm to our research participants. Threats to participants in social research tend to be those involving the release of personal information. By *anonymity*, we mean that no identifying information should be retained in the researcher's files following completion of data collection. *Anonymous* data are just that: There are no identifiers stored with the data, and any particular respondent in a research project cannot be directly identified. *Confidentiality*, on the other hand, suggests that the data are not anonymous—that is, individual respondents can be identified—but that the data will be held securely and not released to unauthorized personnel.

Even without explicit identifiers such as names or addresses, it may be possible to identify specific participants in the study based on other reported characteristics, especially if the data include geographical information. Consequently, to minimize possible harm or embarrassment to the participants, the researcher should make every effort to conceal the identities of the participants when reporting research findings. Although DHHS regulations do not require either anonymity or confidentiality, they do require that the informed-consent agreement describe the extent to which confidentiality will be maintained.

There have been a series of embarrassing releases of confidential information by biomedical and other researchers in recent years. If it is essential to maintain identifying information, then perhaps the most important thing researchers can do is to make sure that there are no identifiers (e.g., names, social security numbers) stored with the data—what the security people call "anonymization." Instead, researchers can create a key that links the identifier to an arbitrary case number. The data themselves are stored with the arbitrary case number so that if the data are lost or stolen, they are still just a series of numbers useless to anyone except the researcher; the key is stored securely and accessed only when absolutely necessary.

Right to Knowledge of the Findings

The researcher has an ethical obligation to share the nature of the research findings with the research participants. In some studies, findings developed during the course of the research may affect the participants' willingness to continue in the project; DHHS regulations require that such findings be provided to the participants in a timely fashion. Most social scientific findings are shared with the public through published work such as journal articles, technically fulfilling the expectation to share the results with participants (although it remains to be seen that participants are aware of how to access the knowledge produced from their participation).

Right to Remedial Services

Applied studies may study the effects of various treatments or programs designed to improve some existing disadvantage or social problem. For experimental designs in which some participants are assigned to a control condition that does not receive treatment benefits, it can be argued that the researcher has the ethical obligation to supply the beneficial treatment or program to members of the control group in a remedial fashion whenever possible.

What Is the Role of the Institutional Review Board?

At the institutional level—say, within a college or university—decisions concerning whether these ethical guidelines have been met for a particular research project are made by what is known as an institutional review board (IRB). To qualify for federal funds, all research institutions must maintain an IRB in accordance with DHHS guidelines. The IRB must consist of at least five members, one of whom is a not a scientist. At least one member must be from outside the institution. In general, all research involving human subjects must be evaluated by the IRB for compliance with the DHHS guidelines. Universities generally require that all research—whether conducted by a faculty member or student—be approved by the IRB before commencing data collection. Thus, IRBs can provide a framework within which we can reduce ethical dilemmas in both how we treat our participants and how we perform our science.

Certain types of research are exempt from the DHHS guidelines. In general, projects involving interviews or observations of public behavior are exempt as long as individuals cannot be identified in the data or if the data are already in the public domain. When in doubt, it's a good policy to submit the appropriate paperwork for review by your local IRB.

Ultimately, the IRB has to weigh the possible benefits accruing from a proposed project against the likely or plausible risks it poses for its participants. These benefits include those of an immediate nature to the research participants as well as the importance of the knowledge that may reasonably be expected to result from the research. The fair, ethical, and compassionate treatment of participants should be paramount in the evaluation of research by the IRB.

Sometimes, however, the IRB fails in its duties. Consider the case of Mani Pavuluri, a child psychiatrist at the University of Illinois at Chicago. Her research studied adolescents with bipolar function using lithium treatments (J. S. Cohen, 2018). A review by National Institute of Mental Health (NIMH; Claycamp, 2017) found four primary violations: enrolling children younger than the approved ages of 13 to 16, including children who had previously used psychotropic medications, which should have made them ineligible for the study; serving as a physician for some of the children in her study; and failing to give some girls pregnancy tests after telling the parents that they would be tested (lithium has been associated with a higher risk of birth defects).

The NIMH review also found "Insufficient initial review by the IRB (e.g., no research protocol was provided at the time of review)" and failure of the IRB to take note of "multiple inconsistencies between and within the research protocol, informed consent documents, parental permissions and assents, initial review application, grant and other documents" (Claycamp, 2017).

A university spokesperson said that "internal safeguards did not fail" but Pavuluri's research was terminated in 2013 and about $800,000 in unspent research funds were returned to NIMH. However, the university named Pavuluri a university scholar later in 2013, an award that included a cash prize of $30,000. She maintains her position as faculty chair and her base salary of almost $200,000, even though the university's chancellor said that "her conduct reflected a 'pattern of placing research priorities above patient welfare'" (J. S. Cohen, 2018).

We're not suggesting here that the institutional review system doesn't work or that IRBs are incompetent; nearly all do their jobs extremely well and flag many inappropriate research protocols before the research can begin. But like all things in this text, we want you to be a *critical consumer* of social research. That means questioning not only the research designs of published studies that you read, it also means paying attention to the processes by which research gets approved and funded.

Fraud in Research on Families and Children

IRBs will work to assure the ethical treatment of participants in research projects and can also weigh in on the extent to which research itself is performed in an ethical manner. However, they are not charged with verifying that data have been collected in the manner described in a research proposal, nor that there is honesty or transparency in the overall performance of the scientific project. Although it is extremely rare, sometimes social researchers report fraudulent data or even entire fraudulent studies. Unless the researcher makes the raw data available to other scholars—something that a few scholarly journals now require—it can be nearly impossible to determine if a particular study is genuine. Sometimes skepticism comes from the inability to replicate a particular study. Other times there are inconsistencies in the research that lead outsiders to question the results. And fraud might be detected when a researcher "can't find" or refuses to provide the data from the study, suggesting that the data never existed.

The Strange Case of Michael LaCour

In 2014, Michael J. LaCour, a Ph.D. student in political science at UCLA, published a paper (LaCour & Green, 2014) titled "When contact changes minds: An experiment on transmission of support for gay equality" in the prestigious journal *Science*. LaCour had conducted a field experiment to see if it was possible to change people's views on gay marriage through a brief discussion about marriage equality (for more detail about the research and its subsequent debunking, see Konnikova, 2015; Singal, 2015). Although persuasive communication studies like these usually produce modest (if any) changes in attitudes, the article reported that there were large, statistically significant effects on the respondents' attitudes as a result of this brief interaction. The story was picked up nationally and was reported in the *New York Times*, the *Washington Post, Wall Street Journal*, and other outlets.

Impressed by LaCour's findings, Berkeley political science Ph.D. student David Broockman attempted to replicate the study. He quickly learned that it would cost approximately *one million dollars* to reimburse the respondents in such a study. It seemed inconceivable that LaCour had received that level of funding, which would be impressive for a tenured professor, let alone a graduate student. Broockman's suspicions led him to publish a report (Broockman, Kalla, & Aronow, 2015) detailing what he called "irregularities" in the LaCour and Green (2014) paper. Apparently, LaCour had used an existing dataset, added the fraudulent measures of attitude change, and presented it as the responses from his field experiment. The *Science* article was later retracted.

Apparently this wasn't an isolated incident of fraud by LaCour. He reported nearly $800,000 in grants on his resumé and several awards that either he didn't receive or simply didn't exist. Shortly after the *Science* article appeared, he was offered a faculty position at Princeton; that offer was later rescinded. He now seems to be out of academia completely.

The Lying Dutchman

Diederik Stapel was professor of psychology at Tilburg University in the Netherlands. Most of what follows comes either from a final report on the case (Levelt, Drenth, & Noort, 2012) or an article reporting an interview with Stapel (Bhattacharjee, 2013). Stapel had an unusual habit of conducting all of his studies himself, even those that were intended for his students' dissertation research, even though graduate students typically conduct their own research. One of his studies with colleague Ad Vingerhoets was intended to examine whether exposure to someone crying elicits empathy or prosocial behavior. The study involved giving school children a coloring task. Half of the children were told to color a cartoon character that was crying; the others were to color a picture of the same character that was not showing emotion. Afterward, the children were asked if they would share candy with other children (an indication of prosocial behavior).

Stapel said he collected the data from a local school and a few weeks later reported to Vingerhoets that they had observed a statistically significant effect on prosocial behavior: the children who had colored the crying character were more likely to share the candy. As he began writing up the article from the study, Vingerhoets wondered if there were gender differences in the effect. Stapel said the data hadn't been entered into the computer yet—but he had earlier shown Vingerhoets statistical calculations which usually require computer analysis. Vingerhoets was suspicious but decided not to press the issue.

Then a graduate student found inconsistencies in three experiments that Stapel had conducted. Confronted with these issues, Stapel claimed that the original data could not be found. Later, another graduate student found anomalies in several of Stapel's datasets, the final straw being where it appeared that Stapel had simply copied data from one row of data to another row.

Eventually two graduate students reported their concerns to the department head. Tilburg, Gronigen, and Amsterdam universities produced a joint report in November 2012 (Levelt et al., 2012) finding fraud in at least 55 of Stapel's published papers and 10 of his students' Ph.D. dissertations (as well as in his own dissertation). The report suggested that the fraud went undetected due to a "a general culture of careless, selective and uncritical handling of research and data" (p. 47). The report also identified what they called "sloppy science," or "a failure to meet normal standards of methodology" (p. 5) including the misuse of statistics. Stapel was dismissed from Tilburg University in 2011.

Power Posing

Amy Cuddy is a lecturer in the Harvard Business School. In 2010, she published a paper (Carney, Cuddy, & Yap, 2010) that claimed that "a person can, by assuming two simple 1-min poses, embody power and instantly become more powerful" (p. 1363). This notion of "power posing"—for example, sitting back in a chair with your arms behind your head—led to Cuddy doing a TED Talk (Cuddy, 2012) that by 2018 had more than 40 million views and a best-selling book, *Presence: Bringing Your Boldest Self to Your Biggest Challenges* (Cuddy, 2015). The power posing apparently not only led people to report that they felt more powerful; there were hormonal changes as well—decreases in cortisol and increases in testosterone, which are linked to power and dominance in humans and other animals.

The finding that such a simple intervention could produce such profound changes captivated journalists around the world. Cuddy became an instant media hit, featured in the *New York Times,* the *Wall Street Journal,* CNN, BBC, and most of the morning TV shows. The power posing results also were viewed rather skeptically by a number of researchers, including Eva Ranehill, a University of Zurich psychologist. In 2015, Ranehill and her co-authors (2015) concluded that their attempt to replicate Carney, Cuddy, and Yap (2010) "failed to confirm an effect of power posing on testosterone, cortisol, and financial risk taking" (p. 656). Two other researchers concluded that "the behavioral and physiological effects of expansive versus contractive postures ought to be treated as hypotheses currently lacking in empirical support . . . the existing evidence is too weak to justify a search for moderators or to advocate for people to engage in power posing to better their lives" (Simmons & Simonsohn, 2017, pp. 690–691). In response, Cuddy wrote "I respectfully disagree with the interpretations and conclusions of Simonsohn et al., but I'm considering these issues very carefully and look forward to further progress on this important topic" (Simmons & Simonsohn, 2015).

Then a most unusual thing happened. Dana Carney, now a professor at Berkeley and the lead author on the 2010 power pose article, posted on her web page that "since early 2015 the evidence has been mounting suggesting there is unlikely any embodied effect of nonverbal expansiveness (vs. contractiveness)—i.e., 'power poses'—on internal or psychological outcomes. As evidence has come in over these past 2+ years, my views have updated to reflect the evidence. As such, I do not believe that 'power pose' effects are real" (Carney, 2015).

In a recent paper (Cuddy, Schultz, & Fosse, 2018), Cuddy and colleagues attempted to rebut her critics. In a review of 55 studies, they concluded that

> findings from the present set of studies provide convincing
> evidence that postural manipulations affected subjects' specific
> emotions, affect, mood recovery, retrieval and recall of positive
> versus negative memories, and self-evaluations, demonstrating that
> the effects of postural feedback on affective variables clearly extend
> beyond causing people to feel more powerful. (pp. 662–663)

Where does this leave us in terms of judging the validity of the power posing hypothesis? First, it's important to note that perhaps the most interesting findings from the original experiment—the hormonal effects and effects on behavior—were not replicated. Second, it's apparent that there's no clear-cut response to the question—reasonable scientists seem to disagree on the matter.

Ethical Issues in Analysis and in the Journal Review Process

Mark Regnerus is a professor at the University of Texas. In 2011, he fielded the "New Family Structure Study" with funding from the Witherspoon Institute and the Bradley Foundation. The project surveyed about 3,000 Americans ages 18 to 39 years "with particular attention paid to reaching ample numbers of respondents who were raised by parents that had a same-sex relationship" (Regnerus, 2012, p. 755). Regnerus compared what he claimed were individuals raised by "lesbian mothers" and "gay fathers" and concluded that, by young adulthood, these children did substantially less well on a number of indicators of well-being, including being more likely to have been arrested, to have pled guilty to non-minor offenses, and having more sex partners. He also concluded that

> the NFSS also clearly reveals that children appear most apt to
> succeed well as adults—on multiple counts and across a variety
> of domains—when they spend their entire childhood with their

married mother and father, and especially when the parents remain married to the present day. (p. 764)

In other words, the gist of the paper was that children are better off being raised by their biological (heterosexual) parents.

Not surprisingly, conservative organizations seized on these findings as ammunition in court battles over same-sex parenting rights—in fact, "the day after publication of the Regnerus study it was cited in an *amicus curiae* brief by a conservative Christian political organization to justify denying marriage rights to same sex couples" (Sherkat, 2012, p. 1349). However, there were a number of issues in the Regnerus paper that raised the concern of other social scientists. There was so much concern, in fact, that when Regnerus came up for post-tenure review at the University of Texas his dean commissioned a detailed report of the issues (Musick, 2014). Some of these issues were purely methodological, dealing with how Regnerus chose to analyze the data; others were ethical and had to do with the funding and publication of the study.

The report began by noting that the Regnerus paper "is probably one of the most, if not the most, scrutinized sociological articles in recent history" (Musick, 2014, p. 1). Regnerus began by classifying the adult respondents as being raised by "lesbian mothers," "gay fathers," or in an intact biological family (and several other categories not relevant here). One problem with this categorization, as Regnerus admitted (Regnerus, 2012, p. 758), was that the categories were not mutually exclusive. To maximize the sample size of children raised by "lesbian mothers" or "gay fathers," Regnerus chose to allow those characteristics to override the other possibilities. While this may sound like an arcane methodological decision, it is actually quite important because it eventually confounds the sexual history of the parents with their marital histories.

In fact, one could reasonably argue that the respondents who were classified into the "lesbian mothers" or "gay fathers" categories weren't raised by same-sex parents at all. To be classified into the "lesbian mothers" group, for example, all that was required was that the respondent report that the mother had at least one same-sex relationship *at some point in their lives*. The result of this seemingly trivial coding decision is that very few of the respondents classified in the "lesbian mothers" or "gay fathers" categories were actually raised by same-sex parents. Nevertheless, many (if not most) non-social scientists reading this paper will come away with the impression that it is about the effects on children raised in same-sex couple households when it clearly is not.

Another curious fact about the Regnerus paper is the strange route it took to publication in a peer-reviewed journal. The paper was actually submitted for publication 3 weeks before data collection was completed, and the total time from submission to acceptance for publication was only about six weeks. This is a substantially shorter time to publication than is usual in social science journals. More interestingly, at least two of the three reviewers of the article had what could charitably be called conflicts of interest, having been paid consultants on the study itself (Sherkat, 2012).

Our take on the Regnerus paper is that it was funded, designed, conducted, analyzed, and presented to make a specific political point. At every step of the process, from formulating the survey to submitting for publication, every decision seemed to be in service of the political goal of opposing same-sex marriage and parenting. As Cohen (2012b) wrote, "I think it's a bad-quality piece of research that should not have been published; and that Regnerus cynically manipulated promotion by the conservative press and anti-equality advocates eager to declare, 'this new research tends to affirm that the ideal for a child is a married mom and dad.'"

The Value of Ethically Sound Research

Research that falls short of ethical standards, either of how to treat participants or of how the science is performed, undermines the ability of other researchers to do their work. Unfortunately, we remember the stories of researchers accused of behaving badly, for example, Milgram's shock studies (Milgram, 1974) and the Stanford prison experiment (Zimbardo, 2007). Most research methods textbooks use the same examples of problematic research for precisely that reason: focusing on the bad behavior will teach others what not to do. Ethically sound research is the standard, although we rarely hear about the precautions used to protect research participants when we hear about the findings of recently published work. However, ethically sound research is the backbone of scientific understanding. If we are to build a body of knowledge about any subject, but particularly the study of human development and families, we need to trust that the study was performed with the utmost care to participants' rights, their ability to participate voluntarily and provide consent (and assent where needed), minimal deception (with debriefing as needed), and confidentiality. Studies that are rigged with predetermined outcomes or are based on inappropriately acquired data undermine our ability to understand the social world and ultimately can do substantial harm through the spread of inaccurate information. The now-infamous study using fabricated data that linked vaccines with autism is the ultimate example of this last problem.

Therefore, it's important to remember that cases of fraud or unethical behavior in social research are the exceptions rather than the rule. The best way for us to detect such cases is to use our methodological skills to critically examine the research we read and not blindly accept the validity of a study simply because it has been published in a reputable journal. One goal of this book is to show you how to evaluate research studies. This chapter has focused on the importance of understanding the structure of the study itself, the protections provided for the research participants, as well as the honesty and transparency attached to the reporting of the scientific process and study outcomes. The rest of the book will expose you to other tools you can use to critically evaluate research, beginning in Chapter 3 with issues of causality.

STUDY QUESTIONS

1. Find a report of family-related research in a daily newspaper or weekly newsmagazine. What information that you think is necessary for your evaluation of the research is not presented?

2. Find a research project using human participants in any of the major journals that publish family-related research. Evaluate the study in terms of the five major ethical concerns in this chapter. How well did the authors of the study adhere to each of these guidelines?

3. Why do you think that people like LaCour, Stapel, and others report fraudulent research? How might family studies and human development scholars combat such research?

CHAPTER 3

Causal Inference in Research on Families and Children

M uch of our thinking about families and children is framed in terms of causality. When we see an outcome—spousal abuse, divorce, increasing age at first marriage, smaller family sizes—a reasonable first question is, "What is causing this outcome?" Implicitly, we are attempting to answer the *why* question in terms of cause and effect: We know the effect, but what is the cause?

To think causally, we must first identify several types of variables that may appear in our analysis. Family size, age at marriage, and marital satisfaction are all variables because they vary. Our analyses involve variables and their attributes, values, states, or levels. Is a particular respondent male or female? Here, gender is a variable with two levels or attributes: male and female. Does the United States have a high or low median age at marriage? Age at marriage is a variable because it can take on many different values, ranging from young to relatively old age at first marriage.

We usually label variables in terms of their **theoretical roles** in our research. Variables typically occupy one of four major theoretical roles in family research: independent, dependent, intervening (mediator or mediating), and control (moderator or moderating) variables.

Variables

Dependent Variables

In research terms, we think of the outcome or the effect as the **dependent variable**. A dependent variable is the factor or characteristic that we think is caused, produced, or affected by some other factors. If we are studying factors affecting marital satisfaction, then marital satisfaction is the dependent variable in the analysis.

Independent Variables

A factor that causes, affects, or produces changes in the dependent variable is known as an **independent variable**. For example, if we think that age at marriage somehow affects marital satisfaction, then age at marriage is the independent variable in the analysis.

A Simple Causal Model

We now have a simple causal model to consider. We think that through some process, age at marriage affects marital satisfaction. We can conceptualize this relationship in many different ways. For example, we could say that age at marriage affects how satisfied people are with their marriages, or we could suggest that those in marriages in which the spouses were teenagers when they married will have lower levels of marital satisfaction than those in marriages in which the partners were in their 30s. In either case, we could diagram this simple causal model as shown in Figure 3.1.

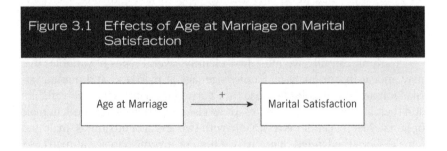

Figure 3.1 Effects of Age at Marriage on Marital Satisfaction

The independent variable (age at marriage) is on the left-hand side of the diagram, and the dependent variable (marital satisfaction) is on the right-hand side. We generally diagram causal relationships from left to right, proceeding from the most fundamental independent variable on the left to the dependent variable of interest on the right. The arrow connecting the two variables is pointed at marital satisfaction, indicating that our model suggests that age at marriage causes or affects marital satisfaction. The plus sign (+) over that line indicates a positive relationship between age at marriage and marital satisfaction; that is, older ages at marriage are associated with higher levels of marital satisfaction, and younger ages at marriage are associated with lower levels of marital satisfaction. A negative relationship (one in which higher levels of the independent variable are associated with lower levels of the dependent variable, and vice versa) would be indicated by a minus sign (−).

Notice in the diagram that we didn't label the dependent variable as high marital satisfaction or low marital satisfaction or the independent variable as teenagers or early 20s. It's important to distinguish between variables themselves and states, levels, or categories of those variables. As an example, let's say we had a model that studies differences between men's and women's scores on standardized tests. The independent variable here wouldn't be male or female; it would be gender.

Intervening (Mediator or Mediating) Variables

This is a simplified model, and nobody really believes that age at marriage is the only variable that affects marital satisfaction. It's possible that age at marriage affects some other variable, which in turn affects marital satisfaction. In this case, that other variable is an **intervening variable** or a **mediator** (or mediating) **variable**. For example, age at marriage might affect emotional stability—because younger people are less emotionally stable than older ones are—and emotional stability, in turn, might affect marital satisfaction. Our causal model now looks like Figure 3.2.

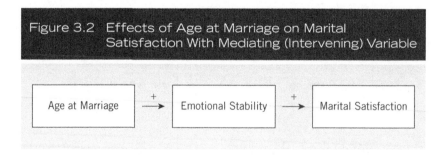

Figure 3.2 Effects of Age at Marriage on Marital Satisfaction With Mediating (Intervening) Variable

The diagram clarifies that our model doesn't suggest that age at marriage affects marital satisfaction directly. Rather, our model says that the effects of age at marriage (our independent variable) on marital satisfaction (our dependent variable) are mediated by emotional stability (intervening variable). In other words, this model says that one's age at marriage affects one's emotional stability, and emotional stability, in turn, affects one's marital satisfaction.

This addition of an intervening variable to our model is important because it tells us a great deal about the process through which age at marriage affects marital satisfaction. It tells us, for example, that not all people who marry at an early age will have low levels of marital satisfaction (young people who are emotionally stable should not have substantially lower marital satisfaction). Similarly, it also tells us that we would expect people who were emotionally unstable to have lower levels of marital satisfaction, regardless of how old they were when they married.

Moderating (Control or Moderator) Variables

Sometimes our theories suggest that the effect of the independent variable on the dependent variable is different for different groups. For example, let's assume that our theory tells us that age at marriage affects marital satisfaction for Protestants and Jews (that is, the younger Protestants or Jews are when they marry, the lower their marital satisfaction), but age at marriage doesn't affect marital satisfaction for Catholics. What's the role of religious affiliation in this model? In terms of a diagram, it would look like Figure 3.3.

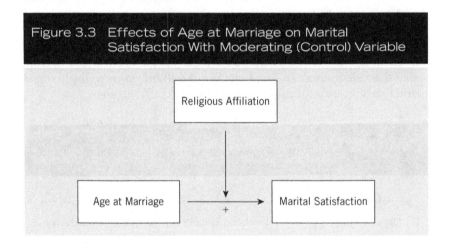

Figure 3.3   Effects of Age at Marriage on Marital Satisfaction With Moderating (Control) Variable

Note that this model doesn't suggest that religious affiliation affects age at marriage; if it did, then the arrow coming out of the religious-affiliation box would be pointing at the age-at-marriage box. And it also doesn't argue that religious affiliation affects marital satisfaction. What this model tells us is that religious affiliation affects the relationship between age at marriage and marital satisfaction (and not either variable individually).

In this model, religious affiliation is a **control variable** or **moderator** (or moderating) **variable**. In this case, we call it a moderator variable because religious affiliation moderates or changes the relationship between the independent variable (age at marriage) and the dependent variable (marital satisfaction). Control- or moderating-variable effects are among the most interesting findings in social research because they suggest that the phenomenon under study works differently for different groups or different types of individuals or families. Such knowledge can lead us to a better understanding of how, exactly, the process works. Why, for example, should age at marriage affect marital satisfaction for Protestants and Jews but not Catholics? The case might be that Catholics have historically married at younger ages than Protestants and Jews; because early marriage is a normatively approved behavior among Catholics, it doesn't have the effect on marital satisfaction that it does for members of other religious groups. Baron and Kenny (1986) and Edwards and Lambert (2007) both presented an excellent treatment of the importance of the moderator and mediator variable in causal models.

Two other uses of the term <u>control variable</u> bear mentioning here. Sometimes, other variables affect the dependent variable, even though we aren't specifically interested in their effects. For example, we know from previous research that age at marriage is the best single predictor of marital stability. Even if we were primarily interested in the effects of some other variable—say, the wife's employment status—we still want to include age at first marriage in our model. Most statistical techniques allow for the inclusion of such control variables, and permit us to see the effects of our independent variable of interest (in this case, the wife's employment) controlling for, or net of, the effects of other variables in the model, including age at first marriage. In principle, one can include as many of these control variables in the model as needed, but generally it is considered inappropriate to include this type of control variable without reasonable evidence to suggest that it affects the dependent variable. This type of model is depicted in Figure 3.4.

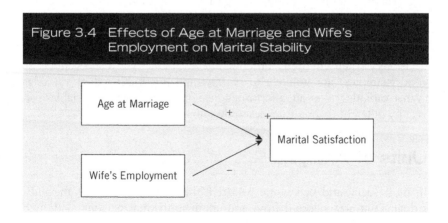

Figure 3.4 Effects of Age at Marriage and Wife's Employment on Marital Stability

Another type of control variable is one that affects both the independent variable and the dependent variable. In research on child well-being, for example, it is often hypothesized that family income has an effect on child cognitive ability: All things being equal, children from higher income families tend to have higher levels of cognitive ability than do children from lower income families. However, mother's education probably affects both the independent variable (family income) and the dependent variable (child cognitive ability). Again, we would probably want to include mother's education in any statistical model so that the effects of family income on child cognitive ability (controlling for, or net of, the effects of mother's education) can be assessed (shown in Figure 3.5).

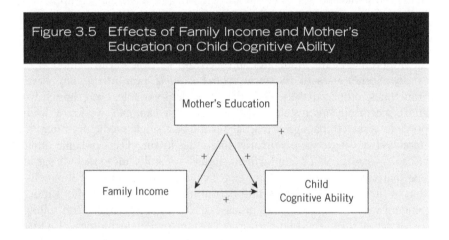

Figure 3.5 Effects of Family Income and Mother's Education on Child Cognitive Ability

Before leaving the subject of the theoretical role of variables, we should point out that just because a given variable occupies a particular theoretical role in one study doesn't mean that it can't occupy a different theoretical role in another study. For example, age at marriage is the independent variable in the marital stability study described here. In a different study, age at marriage might be a dependent variable. For instance, a researcher might want to see how parents' education and income affect the marital-timing decisions of their children. Although a few variables (race and gender are good examples) are unlikely to be anything but independent variables (What variables, after all, affect one's race or gender?), most variables can occupy different theoretical roles in different studies.

Units of Analysis

In most social and behavioral research, the unit of analysis is the individual: Data are collected from and about individual persons. Although these individuals can be combined into groups (e.g., all college-educated individuals, or all individuals older than the age of 65 years), the focus is on the individual. In family research, however, we deal with many different units of analysis. Larzelere and Klein (1987) suggested that family research deals with (a) data on dyads (couples), coresidential families, and extended families; (b) data aggregated at various levels (e.g., community-level data, statewide data, and data at the national level); and (c) data on individuals. The discussion that follows and the accompanying table borrow heavily from their work and that of Levinger and Raush (1977).

In Table 3.1, analyses that examine the effects of individual-level characteristics on other individual-level characteristics are represented in cell 1,1. For example, a study of how personal income affects marriage timing would examine the effects of an individual-level independent variable on an individual-level dependent variable. If our theory hypothesized that regional economic conditions (e.g., the unemployment rate) affected the rate of domestic violence, however, we would be examining the effects of a variable at the aggregate level (regional unemployment rate) on a measure taken at the coresidential family level represented in the table by cell 5,3.

Table 3.1 A Matrix for Generating Research Questions About Families

Unit of analysis: Independent variable	Unit of analysis: Dependent variable			
	1. Individual	2. Dyad	3. Coresidential family	4. Extended family
1. Individual	1,1	1,2	1,3	1,4
2. Dyad	2,1	2,2	2,3	2,4
3. Coresidential family	3,1	3,2	3,3	3,4
4. Extended family	4,1	4,2	4,3	4,4
5. Aggregate level	5,1	5,2	5,3	5,4

Family research often examines the effects of variables measured at the dyadic, coresidential family, extended family, and aggregate levels on individual-level or coresidential family outcomes. For example, we might study the effects of family social class (measured at the level of the coresidential family) on children's occupational aspirations (an individual-level variable); this type of analysis fits in cell 3,1. Less commonly, research might examine the effect of individual-level variables on measures taken at the coresidential or extended family levels (say, the effect of having a child with autism on the coresidential family). Whatever the unit of analysis, the research design must be sensitive to the fact that (unlike most social and behavioral research, which focuses on individuals as the unit of analysis) data can be gathered on many different levels.

Thinking Causally

Few problems in the philosophy of science have stirred so much interest as the issue of cause and effect. This is particularly true in the social and behavioral sciences because often the primary concern is with how to bring about change in some dependent variable. If a theory claims that some independent variable really causes some dependent variable, that suggests that changes in the independent variable should produce changes in the dependent variable. For example, if the amount of parental supervision has a causal effect on delinquent behavior, then increasing the amount of parental supervision should result in decreases in delinquent behavior.

But how do we know when we really have a causal effect? No doubt you've heard the saying, "Correlation does not imply causation," meaning that simply because two variables seem to be associated with each other doesn't mean that one of them causes the other. To take an example, imagine that a researcher has gathered data on family violence (the dependent variable) and is searching for factors that might be causally related to it. The researcher has data on the number of incidents of family violence in major American cities on a monthly basis. By coincidence, the researcher also has monthly data on ice cream consumption in those same cities.

To her surprise, the researcher finds that the number of incidents of family violence is correlated with ice cream consumption. The number of incidents of family violence is lowest when ice cream consumption is low and highest when ice cream consumption is at its peak. Could some ingredient in ice cream possibly make people want to assault their spouses? That is, does consumption of ice cream causally affect the rate of family violence?

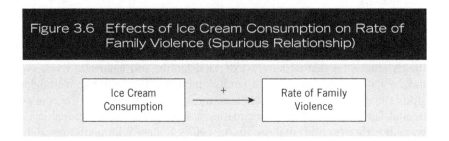

Figure 3.6 Effects of Ice Cream Consumption on Rate of Family Violence (Spurious Relationship)

You've probably already figured out what's going on here. Both the rate of family violence and the consumption of ice cream are affected by a third variable: weather (or, more specifically, the temperature). The rate of family violence and the consumption of ice cream both peak during the warm summer months and are both at their lowest point during the winter. This relationship is diagrammed like the model in Figure 3.7.

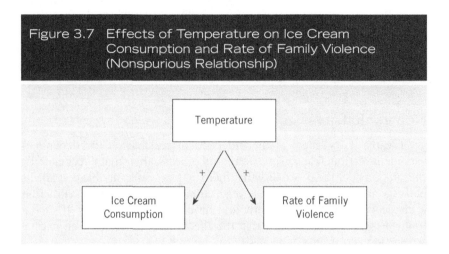

Figure 3.7   Effects of Temperature on Ice Cream Consumption and Rate of Family Violence (Nonspurious Relationship)

This is a classic example of what is known as a **spurious effect**. What initially appeared to be a causal effect of ice cream consumption on family violence is, in fact, caused by the effects of a third variable—temperature—on both the independent and dependent variables. Ice cream consumption has no causal effect on family violence, even though the research may show a correlation or association between the two. In Figure 3.7, notice that there is no line representing a causal effect that connects the variables ice cream consumption and rate of family violence. This is because in the initial model (diagrammed in Figure 3.6), the influence of temperature on both ice cream consumption and family violence creates the spurious effect.

How do we determine if an association or relationship is causal, as opposed to spurious? There are three main conditions that must be met if an effect is to be judged causal: temporal precedence, constant conjunction, and nonspuriousness.

Temporal Precedence

If X causes Y, then X must precede Y in time. Obviously, X can't be a cause of Y if X happens after Y. In the age-at-marriage/marital-satisfaction example, age at marriage precedes marital satisfaction, so the temporal precedence requirement is met.

Constant Conjunction

If X causes Y, then X and Y have to be highly associated or correlated with each other. If age at marriage really affects marital satisfaction, then age at marriage should be highly associated with marital satisfaction—not just in one or a few studies but in many studies over time and across populations. In this case, it is well-known that the relationship of age at marriage to marital satisfaction is consistent in nearly every study of marriages, so the constant conjunction requirement is met.

Nonspuriousness

Clearly, if the effect of the independent variable on the dependent variable is attributable to some spurious process, then that effect can't be causal. Consider the possibility that there may be some variable that affects both age at marriage and marital satisfaction. Maybe some personality trait leads people to both marry early and have unstable marriages. If such a trait exists, it may be the case that the effect of age at marriage on marital satisfaction is spurious, not causal.

Identifying Mechanisms and Specifying Context

While the above three criteria are crucial for assessing causality, the ability to make a causal claim about a relationship between two variables would be improved if we identify the **causal mechanism** and/or specify the context within which the association exists. Earlier, when we discussed the relationship between age at marriage and marital satisfaction, we did not stipulate how or why age at marriage would affect marital satisfaction. One way to strengthen a claim of causality would be to state the mechanism, or the how or why, through which the independent variable affects the dependent variable. In the case of age at marriage and marital satisfaction, why would we expect lower levels of marital satisfaction in marriages that occurred when the spouses were teenagers than in marriages that occurred when the spouses were in their 30s? One possible explanation is that individuals who were older at marriage, as opposed to those in their teens, had more time to date, experience life, and make a determination of what kind of person they would want to marry. Therefore, they might be more likely to be satisfied with the partner they chose and, ultimately, with their marriage. A mechanism is different from a mediating variable, as it is a theoretical process, explaining how or why the relationship occurs, rather than a variable predicted by the independent variable that predicts the dependent variable (review Figure 3.2). We may not be able to directly measure this mechanism in our research design, but if we are able to provide this kind of rationale for how or why the independent variable is associated with our dependent variable, our claim of causality is strengthened.

Families do not exist in a vacuum. Therefore, research on families, especially research trying to explain outcomes in families, could provide better explanations if the specific context in which the proffered associations existed were identified. Context may mean physical context, as in nation of residence or region of the country. But context can also mean part of the "life cycle of an event" (Hallinan, 1998, p. 21) such as identifying different predictors of marital satisfaction in couples with and without children. So rather than trying to universally predict marital satisfaction among all couples, researchers could identify key stages in marriages and then investigate whether the independent variables that influence marital satisfaction in one marital context (e.g., being parents) are the same as in a different context (e.g., not being parents). Remember our discussion of moderator variables? Review Figure 3.3. Specifying the conditions under which an association occurs, or the context, can lead us to the discovery of the mechanism underlying the association, again strengthening our causal claim.

Assessing Causality

To conclude that a relationship or effect is truly causal, we have to be able to (a) establish temporal precedence, (b) assert constant conjunction, and (c) eliminate the possibility that there is some variable (or group of variables) that affects both the independent and dependent variables producing the appearance of a causal effect when in fact the relationship is spurious. To do this, the researcher has to do three things:

1. The researcher has to identify the variables that may be producing the spurious effect.

2. The researcher has to have empirical data on those variables.

3. The researcher has to perform the appropriate statistical analyses to determine whether the relationship appears to be spurious.

Of these three, the first is usually the most difficult. Potentially, there are thousands of variables that might be creating a spurious effect in any particular analysis. Usually, speculation is limited to those variables linked, by a conceptual or theoretical relationship, to the independent and dependent variables in our analysis. Although eliminating all potential sources of spurious effects is probably impossible, we need to eliminate at least the most plausible sources of spuriousness before claiming that the effects are causal.

We will discuss statistical procedures further later in this text. Now that we know something about different types of variables and causality, we're ready to frame a research hypothesis.

Framing the Hypothesis

Most family research begins with a hypothesis. A hypothesis is a forecast or expectation about how variables are associated or how they are causally related. For example, one hypothesis that might be framed about the relationship between age at marriage and marital satisfaction is "Age at marriage has a positive effect on marital satisfaction."

This hypothesis suggests that, all things being equal, people who marry at younger ages will tend to have lower levels of marital satisfaction, whereas those who marry later in life will tend to have higher levels of marital satisfaction. This hypothesis does not mean that every person who marries at an early age will have an unhappy marriage, nor that every person who marries later in life will have a happy marriage. Research hypotheses are typically framed in terms of group averages and tendencies—not the behavior of specific individuals.

Where do hypotheses come from? Ideally, they should come from theories because the unambiguous logical structure of a good theory tells us why, of necessity, a particular independent variable causes or is associated with a particular dependent variable. Practically speaking, however, because relatively few such theories exist in the study of the family, most hypotheses come from either reading the existing body of research literature or from common sense or intuition.

Directional Hypotheses

Hypotheses typically take one of two forms. The framed-at-age hypothesis is a **directional hypothesis**, because it states an expectation about the direction of the relationship between the independent variable and the dependent variable. Increased age at marriage is hypothesized to have a positive effect on marital satisfaction, meaning that those who marry at an early age are expected to have the lowest levels of marital satisfaction, and those who marry at somewhat older ages are expected to have higher levels of marital satisfaction. It follows that age at marriage usually has a negative effect on likelihood of divorce: Those who are younger when they marry are more likely to have unstable marriages, whereas those who are older when they marry are less likely to have unstable marriages.

Nondirectional Hypotheses

In a **nondirectional hypothesis**, the independent variable has an association with, or effect on, the dependent variable, but there is insufficient information to allow an intelligent guess about the direction of that relationship. For example, we might hypothesize that income will affect marital satisfaction, but without some body of knowledge to inform us whether high-income persons will be more (or less) satisfied with their marriages than low-income persons, our hypothesis remains nondirectional.

Whatever the source or structure of the hypothesis, however, it is important to be able to defend it against the critics. You should always be able to justify your hypothesis in terms of theory, existing research, or some type of logical argument. The burden of proof is always on the researcher to demonstrate that the hypothesis is reasonable and that it follows logically from previous theory or research.

Cross-Sectional Versus Longitudinal Designs

Studies that gather data at one point in time are known as **cross-sectional**. If we are attempting to establish that causal effects exist, though, then cross-sectional designs can be problematic. Remember that one of our three criteria for inferring causality was temporal precedence—that is, for X to cause Y, X has to precede Y in time. Sometimes, it's fairly straightforward to establish temporal precedence. For example, studies of adolescent behavior often postulate effects of the child's home environment during infancy. But what about less clear-cut situations?

In Greenstein's (1995) study of over three thousand marriages, he used data from the National Longitudinal Surveys of Youth (NLSY) to study marital stability over time. The NLSY79 is a nationally representative sample of 12,686 respondents who were 14 to 22 years of age when first interviewed in 1979; these respondents were reinterviewed annually through 1994 and on a biennial basis after 1994. Greenstein constructed a dataset where each marriage was represented by, on average, about six annual observations that included information about employment, fertility, and other measures. This kind of design is known as **longitudinal** (and, more specifically, as a **panel** design because it looks at the responses of the same group of respondents—a *panel*—at multiple points in time).

Longitudinal designs in general, and panel designs in particular, can be valuable in establishing temporal precedence. For example, in Greenstein's study, we know exactly when specific events such as entries into and exits from the labor force occur and can study how these events affect the likelihood of separation and divorce over time.

There are many types of longitudinal designs and a full treatment is beyond the scope of this text. For an introduction to different types of longitudinal research see Menard (1991); Frees (2004) provides an excellent treatment of analyzing data from different types of longitudinal designs.

Causal Inference in Qualitative Research

The preceding discussion of assessing causality has implied that the data collected were easily translated into numbers for statistical analysis. Further, we have presumed that the research project is one designed to test hypotheses derived from theories, existing research, or logical inference. However, many family research questions are just that—questions. Family research that is exploratory or descriptive tends to yield broad research questions rather than specific testable hypotheses. The data used to answer these types of questions are typically in the form of observational data and interview transcripts. For example, Risman and Johnson-Sumerford (1998) asked, "What characterizes couples who (almost) equally share the housework?" and Lareau (2011) investigated how race and social class influence parenting behaviors. Assessing causality becomes more difficult in these kinds of studies because of their more narrow focus. Specifically, there is not always variation in both the dependent variable and the independent variable. The Risman and Johnson-Sumerford study above focuses on one attribute of the dependent variable of the division of household labor—(almost) equal—and asks what attributes among many independent variables do the shared housework couples have in common. We cannot assess causality in a study like this one in the same manner that was discussed above because we do not have variation in both the proposed cause and effect.

Rather than trying to test whether there are relationships among variables, these qualitative studies tend to try to understand what is happening on one or two specific cases or attributes of a variable. Lareau (2011) observed and interviewed 12 families, white and black, hailing from poor, working-class, and middle-class backgrounds. Her goal was to try to understand what family life was like for those 12 families. Rather than a priori determining specific hypotheses derived from theories to test, she instead asked, "What is happening in these cases?" She did not hypothesize about class and race differences in child-rearing techniques but instead uncovered them through her observations. Moreover, rather than testing theory, Lareau generated theory regarding the relationship between social class and children's educational outcomes that could be tested in subsequent research. She identified the mechanism through which social class translates into differential educational outcomes for children: child-rearing beliefs and practices. So while she began her research with a causal diagram like Figure 3.8, it became Figure 3.9 as a result of her analysis.

Figure 3.8   Exploring How Race and Social Class Influence Family Life

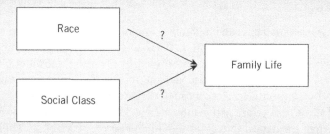

Figure 3.9   Effects of Parental Social Class on Children's Educational Success

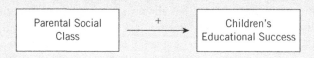

Qualitative research is therefore more likely to identify variables and relationships among them, determine how and why the variables are related (mechanisms), and construct theories describing the social phenomenon that was studied. It would be up to future researchers to follow the steps described earlier in the chapter to determine the veracity of those theoretical claims in other settings and contexts with other samples.

STUDY QUESTIONS

1. Choose two variables related to families or children and (a) give brief definitions of both variables and (b) identify the states, levels, or attributes of both variables.

2. Choose a research article from a family-related journal that uses statistical analysis and identify the independent, dependent, moderating (if any), and intervening (if any) variables in the conceptual model. Draw a causal diagram representing the conceptual model.

3. Choose a research article from a family-related journal that analyzes observational and/or interview data. Identify whether the topic of the paper is being discussed as an independent or a dependent variable. Draw the causal diagram representing the conceptual model implied in the article.

4. Choose a variable related to families or children that is of interest to you and present a conceptual model that shows that variable as an independent variable. Then, repeat the process with three more models that show that variable as a dependent, moderating, and mediating variable, respectively. Draw a causal diagram for each. Note: Because not all variables (race and gender are good examples) can occupy all the different theoretical roles, you should choose your variable carefully.

5. Describe a relationship in the family or human development literature that appears to be a causal effect but is in fact spurious. Clearly identify the variables involved and draw a causal diagram representing this process.

6. Choose some process or relationship in the family or human development literature and frame a hypothesis about that process or relationship. Clearly identify the independent and dependent variables in your hypothesis, and the direction (if appropriate) of the relationship.

4

Searching and Reading the Literature

O nce you've constructed a research question to answer (and maybe even identified a dependent variable), you need to examine the prior research literature on your topic. It's always surprising that people think that they're the first to be interested in a particular topic. We get phone calls and e-mails from people who want to conduct a study of some family-related phenomenon—say, first-time mothers returning to work or cohabiting couples with children—who assume that nobody has ever studied the topic before. The fact of the matter is that in any given year, several thousand studies relating to families and children are published in professional journals. So, regardless of whether you're planning a study of your own or you simply want to know what's already been done, you need to begin by searching the literature.

Although some of this research is published as research monographs (what most of us think of as books), most research on families and children is published as articles in professional journals. *Journal of Marriage and Family, Journal of Family Issues, Child Development, Developmental Psychology, Journal of Family Psychology,* and *Family Relations* are some of the best known journals specializing in research on families and children.

To find out what research has been published on a given topic, you'll need to search these and other journals. Because scholars who do research on families may have backgrounds in a variety of academic fields, the articles you seek might be published in sociological journals, psychological journals, or other sources. Fortunately, there are several excellent indexing systems available to take much of the work out of this task. Sociological Abstracts indexes virtually all the sociological journals, whereas PsycINFO indexes publications in psychology. A third indexing system is Web of Science, which scans journals across many different sciences. Web of Science's predecessor, the Social Science Citation Index, was the first database, or indexing system, to report how frequently a given article is cited by other research, thus giving a crude measure of the *impact* of a particular article on the discipline. Another recent addition is Google Scholar, a search engine available online that indexes scholarly publications.

Although the exact details of using these indexing systems vary, the general procedures are similar. Your local reference librarian can show you the specifics of how to access these services in your library. Many libraries also make these services available to their patrons over the Internet.

There are also indexing systems specifically for literature on family research. The Family Studies Database is the electronic version of Inventory of Marriage and Family Literature and FAMILY (Australian Family & Society Abstracts). It indexes more than 1,000 journals, books, chapters, newsletters, government documents, and dissertations and covers the educational, medical, psychological, and sociological aspects of family literature.

Whichever index system you select, begin by choosing some keywords that are appropriate for the research that you're seeking. For example, if you wanted to study the relationship of child abuse to school performance, the keywords might include *child abuse, academic outcomes,* and *school.* You probably will want to review any articles listed under *child abuse* and either *academic outcomes* or *school.* Once these keywords are entered, the program will display a list of journal articles that studied these issues. If this step generates hundreds of references, you probably need to narrow your focus by adding additional keywords as limitations on the search. If you get only a few references, however, the search keywords probably are inappropriate and you need to change them.

The next step is to read the articles' abstracts. An **abstract** is a brief summary of what a study was about, how the research was conducted, and what the findings were. As you read these abstracts (which are typically displayed along with the reference items by the indexing program), you will find that only some of the articles are really relevant to your work. You will probably then want to find the actual journal containing the articles and scan the articles to see if they are indeed relevant. Many journals are now available online, making your search both easier and more difficult. Instant access to the article in an electronic format allows you to save a copy of the article and then move almost immediately to the next article on your list. However, do not be tempted to read only articles that are available online, as you may have access through your library only to the print copy of a journal. A key article about your topic may just have been published in one of those journals. Another possible pitfall is information overload. Because electronic storage is so cheap, you may be tempted to download any article that looks like it could be related to your research topic. Don't. Focus in on articles whose abstracts leave no doubt in your mind of how they are connected to your topic. You can always expand your reading list later. Sometimes, journals publish a **review article**, which summarizes the research literature on a particular topic. Such articles will save you a lot of work because much of the pertinent literature will already be cited and summarized for you.

Reading a Journal Article

Once you're satisfied that you have the most important articles about your topic, sit down and read them in detail. Articles in professional journals are probably unlike anything you've read before. They are concisely written—journal articles are rarely longer than 25 pages—and they tend to use many abbreviations, technical terms, and jargon. Fortunately, they also tend to follow a rather strict style with a number of clearly defined sections. The following discussion of the various sections of a typical journal article will help you to read the articles you've located and write your own research article.

Title

Of course, each article has a title, and the content of the title is highly informative. It will probably identify the dependent and independent variables and perhaps the nature of who was studied. For example, a title such as "Effects of Classroom Composition on the Development of Antisocial Behavior in Lower Secondary School" (Muller, Hormann, Fleischli, & Studer, 2015) immediately tells you that the independent variable is classroom composition, the dependent variable is development of antisocial behavior, and students in lower secondary schools were studied.

Author and Institutional Affiliation

Immediately below the title will be any author names and their institutional affiliations. You'll notice that most research articles are written by individuals affiliated with universities.

Abstract

As we mentioned earlier, an abstract is a brief summary of the research study. It should include the research questions and/or primary hypotheses, the nature of the sample, a brief mention of the research procedures and analyses, a brief statement of the findings, and a sentence about the implications of the study—all in 150 to 200 words. Always read the abstract first—if the article isn't relevant to your interests, then you can save yourself a lot of time.

Introduction

The introduction section (which typically will not have a heading indicating as much) introduces the problem and justifies its importance. This section should answer the question, "Why should anyone care about this problem?" On one hand, the importance of the paper might be justified in practical or policy terms. For example, in their 2007 paper, "Parental Deployment and Youth in Military Families: Exploring Uncertainty and Ambiguous Loss," Heubner, Mancini, Wilcox, Grass, and Grass (2007) note that given the increasing number of children whose parents are deployed, it is important to understand whether and how parental deployment influences adolescent mental health. In other words, they argue that the topic is important and worth studying because of its practical significance. Another example of justifying the research for practical reasons is provided by Fortune and McKeown (2015) who studied people with dementia and their spouses. They noted that these people often feel marginalized and excluded in their communities, making a case for social inclusion and justice through their examination of a targeted social program.

On the other hand, an author may argue that a paper is important because of its theoretical or conceptual significance. In "Effects of Union Type on Division of Household Labor: Do Cohabiting Men Really Perform More Housework?" Davis, Greenstein, and Gerteisen Marks (2007) explicitly sought to use several different theoretical traditions to explain differences between cohabiting and married couples in their division of household labor. Although there may be indirect policy or practical implications of the research, the paper was aimed primarily at an application of theories. Similarly, Simmons, Steinberg, Frick, and Cauffman (2017) explicitly sought to use different theoretical traditions to explain differences between harsh and absent fathers in juvenile delinquency. Although there may be indirect policy or practical implications of the research, the paper was aimed primarily at an application of theories.

Generally speaking, a research article might be published for any of several reasons. First, it's possible (although unlikely) that a particular problem has never been studied. Assuming that the problem is one of interest to those studying families, the article will fill a gap in the research literature.

Second, it's possible that, although the particular problem has been studied, the author finds shortcomings or problems in the existing literature. For example, the author might offer methodological improvements over previous research—perhaps with a better sample or more precise measurement.

Previous research might have methodological flaws that the author claims a new study can correct; sometimes incorrect statistical procedures or biased instruments can produce faulty or misleading conclusions. Also, previous research might contain conceptual flaws; perhaps the author feels that a different theoretical approach is necessary or that a previous author incorrectly applied some body of theory. An article might **replicate** previous research in a different population with more recent data, better controls, or better measures of key variables.

Regardless of how the authors choose to justify the importance of the paper, their goal is to convince the reader that the topic is worth studying. The introduction should convince the reader that the problem under study is important and should indicate where the authors are going in the article, how they're going to get there, and why the research is being done.

Literature Review

Again, there may not be a *literature review* heading, but at some point, the authors discuss previous studies relevant to the current research. There is a simple rule for which items should be discussed in the literature review: Discuss all that is relevant and nothing that isn't. The authors will want to include the major studies that have looked at the same independent and dependent variables as their study. It's unnecessary to cite every study ever conducted on the topic—only the important ones. The authors' goal in the literature review is not only to show what's already been done on the topic but, more importantly, to show what hasn't been done and why their study must be done. This is especially key if the study is exploratory. The literature review will situate the research question in the appropriate body of research. The researchers will then situate themselves within those previous findings and should show how and why their exploration is useful and needed.

If the authors have hypotheses to present, they will usually present them immediately following the literature review. The hypotheses should be stated as explicitly as possible. Often, hypotheses are stated first in conceptual or abstract terms, then in concrete or operational terms. The hypotheses should tell exactly which outcomes will confirm (be consistent with) the hypotheses and which outcomes will disconfirm (be inconsistent with) the hypotheses. Some studies—particularly those that collect and analyze qualitative data—will not present specific hypotheses but will frame their inquiry through broad research questions. For example, in her study on identity development among transgender or gender nonconforming students, Austin (2014) wrote,

> Given the evolving conceptualization of gender identity in society, as well as the recognition of a diversity of experiences of gender among TGNC [transgender and gender non-conforming] individuals, particularly TGNC young people, it is important to gain a more in depth and nuanced understanding of these experiences . . . The primary aim of my study is to use grounded theory methodology to extend the discussion of navigating an emerging TGNC identity during the complex journey toward adulthood in a society in which TGNC identities remain invisible and marginalized. (pp. 216–217)

Methods

There will probably be a section labeled methods or methodology (the term should usually be *methods* because methodology is the study of method, and what the author is presenting here is a description of a specific method, not the study of methods). The purpose of this section is twofold: first, to describe exactly who was studied (the sample) and how they were studied (the procedures); and second, to describe what was studied (the measurements or instruments). Ideally, this section should provide enough information for the reader to judge whether the sample and procedures were appropriate for the problem and the outcomes.

Sample

Nearly all methods sections will begin with a discussion of the sample. This should tell the reader exactly who was studied, how many were studied (the sample size), when the data were gathered, how respondents were selected, and so forth. We discuss sampling procedures in detail in Chapter 5. If another researcher or organization originally collected the data (for example, the U.S. Census Bureau), there should be a citation to the original source documentation for the data.

Measurement

This subsection should identify all the key variables in the study and explain how they were operationalized or measured. If sample surveys were used, this section should provide the exact wording of key items or questions that are used in the study. If standardized scales or indices were used, then this subsection should cite the original sources and briefly report any known problems with validity or reliability of the measures. Any recoded items (categories combined for analytic purposes) should be clarified. We discuss measurement issues in Chapter 6.

For qualitative studies, this section can be problematic. Many qualitative studies are exploratory in nature; prior to beginning the research, it's not always clear what the key variables are or how they should be measured. Rather, this information may emerge from the data collection process. Qualitative studies, therefore, rarely have this subsection.

Procedures

This subsection should explain in detail exactly how the data were gathered. There are two main purposes of this subsection: first, to describe exactly what techniques were used to collect the data; and second, to provide enough detail to allow an interested researcher to replicate the study. Common techniques for collecting quantitative data are presented in Chapter 8, while our discussion of techniques for collecting qualitative data is in Chapter 9.

Findings or Results

Sometimes, this section will be labeled *analyses*. The actual results of the study should be reported here without interpretation (interpretation of the results follows in the *discussion* section). The beginning of this section should consider general issues such as response rates and estimates of reliability and validity. Any statistical techniques used should be described here and their use justified. The authors must convince the reader that their techniques were appropriate and the best available for the particular types of data and research questions. If the techniques were unusual or are not commonly used, the authors may take a few paragraphs to explain them.

In most quantitative studies, the first results reported will be descriptive statistics about the respondents. Typically, the analyses will include a table of statistics about the variables in the analyses. This table is important because it tells the reader much about the characteristics of the respondents in the study: Age, gender, race, education, marital status, and other relevant variables are typically reported. Other tables will probably report results relating to the hypotheses or goals of the study. Additional information about tables follows. We present detailed discussions about analytic techniques for quantitative data in Chapters 12 and 13.

Qualitative studies typically organize their results around the themes that emerged from the data analysis. Rather than tables, data are often summarized with key quotes or observations used to punctuate important points.

Discussion

The *discussion* section in a quantitative study usually begins with a restatement of the research problem followed by a listing of the major hypotheses. Next, the evidence supporting the hypotheses will be presented and interpreted. Any weaknesses or problems with the design of the study or the quality of the data should be mentioned and explained. For example, the data might be relatively old, or the sample might be unusual or biased in some way. Perhaps it was not possible to control for some important explanatory variable. These issues need to be made clear to the reader, and the authors will generally try to show why these concerns don't interfere with their ability to draw reasonable inferences from the study.

Any alternative interpretations of the findings—that is, different ways of interpreting the results—should be discussed. All findings should be related back to previous theory or research with the emphasis on how the research accomplished the goals set out in the beginning of the introduction. If the conclusions of the article are not presented in a separate section, then they are normally at the end of the discussion section.

Qualitative studies follow a similar structure, though they focus on the broader conceptual contributions of the paper rather than on an evaluation of specific hypotheses. The main purpose of the discussion section in those studies is articulating the theoretical contribution of the paper to the research literature.

Conclusions

The *conclusion* is the wrap-up of the article where the authors tell us what they have contributed to the literature. They may also link the research findings to specific social-policy issues or to further developments in theory. They will often propose directions for further research that are suggested by the current study's findings. Sometimes, the conclusions are the last few paragraphs of the discussion section without a separate heading.

References

The documents cited in the article are listed in alphabetical order by the last name of the first author of each document. Only documents that are specifically cited in the paper should appear in this reference list.

Reference items are formatted according to the style of the journal in which the article appears. Journals published by the American Psychological Association (APA)—*Developmental Psychology* and *Journal of Family Psychology,* for example—and many other journals use the style described in the *Publication Manual of the American Psychological Association* (American Psychological Association, 2009). Journals published by the American Sociological Association (ASA) (such as *American Sociological Review*) use a style that is similar to that of the APA and is described in the *American Sociological Association Style Guide* (American Sociological Association, 2010). Journals published or sponsored by the National Council on Family Relations (*Journal of Marriage and Family, Journal of Family Issues,* and *Family Relations,* for example) generally use the APA style.

Tables

A good table supplements (but does not duplicate) the textual material in the body of the article. Generally, it's better to use as few tables as possible to convey the information found in the research. The tables should be organized around the primary hypotheses of the study. The titles of the tables should be clear and unambiguous; ideally, the table titles will identify the primary dependent variable and, if practical, the independent variables as well. Tables are numbered so that the author can refer a specific table by number without having to mention the entire title.

Figures

Most journals prefer that authors keep the number of figures to a minimum (*tables,* by the way, consist only of numbers and text; *figures* contain graphics and are less precise than tables). Like tables, figures are numbered consecutively.

Where Do I Go From Here?

At this point, you've probably got an electronic file of articles (or maybe just the abstracts from an indexing system) that seem relevant to your topic. You will want to begin by skimming all the articles. At this stage, it may help to ignore the *methods* and *results* sections, and focus on the *introduction* and *discussion* sections. As you read the articles, you can begin to cull the stack a bit by deciding which articles are relevant to your topic and which are not. Move the articles that you've decided aren't directly relevant to your current project to another electronic folder in case you reconsider them later.

Now consider the articles that you've decided are relevant to your project. Read them again but this time without omitting any sections. Note any patterns or inconsistencies in the theories, methods, findings, and conclusions of the studies. Does a single theory seem to guide all these studies, or do they work within differing theoretical traditions? Do these studies tend to use the same or different methods of data collection? Are their findings in agreement, or do they conflict? How do the authors interpret these findings?

At the same time, be alert to gaps in the literature. What types of issues or variables are seldom or never addressed by the research? What populations haven't been studied? Are the studies relatively recent or are they old? Might some body of theory be relevant that hasn't been applied to this particular problem? Often, the last few paragraphs of the discussion or conclusion section can tip you off to problems or possibilities in the literature. Authors will frequently discuss possible limitations in their own work or suggestions for future research.

You should also examine the reference lists at the end of each article. Notice which items tend to be cited by the articles you've collected; if those often-cited items aren't already in your file of articles, they should be. Such often-cited or seminal papers are important for several reasons. First, if many of the current studies in your topic cite a particular paper, it must be important to the development of research in your area. Second, authors often assume that their readers are familiar with the classic or seminal works in their area; if you haven't read these papers, you may not be getting the full sense of what's going into the research. Third, these works may suggest possibilities or directions for research that, for whatever reason, no one ever pursued.

Web of Science index has some unusual capabilities that provide an effective way to build up a bibliography. After identifying the classic or seminal works in a particular area, you can use Web of Science's "Cited Reference Search" to identify all the items in the database that cited those works. This technique is called *citation mining*. Citation mining often can identify articles that are relevant to your topic that might not have been uncovered through other methods. Citation mining can be done in two different ways. The first way is to simply go back through the current article and comb through all the citations within it, to see if any other older article might be useful. The other way is to go forward in time to see who has cited the current article in more recent research. Search engines such as Google Scholar give you this option.

How Do Journal Articles Get Published?

We sometimes hear about the publish-or-perish syndrome for academic researchers, but most people don't realize how difficult it is to publish an article in a major journal. The process varies somewhat across journals, but most follow a basic pattern.

First, the author or authors (most research articles have multiple authors) submit the manuscript to the journal. The journal editor then sends copies of the manuscript to two or three reviewers, usually individuals chosen for their expertise in the field. The reviewers read the manuscript and send the editor two sets of comments: one set to be sent to the author and a second for the editor's eyes only. The reviewers can critique any aspect of the paper: review of the literature, hypotheses, methods, analytic techniques, and conclusions—even the writing style.

The reviewers are especially concerned with two issues. First, is the research important enough to merit taking up valuable pages in the journal? Because of page limitations, most journals reject more than 50% of submissions, and major journals often approach 90% rejection rates.

Second, was the research conducted in such a way that the conclusions drawn by the authors are valid? Publication of an article by a major journal implies approval of the research design by the reviewers and the journal's editorial staff, so most journal editors are concerned about the quality of the research design and analytic techniques.

Once the editor has the reviewers' comments in hand, one of three decisions must be conveyed to the author. First, the editor can decide to publish the manuscript in its current form (or perhaps with minor editorial revisions). This is extremely rare, because most reviewers raise at least one or two major concerns that have to be dealt with in a revision. The second possible decision by the editor is to ask the author to revise and resubmit the manuscript for further review, taking into account the criticisms and suggestions of the reviewers. The revised manuscript will be reviewed again, usually by the original reviewers. The third decision the editor can make, of course, is to reject the manuscript outright. The rejection might be based on the topic's irrelevance or on fundamental flaws in the conceptualization, research design, or analytic techniques that cannot be fixed with a revision.

The time lag from submission to the editor's decision varies greatly across journals, but often it is 12 to 20 weeks (in 2016, the *Journal of Marriage and Family* reported an average time from submission to decision of about 52 days, or about 7 ½ weeks). If the author receives a revise-and-resubmit decision, the review process will take another 12 to 20 weeks (plus the time spent revising the manuscript). You can see that even under ideal circumstances, 6 to 12 months can pass between the time of the original submission of a manuscript and the editor's final acceptance of that manuscript for publication. Add about a 6-month lag between acceptance and actual appearance in print, and you have at least a year's span, if not much longer, between submission and actual publication.

This reviewing process, or **peer review**, is one of the great strengths of scientific disciplines. Most journals do blind reviews, meaning that all identifying information is removed from the manuscripts that the reviewers read. The goal is to publish the best conducted and most important research, regardless of who has written it.

Does this rigorous reviewing process ensure that every article published in a major journal is of uniformly high quality? Unfortunately, no. The reality is that journal editors and reviewers make mistakes. Fortunately, the public nature of the scientific enterprise permits members of the scientific community to publish critiques of the articles (known as *comments*) that point out what they believe are flaws in the original article. An interesting example of this self-correcting process of science in the study of families is demonstrated in Wood's (2013) criticism of Regnerus's (2012) conclusion that there were substantial differences between children with lesbian and gay parents as compared to children of parents in heterosexual relationships.

Research Monographs

Some research on families and children is published in the form of books (usually called *research monographs*). Much greater in length, monographs allow more extensive presentations of theory and research findings than do journal articles. The structure of research monographs will vary widely, but all of the sections and material described above should be present. Some information, like specific measurement or sampling details, may be located in an appendix.

Research monographs also go through a review process. The reviewing of monographs is not blind because the reviewers—being experts in the field—usually are aware of who is doing research on what topics, so even if identifying material is removed from the draft of the monograph, the reviewer probably can identify the author or authors. Because of this, and because contracts for monographs are typically offered before the draft is completed, research monographs may not be as critically reviewed as an article appearing in a major journal.

Another difference between journal articles and research monographs is the time lag until publication. Several years typically elapse between the beginning of work on a research monograph and its appearance in print. Harrington-Meyer's (2014) study of grandparent caregiving and grandparents providing care while employed began in 2009. Tichenor's (2005) study of women who outearn their husbands began in 1991. As a result, if you're looking for the most current research on a particular topic, you will probably want to begin by searching the indices (such as Web of Science,

Sociological Abstracts, and PsycINFO) to produce a list of recent journal articles, then move on to the research monographs on that topic.

Edited Volumes

A special type of scholarly book, the *edited volume*, is a journal–research monograph hybrid. These collections are typically books organized around a theme and include original (usually) article-length papers. The papers are reviewed by the editor of the book (typically the scholar who came up with the idea for the edited volume in the first place). The edited volume as a whole seeks to move science forward broadly on a particular topic: Each paper or chapter is focused on one narrow question related to that topic. Roskos and Christie's (2017) *Play and Literacy in Early Childhood*, an edited volume that determines cognitive, ecological, and cultural perspectives formed from the play–literacy relationship, is a good example of this type of book. Treas and Drobnič's (2010) *Dividing the Domestic: Men, Women, and Household Work in Cross-National Perspective,* an edited volume making the case for what can be learned through cross-national studies of housework, is another example.

Other Types of Publications

Although primarily published as journal articles or research monographs, research on children and families also appears in other forms as well. Each year, the professional organizations of scholars that study families and children (e.g., the National Council on Family Relations, the ASA, and the APA) hold national conferences at which hundreds of conference papers are presented. Many of these eventually appear in professional journals, but some do not. Because most of these papers do not go through an elaborate peer-review process, their status in the scientific world is somewhat less than that of published articles. Moreover, these papers haven't appeared in print, making them somewhat difficult to obtain. The major indices, such as Sociological Abstracts and PsycINFO, will have entries for most of these papers, along with instructions on how to obtain copies.

Doctoral dissertations and master's theses are another source of research on families. Sociological Abstracts and PsycINFO index dissertations completed at U.S. universities; Dissertation Abstracts International also provides listings and abstracts of dissertations and information on obtaining copies of the dissertations themselves.

Government agencies, such as the Department of Health and Human Services, the National Institutes of Health, and the U.S. Census Bureau, as well as private foundations and organizations such as the Children's Defense Fund, the David and Lucille Packard Foundation, and others, publish agency reports of research funded by their organizations. The reports themselves are not usually peer reviewed, but papers based on their data sometimes appear in journal articles or research monographs. Internet searches are apt to turn up such reports.

Organizations also publish "white papers" that are specifically designed to inform public discourse and public policy. These papers range from literature reviews to original data analysis. The key difference is that the goal is not for a version of these papers to be placed in a scientific venue in order to contribute to the construction of scientific knowledge. Instead, the goal is to disseminate specific information to the public as quickly as possible. The Council on Contemporary Families is one organization that relies extensively on white papers to highlight new scientific findings or to speak to a particular issue rapidly. Unpublished manuscripts are the most difficult documents to locate and obtain. These are usually works in progress that researchers have circulated before submission for publication or presentation at a conference. Because they have not been reviewed, one must be cautious in how much credence to lend to their findings. As a general rule, you should try to avoid citing unpublished materials unless it is essential.

The Internet has facilitated the rapid expansion of knowledge about many things, including families. Hundreds of organizations interested in families have created sites on the World Wide Web. All the major professional organizations for family researchers, teachers, and practitioners have websites. The National Council of Family Relations has a site at www.ncfr .org. The American Sociological Association is at www.asanet.org; its Family Section is located at www.asanet.org/asa-communities/sections/family/, and its section on Sociology of Children is at www.asanet.org/asa-communities/ sections/children-and-youth. The American Psychological Association's (APA) website is www.apa.org; and its Children, Youth, and Families office site is www.apa.org/pi/families/index.aspx. The National Association of Social Workers can be found at www.naswdc.org, the American Association for Marriage and Family Therapy is at www.aamft.org, and the American Association for Family and Consumer Sciences is located at www.aafcs .org. The National Association for the Education of Young Children can be found at www.naeyc.org, and the Council on Contemporary Families maintains a website at www.contemporaryfamilies.org.

Many federal government agencies are involved with families and children. Some of the federal agencies that fund research and programs on families and related topics include the National Science Foundation's Directorate for Social, Behavioral, and Economic Sciences (www.nsf.gov/ sbe); the National Institute of Child Health and Human Development (www.nichd.nih.gov); the National Institute on Aging (www.nia.nih.gov); and the U.S. Department of Agriculture's Cooperative State Research,

Education and Extension Service (www.usda.gov/topics/rural/cooperative-research-and-extension-services).

Many foundations support research and programs involving families, such as the Annie E. Casey Foundation (www.aecf.org), which sponsors the online KIDS COUNT database (www.aecf.org/work/kids-count/kids-count-data-center/); the Ford Foundation (www.fordfound.org); the Russell Sage Foundation (www.russellsage.org); the Robert Wood Johnson Foundation (www.rwjf.org); and the Children, Families and Communities program of the David and Lucille Packard Foundation (www.packard.org/what-we-fund/children-families-and-communities/) to name just a few. A comprehensive list of charitable foundations can be found at The Foundation Center (fdncenter.org).

Many advocacy groups have websites. A small sampling of these includes Children Now (www.childrennow.org), the Children's Defense Fund (www.childrensdefense.org), ZERO TO THREE (www.zerotothree.org), Focus on the Family (family.org), the National Center for Fathering (www.fathers.com), the Family Research Council (www.frc.org), and the Institute for American Values (www.Americanvalues.org).

As most Internet users are aware, web content is subjected to negligible quality control. Anyone can create a website and post whatever they please without regard to the information's accuracy. Often, individuals or organizations will create websites to support their own agendas, and separating factual (or even meaningful) information from rhetoric and downright deception can be difficult. Further, individuals and organizations may blog about research, complicating web users' ability to discern the distinction between research findings and someone's opinion or interpretations of the findings. Because many sites are relatively short lived, citing a website address can sometimes create problems in a manuscript. By the time the manuscript appears in print, the website may have changed addresses or disappeared completely. For further information about using the Internet in your research, you may wish to consult Fielding, Lee, and Blank (2008).

STUDY QUESTIONS

1. Choose a research topic (e.g., child abuse, marital satisfaction, or elder care). Learn how to use Sociological Abstracts, Web of Science, or PsycINFO and conduct a search on your topic. List five articles that you find that are relevant to your topic.

2. Choose a well-known family researcher and use the index system of your choice to find articles published by that person over the last 10 years.

3. Find an article in a major family research journal, such as *Journal of Marriage and Family* or *Journal of Family Issues*. Compare the structure of the article to that in this chapter. What sections are missing? Are there any key pieces of information absent from the article?

4. Pick any one of the journal articles listed in the References section and report how many times it was cited in the literature for each of the last 3 years.

Sampling Issues

I f we're going to conduct research, we need data. As a researcher, one of the first things you will notice is that we can't possibly collect data on every single person of interest to us. For example, if we wanted to study children in group day care, we couldn't possibly observe each of the more than eight million preschoolers enrolled in group day care centers in the United States today. **Sampling procedures** are the techniques through which we determine which and how many persons, couples, families, organizations, or communities to observe.

Let's begin by defining some sampling concepts. The unit about which information is gathered is known as an **element**. Elements and units of analysis are often (but not necessarily) the same in most studies; elements are linked to the sample-selection process, whereas units of analysis refer to the analysis of the data. For example, a researcher sampling households in a given metropolitan area would select specific households to study; the unit of analysis would be the household, and the focus of the analysis would be some aspect of the household—for example, household income or household size. Alternatively, the analysis might focus on characteristics of the married couples in those households (in which case, the unit of analysis would be the couple) or their children (so that the unit of analysis is each individual child).

A **population** is the complete and inclusive collection of all theoretically defined elements. If the population of interest is all children enrolled in group day care, each child enrolled in group day care is an element in that population. A **sample** is the collection of elements drawn from the population that are actually studied. If we decide to study just those children enrolled at Happy Times Childcare, these children constitute the sample under study.

Of course, if you study only the children enrolled at Happy Times Childcare (an expensive child-care center located in a wealthy suburb), a critic of your study might (with some justification) argue that your results would have differed had you instead studied the children at Dinoland Day Care (which is located in a disadvantaged section of town). After all, suburban child-care centers are likely to charge more, permitting a lower child-to-caregiver ratio and better facilities. In many cases, the research results can be expected to be heavily influenced by who, exactly, is studied.

Sampling procedures help us decide who is studied and how to select those individuals (or households or couples or families or groups or organizations—whichever is our unit of analysis) to produce valid results that can be generalized to the entire population under study. The first step in this process is deciding on the unit of analysis. In Chapter 3, we suggested that family researchers examine data at many units of analysis (e.g., individuals, dyads [couples], coresidential or nuclear families, and extended families) and at various levels of aggregation (individuals, couples, households, communities, states, or nations). For research on families and marriages, this is a particularly important issue; and a great deal of thought has to go into deciding on the unit of analysis. If the unit of analysis is the marriage, does that require that we gather data from both spouses? If the unit of analysis is the nuclear family, do we need to collect data on all members of the nuclear family? Or can we rely on the responses of only one member of the family to provide us with the information we need? If we ask only one spouse, how can we be sure that the information about the other spouse and the rest of the family is valid?

Many family researchers (such as Maguire, 1999; Sayer & Klute, 2005; Szinovacz, 1983; Thomson & Williams, 1982) have wrestled with these issues. Let's take an example. Imagine that a researcher wishes to study the effects of family social status on adolescent drug use. The unit of analysis here is the family (because we are interested in family social status), but how do we measure this construct? Because husbands tend to have higher status jobs than their wives, do we look only at the husband's occupational prestige? Do we somehow combine the husband's and wife's occupational-prestige scores in dual-earner marriages? What about single-parent households? What do we do with divorced couples who have joint custody of their children? These are all issues that the researcher must consider when designing the study that is discussed by Maguire (1999) and by Sayer and Klute (2005) and later in this text in Chapter 13 where we discuss analysis of data from couples or families are the unit of analysis.

Defining the Population

A key issue is defining the population of interest. This process has two steps. First, the target population—the population to which we want to generalize our findings—must be defined. To define the target population, we must specify the characteristics that identify the members of the population. Characteristics such as age, income, education, ethnicity, region of residence, and marital status are typically used. For a study of children enrolled in group day care facilities, the target population might be defined as "all children younger than age 6 years who regularly spend at least 30 hours per week in a child-care facility that houses a minimum of 60 children."

Next, the **sampling frame** must be constructed. The sampling frame is the set of all elements from which the members of the sample—that is, those persons or groups who will actually be studied—are drawn. The sampling frame is constructed in two ways: We can create (or locate) a list that identifies all the relevant elements, or we can construct a rule that defines membership in the population. Unfortunately, there aren't lists of all residents of a particular community, state, or nation. There are lists of taxpayers, but such lists are limited to those who own real estate. There are voter registration lists, but a sizeable percentage of the eligible population isn't registered to vote. There are lists of utility (electric, water, gas, etc.) customers but these omit people who don't pay their own utility bills (e.g., many renters).

On the other hand, if you are doing research on a particular corporation (and you have obtained the relevant permissions) there are lists of that corporation's employees. If you are surveying elected officials, their names are public information. But while school districts certainly have lists identifying their students, such lists are not public record. So, finding a list of the members of the population you want to study is going to be problematic.

For a telephone interview of the residents of a given city, the local telephone directory is an example of a list that identifies all the residents of a particular area with listed telephone numbers. Of course, as cell phones have gradually replaced landline phones, the local directory has become an inefficient method, but these techniques provide an excellent example of using a rule to develop a sample. The set of area codes and telephone exchanges (the three-digit prefixes) in a particular area provides a rule. Unless the list is known to be accurate and up-to-date, using a rule to construct the sampling frame is often preferable. For example, we know that the telephone directory is an incomplete list of persons living in a given area. Not all households have telephones, and not all telephone numbers are listed in the telephone directory. These factors are tied to social class: Working-class households are less likely to have telephones, and middle- and upper class households are more likely to have unlisted numbers or wireless phones that aren't listed in a directory. In addition, the telephone directory is printed only annually, so highly mobile individuals are going to be underrepresented.

A better strategy might be to use the three-digit exchanges and then randomly generate the final four digits of the seven-digit number. This removes the bias of unlisted numbers, includes those with cellular phones and those whose households are too new to appear in the directory, but it doesn't solve the problem of differential telephone ownership by social class. Now, of course, mobile phone numbers are linked to individuals. People keep their phone numbers (including the area codes and three-digit exchange) when they change residences, so using three-digit exchange codes or even area codes to geographically limit a sample probably won't be effective. There is also evidence that response rates are higher for landline phones than for cell phones (Brick et al., 2007), so it is apparent that new strategies need to be developed.

More detail on telephone survey sampling and procedures can be found in Lavrakas (1993) and in Blair, Czaja, and Blair (2013). For an interesting comparison of response rates to mailed questionnaires versus telephone interviews, see Rocheleau et al. (2012).

Ideally, the target population and the sampling frame are identical. In practice, however, this is rarely the case. One problem is that often we want to study persons, families, or couples for whom no lists exist. Moreover, using the rule doesn't identify particular children for study; we still have to go out and find children in the right age group and then determine whether or not they belong in the population of interest. No list exists of "all children younger than age 6 years who regularly spend at least 30 hours per week in a child-care facility that houses a minimum of 60 children." We might be able to obtain lists of children in particular child-care facilities and use them as a sampling frame (though with the concerns raised earlier). However the sampling frame is constructed, the researcher must always be aware of possible biases that might affect the study's results.

Sampling Designs

The next step is to choose a particular sampling technique that will indicate precisely which elements of the sampling frame will be selected for observation (i.e., how to select the elements that will be included in the sample). The goal is to obtain a sample whose data will yield results similar to those that would have been obtained if data were collected on the entire population of interest. Sampling designs may be grouped into two broad categories. In probability sampling, every member of the target population has a known and nonzero probability of being included in the sample; selection must be random. In nonprobability sampling, the probability or likelihood of any given element being included in the sample is unknown, and the selection process is not necessarily random.

Probability Samples

Probability sampling offers two crucial advantages over nonprobability sampling. First, because the sampling uses random procedures based on known probabilities of inclusion, the likelihood that the researcher's intentional or inadvertent biases might affect the nature of the sample is reduced. Second, the use of random sampling allows for the use of powerful statistical techniques to estimate the accuracy of the sampling process. Differences between the characteristics of the sample and those of the population are known as **sampling error**. For example, census data (which includes all the households in the metropolitan area) might reveal that 64% of the households in a particular metropolitan area are headed by married couples. Because the population of interest is the set of all households in that metropolitan area, the 64% value represents what is known as a **population parameter**—that is, the actual value of some statistic for the entire population.

Let's say that we find that in a sample drawn from the population of all households in that metropolitan area only 58% of the households are headed by married couples. This 58% value represents the **sample statistic**—the empirical value determined for the elements included in our sample. The difference between the *population parameter* and the *sample statistic* represents the amount of *sampling error* for that particular sample and measurement procedure. Because in a probability sample the probability of including any specific element in the sample is known, researchers can calculate in advance the expected sampling error for any probability sampling procedure. Therefore, all things being equal, probability samples are preferred over nonprobability samples.

There are three major types of probability sampling procedures. In **simple random sampling**, every element in the sampling frame has a known and equal probability of being included in the sample. If a sampling frame contains 1,000 elements and we are going to draw a sample of 100, then the probability of any given element being included in the sample is 100/1,000, or 1/10. Furthermore, we also know the probability of any combination of elements being included in the sample. A key requirement of simple random sampling is that a list or enumeration of every member of the population must exist from which the sample is to be drawn. Because we rarely have a complete list of all the members of a population, simple random samples are uncommon in social and behavioral research.

In **stratified random sampling**, the population is divided into **strata** (mutually exclusive segments based on some readily observable characteristic such as zip code, county, or gender). Simple random samples are drawn within each stratum, and these subsamples are combined to form the stratified sample.

As an example, let's say that we want to do a statewide survey on the use of corporal punishment by parents. We know that social class, which is often operationalized as family income, correlates with the use of corporal punishment—parents from higher social class families are less likely to use corporal punishment. To ensure that we get a sample of families across a broad range of incomes, we might decide first to classify the counties of the state in terms of median family income (high, medium, low). We then select five counties at random from each of the three groups. Median family income, then, is the stratifying variable in this procedure. We can even have multiple stratifying variables; for example, we might further stratify the counties in terms of how rural they are.

Once the counties have been selected, we can sample families at random within each county. The major advantage of stratified random sampling is that when the stratifying variable is statistically associated with the key dependent variable in the study, the precision of the estimates of the values under study is increased. Under these conditions, a stratified random sample can actually be as precise as a simple random sample of larger size; consequently, stratified random sampling is cost efficient. The drawback to stratified random sampling is that you need to know the values of the stratifying variables before drawing the sample, which is not always possible.

Another advantage of stratified random sampling is that it allows for more precise estimates of values for relatively small groups. In a simple random sample of the population, we find relatively few single-parent households headed by fathers. With a technique called **disproportionate stratified random sampling**, the researcher can obtain a greater proportion of single-father households than occur in the population.

One major drawback of simple random sampling and stratified random sampling is that both require a list of all members of the population. Lists exist of members of various organizations (e.g., voters registered with a particular political party), but lists of the general public are generally unavailable for research purposes. Most government lists of the general public (e.g., the decennial census, income tax returns, social security registration) are confidential, and public lists (voter rolls, driver's license lists, telephone directories, city directories) are often selective or quickly become out of date.

Cluster sampling may be used when it is difficult or impossible to list the members of the target population. For example, lists of "all children younger than age 6 years who regularly spend at least 30 hours per week in a child-care facility that houses a minimum of 60 children" are unavailable, but lists exist of the children enrolled in each facility. In addition, complete lists of all such licensed facilities are available through the state agency responsible for regulation of child-care providers. To select which facilities we would study, we might begin by sampling (perhaps using a stratified random sample based on the number of children in each of the facilities) from the list of all child-care facilities. Then, we could sample within the selected facilities to create our sample. For example, the Longitudinal Study of Australian Children was constructed using two-stage cluster sampling procedures (Misson & Sipthorp, 2007; Soloff, Lawrence, Misson, & Johnstone, 2006).

The major advantages of cluster sampling are that it allows us to draw probability samples even when a list of the target population is unavailable, and its cost is relatively efficient compared to stratified random sampling. The disadvantage is that cluster samples typically have larger sampling errors than stratified random samples of comparable size. Increasing the sample size can offset this drawback (but this, of course, means higher costs). For probability samples, error generally decreases with increasing sample size, but cost increases with sample size. As a result, researchers are almost always faced with a trade-off between reducing sampling error and reducing costs. Usually, cost is the limiting factor; we know how much money is available to spend gathering data and we choose our sample size accordingly. More about choosing a sample size later.

Nonprobability Samples

As mentioned earlier, in nonprobability samples, the probability, or likelihood, of any given element's inclusion in the sample is unknown. Unlike probability samples, nonprobability sampling procedures do not provide control for possible researcher bias in selecting elements for inclusion in the sample, and they offer no means of assessing the amount of sampling error. Despite these drawbacks, nonprobability methods become the preferred alternative in at least four situations where probability sampling is inappropriate, unnecessary, or not feasible.

First, as Marshall (1996) points out, the "probability sampling techniques used for quantitative studies are rarely appropriate when conducting qualitative research" (p. 522). In exploratory or qualitative research, researchers are typically unconcerned with generalizing to a population. In such cases, a nonprobability sampling procedure can be adequate. See Roy, Zvonkovic, Goldberg, Sharp, and LaRossa (2015) for a detailed discussion on sampling in qualitative research. Second, probability sampling is impractical and may even be undesirable when the sample is extremely small. Perhaps the researcher is doing a qualitative study of family dynamics involving intensive observation of families over a period of weeks, thus, necessitating a relatively small sample of families. Creating a random sample of size 10 or fewer is not feasible (and even if you could, the sampling error would be so large as to render any statistical generalizations meaningless). A similar situation arises when conducting single-case studies, where only one case is of interest. A third situation occurs when the population contains only a few elements. Perhaps you wish to do a comparative study of major American religious denominations and their family-life teachings. This population is relatively small, so studying all the elements in the population, rather than a sample from it, is probably worthwhile. Finally, research is often limited to available data. Data and records might be available on only three 19th-century communes in the United States, making any kind of probability sampling meaningless.

Given these situations, four major types of nonprobability sampling procedures might be employed: convenience sampling, quota sampling, purposive sampling, and snowball sampling.

As its name suggests, **convenience samples** are composed of those elements that are convenient for the researcher to study. As an example, suppose we wanted to study preschoolers' reactions to strangers. For practical reasons, we probably wouldn't be able to sample from the population of all preschoolers, but because we know the owner of a local day care center, we might get her approval to study the reactions of the children enrolled there (assuming parental permission, of course) to strangers in a controlled situation. This is an example of a convenience sample because this day care center was chosen primarily because it was readily available ("convenient") to study. Although the results of the study might be interesting and informative, the problem with a convenience sample is that it's never clear to what population (if any) the findings might apply. And, as in all nonprobability techniques, estimating the amount of sampling error (or the value of a population parameter) involved in the procedure is impossible. Most often, convenience samples are used during the exploratory stages of research or when probability samples are impractical to obtain. In their study of sibling abuse, Rapoza, Cook, Zaveri, and Malley-Morrison (2010) drew a convenience sample by having each student in research methods classes recruit two respondents (one male, one female). The sample created in this way was clearly a nonprobability sample because the likelihood of inclusion of any given individual was unknown; respondents were simply willing individuals who were known to the students.

In **purposive sampling**, researchers deliberately attempt to select cases that, in their professional judgment, represent the population of interest. Specific cases are selected precisely because they are believed to be typical. In the reactions-to-strangers study mentioned previously, a researcher might deliberately select one day care center in a suburban area, another in a rural area, and a third in an inner city to study differences in reactions to strangers by children from different types of residential areas. Although purposive sampling may appear to be more scientifically valid than convenience sampling, it is heavily dependent on a comprehensive understanding of the processes under study by the researcher. Marsiglio, Hutchinson, and Cohan (2001) studied young men's procreative identities by using a purposive sampling strategy to deliberately create a sample of men with varying fertility experiences.

Quota sampling involves creating a sample whose characteristics mirror those of some population of interest. Because it is difficult to draw a probability sample of preschoolers, the researcher might instead opt for a quota sample. As in a stratified random sample, the researcher begins by dividing the population of interest into relevant strata such as ethnicity and family income. Then, the proportion of the population that falls into each category of the stratifying variables (e.g., the percentage of families who are below the poverty line) is determined. The goal is to create a sample with the same percentage of preschoolers from families below the poverty line as occur in the population.

Unlike stratified random sampling, however, quota samples do not necessarily select cases randomly; instead, the cases can be selected through any method that the researcher finds feasible. One way to think about a quota sample is to realize that it is really a convenience sample whose composition matches the population along the dimensions of the stratifying variables.

Quota sampling procedures can also be constructed to oversample groups of interest. In their study of interaction among siblings, Connidis and Campbell (1995) developed a multistage quota sampling technique that deliberately oversampled single, divorced, and childless men and women and widowed men who had living siblings.

Snowball sampling is often used to study groups or individuals that are hard to identify or locate. Risman and Johnson-Sumerford (1998) wanted to study issues relating to the division of household labor in dual-career couples who shared household tasks evenly. Because such couples constitute only a tiny fraction of all married couples and because no list exists of such couples, the researchers built their sample by asking each couple that met their criteria to suggest other such couples that might fit the study's requirements. In this sense, the continuing growth of their sample resembled a snowball rolling down a hill, increasing in size as it picks up more snow in its path. One drawback of snowball samples is the fact that there is the possibility for potential bias in the sample because members of a snowball sample often know each other.

How Large Does the Sample Need to Be?

A common question raised by readers of family research has to do with sample size. How small a sample is too small? How can we determine whether a sample is sufficiently large? For simple random samples, the process of determining sample size is relatively straightforward. Generally speaking, determination of sample size boils down to three major considerations: the amount of sampling error that can be tolerated, the amount of variability in the dependent variable, and the cost of gathering data about additional observations. As sample size increases, the amount of sampling error decreases (which is good); but as sample size increases, so does cost (which is bad). Researchers, therefore, are faced with a trade-off: They can draw large samples with relatively small amounts of sampling error but at a high cost; or they can draw smaller samples that cost less but have relatively higher amounts of sampling error. Jacob Cohen (1988) presented a detailed introduction to sample-size determination. For simple random samples, if the amount of sampling error can be determined (or estimated), a simple equation can be used to calculate required sample size.

Here is one basis for comparison: Most national samples of 1,000 to 1,500 cases have sampling error in the plus-or-minus 3% to 4% range. This means we can be relatively confident that the population values—that is, the response we would have obtained had we the resources to collect data on all the members of the sample population—are within 3% to 4% of the sample estimates. Sampling error and sample-size determination for large national samples are complicated by the fact that such surveys almost never use simple random samples; they are more likely to use some type of multilevel combination of stratified random and cluster sampling. Of course, these rules apply only to probability samples; there is no way to estimate sampling error for nonprobability samples.

How Do We Go About Choosing a Sampling Technique?

Given their shortcomings, you might wonder why anyone would use nonprobability samples. Ideally, every research project would use a large, stratified random sample with relatively small sampling errors that render the findings of the study readily generalizable to the population of interest. In reality, however, pragmatic considerations often make it difficult for researchers to work with such samples. Much research is conducted directly by individual researchers without additional assistance, making it impractical to build large samples. The costs of doing stratified random samples make them nearly impossible to use without substantial funding from government agencies or private foundations. And certain kinds of research strategies—in-depth interviews, participant observation, and most qualitative studies, for example—don't lend themselves well to probability sampling.

As a result of these factors, you will find many nonprobability samples as you browse the family science and human development research literature.

Although the findings of these studies may not be readily generalizable to any particular population, they still may be of great value in understanding how social processes operate, especially on topics where relatively little research has been conducted or theory is poorly developed.

STUDY QUESTIONS

1. Find a published report in a newspaper or magazine of a public opinion poll. What information is given about how the sample of respondents was selected? What information do you need to judge the representativity of the sampling procedure?

2. Choose three quantitative research studies on families from professional journals that use different sampling procedures. For each study, identify (a) the population, (b) the type of sampling procedure, and (c) the unit of analysis. For each study, consider whether the sampling procedure appears to be representative of the population.

3. Give examples of three different populations (e.g., the set of all registered sex offenders in New Hampshire) that could be readily sampled using a simple random sampling procedure or other type of probability sampling. Then, give examples of three different populations (e.g., the set of all persons who have nightmares about sharks) that most likely could not be sampled using probability procedures and suggest a possible nonprobability sampling procedure for each case.

CHAPTER

6

How Do
We Measure
Concepts?

S ocial researchers are faced with something of a dilemma when they attempt to measure concepts. Take, for example, a concept such as marital satisfaction. This concept is abstract; you cannot touch, feel, or see marital satisfaction. Yet we somehow have to translate this abstraction into some kind of concrete measurement. We have to figure out a way to get people to tell us, as accurately as possible, how satisfied they are with their marriages.

Much of our thinking about families and children begins with what Babbie (2010) calls *conceptions*. We each have a conception of what defines marital satisfaction. But it's clear that marital satisfaction is not a physical object or quantity that can be readily observed and measured. How do we translate the relatively abstract and unobservable concept of marital satisfaction into something that we can measure and study?

Kaplan (1964) suggested three types of things that can be measured. A **direct observable** is a physical characteristic that can be observed directly, such as the number of people present at a meeting. A person's response to a questionnaire item about the number of people in a household is an **indirect observable**—an indirect representation of a characteristic or object.

A **construct** is a creation based on observation, but it cannot be observed directly or indirectly. Marital satisfaction is an example of a construct. We may be able to observe consequences of marital satisfaction (e.g., marital stability), and we may be able to observe causes or antecedents of marital satisfaction (e.g., an equitable division of household labor between partners), but we cannot observe marital satisfaction itself.

Operationalization is the name given to this process of translating abstractions into concrete measurement processes. In this process, we need to make a number of decisions about how to translate an abstract construct, such as marital satisfaction, so we can measure the marital satisfaction of our selected respondents.

Characteristics of a Good Measurement Procedure

In Chapter 3, we distinguished between variables and their states, levels, or attributes. Parental status is a variable; having no children is an attribute of parental status. Income is a variable; $45,000 is a state or level of income. One important decision to make in the operationalization process is what and how many attributes, states, or levels a variable will have in the measurement process.

A good measurement procedure is characterized by three key qualities. First, the set of attributes representing a variable must be exhaustive and inclusive. That is, all possible responses or states must be represented by a state, level, or attribute of the variable. If we were operationalizing the variable relationship status, we would find that using only the categories *married* and *single* would produce many blank stares from our respondents. We would probably need to include *never married and not cohabiting, divorced but not repartnered, married but separated,* and *widowed* as well as a category for cohabiting couples, *partnered and living together as married.*

Our second concern is that the attributes, states, or levels chosen to represent a variable must be mutually exclusive. No respondent should be able to be placed in more than one category. In the six-category scheme to measure relationship status (never married and not cohabiting, currently married, married but separated, divorced but not repartnered, widowed, and partnered and living together as married), no person could meaningfully claim to fall in more than one category.

Finally, we need to be concerned with our attribute scheme's precision. Ideally, our category scheme should use more, rather than fewer, distinctions when feasible. For example, rather than coding certain respondents as Protestant, it is probably more useful to include the choices Baptist,

Episcopalian, Methodist, and so on. In this way, you can determine how many respondents are of each denomination. But if you fail to allow respondents to identify themselves as Baptist, Episcopalian, or Methodist, you will never know.

Levels of Measurement

These three qualities of measurement processes—inclusive and exhaustive, mutually exclusive, and precision—are important to consider for all variables. The variables themselves, however, may be measured in vastly different ways. Level of measurement refers to the properties that define the measurement process itself. Most social and behavioral data are measured at one of four levels of measurement: nominal, ordinal, interval, or ratio.

Levels of Measurement: Nominal

Some variables have attributes that meet only the minimal requirements of being exhaustive and mutually exclusive. Some examples of variables at the **nominal level of measurement** are religion, race, city of residence, and marital status. Each of these variables, when properly defined, has a set of logically exhaustive and mutually exclusive categories or attributes. In other words, nominal variables identify the attributes associated with a variable without making any statements about whether one state or level is more or less than any other state or level. With variables measured at the nominal level, it's not possible to rank categories along any particular dimension, nor is it possible to state with great precision how much of the attribute is present.

It's also important to note that for nominally scaled variables, the differences between categories are not mathematically meaningful. For example, let's say that we gave the following response choices to the question, "What is your current relationship status?":

1. Currently married

2. Currently partnered and living together as married

3. Married, separated

4. Divorced, not repartnered

5. Widowed

6. Never married and not cohabiting

The fact that we assigned the number 6 to the response "never married" doesn't mean that it's one point better than "widowed" or six times as much as "currently married." For variables scaled at the nominal level, only the categories are meaningful—not the distances or gaps between categories or the numerical values we might arbitrarily assign to the categories for coding purposes.

Levels of Measurement: Ordinal

Variables that are scaled at the **ordinal level of measurement** have all the properties of nominally scaled variables, but they add an important characteristic: The categories are ranked or ordered along some evaluative dimension. That is, unlike nominally scaled variables, ordinally scaled variables are assumed to represent some underlying continuum (e.g., from least to most or least desirable to most desirable). Some examples of variables that are typically measured at the ordinal level are social class (working class, middle class, upper class), marital happiness (not very happy, somewhat happy, very happy), or highest degree obtained (less than high school, high school diploma, college degree, graduate, or professional degree).

Another type of measure that is often considered at the ordinal level is a **Likert scale** item (discussed further in Chapter 7). For example, we might ask respondents to indicate how they feel about this statement: "If a husband and wife both work full time, they should share housework tasks equally." How do you respond?

1. Strongly disagree

2. Disagree somewhat

3. Undecided, not sure

4. Agree somewhat

5. Strongly agree

Notice that such a variable has an exhaustive and mutually exclusive set of categories and that the categories clearly are ranked or ordered along the dimension of agreeing with the idea of sharing the housework. Those who say they "agree somewhat" with the statement are more strongly supportive of husbands and wives sharing housework than someone who says they "disagree somewhat." However, we can't say how much more supportive these people are, and we undoubtedly can't say that someone who agrees somewhat is twice as supportive of husbands and wives sharing housework as someone who disagrees somewhat. For ordinally scaled variables, the differences between categories are not mathematically meaningful because the numbers we assign to the categories merely reflect the ordering of the response choices.

One advantage of ordinal measurement is that people can often make comparative judgments relatively easily, whereas making an absolute judgment is far more difficult. For example, although respondents could probably tell us which aspect of their family lives gave them the most satisfaction, they would be hard pressed to tell us exactly how much more satisfaction they got from their family leisure time than from doing housework chores.

Levels of Measurement: Interval

Besides including all the characteristics of nominal and ordinal variables, variables that are measured at the **interval level** have differences between scale units that are meaningful and constant. A commonly used interval level measure employed in the social sciences is any standardized intelligence test. The scale is designed so that the 10-point difference between an intelligence quotient (IQ) score of 120 and one of 110 has the same meaning as the 10-point difference between scores of 140 and 130 (or, for that matter, any 10-point difference anywhere along the scale).

Although, strictly speaking, Likert-style items don't meet the requirements for interval-level measurement, they are often treated as if they do. Methodologists and statisticians don't seem to agree on whether this type of treatment is appropriate. One way to circumvent this criticism is to combine a number of Likert-style items into a composite index of some construct and treat the scale total as an interval-level measure. There is more on this in Chapter 7.

Levels of Measurement: Ratio

Variables that are measured at the **ratio level of measurement** include all the characteristics of nominal, ordinal, and interval variables. What distinguishes the ratio level of measurement from the other levels is that the scale of measurement has a theoretically defined origin, or zero point. Income in dollars is a ratio-level measure because zero dollars means the absence of money. Number of children in a family is a ratio-level measure because zero children indicates the absence of children in the family. For comparison, note that temperature in the Kelvin scale (K) is a ratio-level measure (because the zero point is theoretically defined as the absence of all molecular motion), but temperature in degrees Fahrenheit (°F) is not a ratio-level measure (because 0°F is an arbitrary point on the scale).

For ratio variables, as for interval variables, the scale intervals mean the same thing at all points on the scale (e.g., a $1 increase in income means the same at all points along the income continuum). For ratio variables, however, it also makes mathematical sense to compare different levels in a multiplicative sense. For example, a family with four children has twice as many children as one with two children; someone who earns $50,000 has twice as much income as someone who earns $25,000. But although 200 K is twice as warm as 100 K, an 80°F day is not twice as warm as a 40°F day.

Summary of Levels of Measurement

It may have occurred to you that the same concept might be measured at several different levels of measurement. Marital satisfaction, for example, can be measured at the nominal level by asking respondents, "Are you satisfied with your marriage?" and offering response choices of "Yes, I am satisfied with my marriage" and "No, I am not satisfied with my marriage." Marital satisfaction can be measured at the ordinal level by asking, "How satisfied are you with your marriage?" and offering choices of "very dissatisfied," "somewhat dissatisfied," "unsure," "somewhat satisfied," and "very satisfied." Similarly, family size might be measured at the ordinal level by classifying families as small, medium, and large or at the ratio level by finding out exactly how many members there are in a given family.

A key reason that level of measurement is so important is that different statistical techniques require measurement at particular levels. Some procedures, for example, are only appropriate for interval- or ratio-level data. Other techniques are appropriate for both nominal- and ordinal-level data, but some are specific to ordinal-level data. We'll talk more about level of measurement and the selection of a statistical test in Chapter 12. Whichever level of measurement is used, however, the key issues in data quality are reliability and validity.

What Are Reliability and Validity?

No measurement procedure is perfect. In statistical terms, no measurement procedure is error free. We know that some respondents will provide incorrect responses because they don't know the answer to our question. Others will deliberately give wrong answers to appear more socially acceptable or answer the questions in the way they think the researcher wants them answered. Still other respondents will be confused by the phrasing or content of the question and answer incorrectly. Some respondents will give different answers to our questions at different times.

Social scientists gauge the amount of error in measurement in terms of reliability and validity. **Reliability** refers to the stability or consistency of a measurement operation. **Validity** refers to whether we're really measuring the concept that we intended to measure. More detailed discussions of each follow.

Reliability

If a measurement is really a good way of operationalizing a construct, then that measurement procedure should yield the same result each time it is used (assuming, of course, that the value of the underlying construct hasn't changed over time). We refer to this type of reliability as **stability**. Another type of reliability deals with whether different observers using the same measurement procedure come up with the same result. This second type of reliability is known as **consistency**.

Stability

In the National Longitudinal Survey of Youth (NLSY; Chase Lansdale, Mott, Brooks Gunn, & Phillips, 1991), a sample of men and women were asked a series of questions about their work, education, and their lives in general. In two separate interviews in 1983 and 1984, women were asked, "At what age did you first have sexual intercourse?" Obviously, a woman's age at first intercourse can't change over time. The response from any particular woman should not change from year to year if the measure is perfectly reliable.

If this measure were perfectly reliable, we would expect to get exactly the same response from each woman at each interview. Typically, however, some responses do change over time. Of the 5,788 women responding to this question at both interviews, only 57% gave the same response both times! Yet of the women who gave different responses, nearly all (90%) gave a response in 1984 that was within 2 years of their 1983 response.

So is this measure reliable or not? One way to think about this issue is to look at the difference between the average age given for first sexual intercourse at the 1983 response and compare it to the 1984 average. Overall, the average difference between the two responses is 0.03 year (about 11 days!). On that basis, we can conclude that the measure has very good reliability. Another way of looking at the reliability of this measure is to think in statistical terms. If this measure were perfectly reliable, the correlation coefficient (a numerical index of similarity) between the 1983 and 1984 responses would be equal to 1.0. For these data, the correlation is about 0.97, suggesting high reliability in the sense of stability.

Consistency

Another way of thinking about reliability is in terms of consistency. Whereas stability refers to the reliability of a measure over time, consistency refers to its reliability across observers or across items. Reliability in the first sense is known as **interobserver reliability**, or agreement; reliability across items is known as **internal consistency**, or internal reliability. In Chapter 7, we discuss the issue of internal reliability in the context of index construction.

If we were doing a study of marital quality, we might have six family therapists observe 10 married couples discussing their marriages. We then ask each therapist to rate the quality of each couple's marriage on a scale of 1 (*very poor*) to 10 (*very good*). We would expect that if all six therapists are using the same criteria to judge the quality of the marriages, they would have a high degree of agreement. If the counselors agree on the marital quality for each couple, the measure of marital quality has reliability in the sense of consistency. We could even calculate an index of agreement where 0 equals no agreement whatsoever between the six therapists and 1.0 equals perfect agreement. Of course, just because six marriage counselors agree on how happy the couples are doesn't mean that their estimates are meaningful or valid.

Validity

In its truest sense, validity refers to how well we're measuring some underlying construct. Are we measuring what we think we're measuring? The ideal way to measure the validity of a measurement operation is to compare the results of the measurement to the actual (real) value of the construct. Unfortunately, this usually isn't possible, because for most of the constructs we want to measure, actual value can't be determined. How can you learn a person's real attitude toward interfaith marriage? How could you know the real level of a person's marital satisfaction?

Consequently, most of our measures are indirect. We rely, for example, on a person's response to our questions about abortion to determine how that person feels about interfaith marriage. When we attempt to get an indication of the real value of the construct, we are aware that our measurement process may be imperfect. Methodologists call a person's real attitude about interfaith marriage the *true* score; responses to our questions about interfaith marriage are the *observed* score. Every observed score is the sum of two parts: the true score plus an error component.

The difference between the true score and the observed score is known as **measurement error**. Some of this error may be **random measurement error**: It is unrelated to the real value being measured. These random errors tend to cancel each other out and won't bias a measurement in any particular direction.

More serious for social and behavioral researchers is **systematic measurement error**, which can bias the result of the measurement process in one direction or another. For example, in a survey of parenting strategies, we might ask parents how many times in the past month they have had to physically punish their children. We expect to find that the responses are going to be biased downward—that is, we expect that parents systematically underreport the use of physical punishment—because many parents feel that use of physical punishment is indicative of a bad parent (even if they themselves use physical punishment). Moreover, parents who frequently use physical punishment are more likely to underreport such activity than those who rarely use physical punishment. Similarly, responses to a question on marital happiness might be systematically biased upward, because people often aren't willing to admit that they are unhappy with their marriages. In other words, the measurement error on these measures is probably not random. Singleton and Straits (2017) present a clear discussion of measurement error in the more general context of reliability and validity.

To deal with these problems, social scientists have developed a number of alternate indicators of a measure's validity.

Face Validity

When we talk about **face validity**, we mean whether the instrument *looks* like it's measuring what it's supposed to be measuring. For example, you wouldn't expect that a measure of marital satisfaction would contain items about the legalization of marijuana or attitudes about gun control.

Of course, just because a measure of marital satisfaction contains items that *look like* they're measuring marital satisfaction doesn't necessarily mean that the instrument is actually measuring what it's supposed to be measuring. For example, we might ask a sample of married persons, "How satisfied are you with your marriage?" with response categories "not very satisfied," "somewhat satisfied," and "very satisfied." Such a measure looks valid from a face validity standpoint; clearly, the question is about marital satisfaction, and the response choices seem to capture the range of possible satisfaction levels. However, the item might have questionable validity if people tend to overreport their actual levels of marital satisfaction.

Criterion Validity

Criterion validity deals with how well a measure correlates with (or predicts) external criteria, including behaviors. There are two major forms of criterion validity. **Predictive validity** reflects the ability of a measure to predict future behaviors or conditions. We could expect our measure of marital satisfaction to correlate highly with how many violent arguments the couple had in the last 12 months. After all, you could assume that if a couple has violent arguments, they are probably not too satisfied with their marriage. Similarly, you would expect a valid measure of marital satisfaction to predict with some accuracy which couples would most likely divorce over the next 5 years.

Criterion validity can also reflect how well a measure correlates with alternative measures of the same phenomenon taken at approximately the same point of time; this type of criterion validity is known as **concurrent validity**. A new measure of spousal communication skills, for example, should correlate well with existing measures of such skills, especially those known to be well validated.

Construct Validity

Construct validity refers to how well a measure correlates with other theoretical constructs. We can expect a measure of marital satisfaction to correlate well with measures of such constructs as marital happiness, affection for one's spouse, and perceptions of fairness of the division of household tasks. If the measure of marital satisfaction did not correlate well with such measures, we would be suspicious that maybe it wasn't really measuring marital satisfaction.

Some writers argue that predictive validity is the most important indicator of a measure's overall validity. When measures of external criteria such as behavior are unavailable, however, construct validity can be a useful indication of how well we're measuring our concept.

Content Validity

Marital satisfaction probably has many different aspects or dimensions. Married persons might be satisfied or dissatisfied with their sex lives, how much work they have to do around the house, how much free time they have, how their paid work relates to their family life, how well they communicate with their spouses, and other dimensions as well. **Content validity** refers to how well the measure taps the full range of dimensions or meanings of the underlying construct.

Some Thoughts on Reliability and Validity

Imagine four different clocks. One of them is broken and always reads six o'clock. Another clock works perfectly but is set exactly 2 minutes ahead of the actual time. A third clock is fast and gains 1 minute every hour. The fourth clock keeps perfect time and is set correctly. Obviously, the fourth clock is both perfectly reliable and perfectly valid. But what about the other clocks?

The broken clock is perfectly reliable. No matter how many times we look at it, it always says the same time: six o'clock. What about the validity of this clock? The clock is exactly right—it is a perfectly valid measure of the current time—twice a day (at six o'clock in the morning and again at six o'clock at night). In fact, if we took our measurements at six o'clock each day, we might conclude that it is perfectly valid. Overall, however, this clock is not a valid measure of the current time, because it is correct only twice in each 24-hour period.

The second clock—the one that is always 2 minutes fast—is also perfectly reliable. If we check the clock each day at six o'clock, it will always read 6:02. As far as validity is concerned, this clock will never have the correct time, but it is an excellent indicator of the correct time.

The clock that gains 1 minute every hour is unreliable. If we check it at six o'clock each day, the clock's reading could be almost anything. Occasionally, this clock would have the correct time, but most of the time it's wrong.

The moral of this story is straightforward. A measure that is perfectly reliable is not necessarily perfectly valid. Yet a measure that is perfectly valid is perfectly reliable; a measure that always gives the correct answer must always give the same answer (assuming that the underlying construct hasn't changed).

Sometimes, a measure that we know is not perfectly valid may nonetheless be useful. None of our measures in the social and behavioral sciences are perfectly valid, but they don't have to be perfect to be of some value to us. Think about that the next time someone is critical of opinion poll results—while the numbers aren't perfect, they are probably a pretty good indication of how people feel.

Finally, keep in mind that the time to have these concerns about reliability and validity is before the instrument is constructed and before the data are collected. Once you've collected your data, it's too late to amend the research protocol. Whenever possible, it is important to assess the reliability and validity of the measures in our research *before* gathering our data. This may necessitate pilot studies or pretests where we gather a small amount of data and evaluate the reliability and validity of our measures before the full-scale data collection begins. It can be invaluable to simply ask someone not connected with the research to read over the questionnaire or other instruments and make some general comments.

STUDY QUESTIONS

1. Give four examples of family-related variables measured at each of the four levels of measurement.

2. Select an article from a recent family or human development journal (e.g., *Journal of Marriage and Family, Journal of Family Issues, Child Development*), and identify three of the major variables in the study. Then, for each variable, identify the level of measurement used in the study.

3. Using the same article you selected above, for each variable, discuss the reliability and validity concerns raised by the authors. If the authors don't make any statements about reliability and/or validity, make sure that you report this.

CHAPTER 7

Working With Scales and Indices

S ome concepts can be easily measured using a single questionnaire item. Marital status, for example, is typically measured with a single item. Other concepts or constructs—particularly those measuring attitudes, psychological traits, or complex behaviors—require multiple questionnaire items to be operationalized in a meaningful way.

There are two reasons why a specific concept might require more than one questionnaire item to be operationalized in a valid fashion. Consider the measurement of marital satisfaction. Most researchers agree that the construct of marital satisfaction is probably **multidimensional**—that is, there are multiple aspects or dimensions of marital satisfaction that are interrelated yet distinct. For example, we might think of how satisfied married persons are with their marital sex lives, how satisfied they are with how well they communicate with their spouses, how satisfied they are with the allocation of power in their marriages, and so on. People who are satisfied with their sex lives might not be satisfied with the allocation of power; those who are satisfied with the quality of communication might not be too happy about their sex lives. Clearly, a valid and reliable measure of marital satisfaction is going to require several questionnaire items to tap these multiple dimensions.

A second reason that multiple questionnaire items might be necessary to measure a single concept is that multiple items are often necessary to create an ordinal measure of the concept. For example, a researcher studying the behavior of dating couples might require an ordinal measure of physical intimacy. Level of physical intimacy might range from no physical contact at all to frequent sexual intercourse, with many levels in between—holding hands, kissing, fondling, petting, and so forth. To measure this concept, the researcher might include a series of questionnaire items about each form of intimate behavior. Note that the concept of physical intimacy is probably **unidimensional**—a single continuum or dimension of sexual intimacy, ranging from least to most intimate.

Scales and indices are the two primary techniques that social scientists employ for handling concepts and constructs that must be measured with multiple items. Babbie (2010) suggests that although they appear to be similar, scales and indices are two different kinds of composite measures (pp. 161–162). An **index** is the result of the simple accumulation of scores to measure the extent or quantity of some attribute. An index of the level of conflict in a marriage, for example, might use multiple questionnaire items to ascertain the level or degree of conflict. A simple index might simply add up the number of *yes* responses to questions about whether the couple argues about various issues in their marriage. Such an index, however, implicitly assumes that each of the conflict areas is of roughly equal importance. Standardized tests such as the Scholastic Assessment Test (SAT) or intelligence quotient (IQ) tests are indices; their scores reflect the extent to which the respondent could correctly answer the questions in the test.

A **scale**, however, is intended to reflect a pattern of responses and can include aspects of the intensity of beliefs or behaviors that may exist. Scales also can take into account the possibility that some beliefs or behaviors are more important or more consequential than others. In the literature on families and children, there are three major types of scales: Guttman scaling, semantic differential, and Likert scales.

Types of Scales and Indices

Guttman scaling, introduced by sociologist Louis Guttman (1950), is based on the notion that attitudes and other concepts may be measured as hierarchical structures. Consider our example of the concept of level of physical intimacy in dating couples. We conceptualize level of physical intimacy as a dimension or continuum ranging from least intimate to most intimate. At the least intimate end of the continuum, we might think in terms of whether a couple holds hands; we might place having sexual intercourse at the most intimate end of the continuum. Between these extremes, there are a range of other behaviors: hugging, kissing, fondling, and so forth.

The idea underlying **Guttman scaling**, as applied to our example, is that if these different types of behaviors really comprise a scale, couples who report the highest level of physical intimacy (sexual intercourse) are likely to be engaging in all or most of the less intimate behaviors as well.

Those who report that they are not having sexual intercourse but fondle are probably kissing and hugging and so forth. Diagrammatically, the response patterns might look like the depiction in Table 7.1.

Table 7.1 Response Patterns for a Perfect Guttman Scale

Level of Intimacy	Response Pattern				
Holding hands	Yes	Yes	Yes	Yes	Yes
Hugging	No	Yes	Yes	Yes	Yes
Kissing	No	No	Yes	Yes	Yes
Fondling, petting	No	No	No	Yes	Yes
Sexual intercourse	No	No	No	No	Yes
Scale score	1	2	3	4	5

A couple with the highest level of physical intimacy would report engaging in all five of the behaviors and receive a scale score of 5; those engaging in only the lowest level of physical intimacy—holding hands—would receive a score of 1. (You could also argue that there should be a scale score of zero for those who didn't answer *yes* to any of the items.) One interesting quality of a Guttman scale is that the scale score reveals exactly where the respondent stands on the continuum being measured: A couple with a score of 2, for example, hugs and holds hands but doesn't kiss, fondle, or have intercourse. Guttman scales are clearly *ordinal*—each score on the scale represents a higher level of intimacy than any lower score—but not *interval,* because the meanings of the intervals between scale scores can be inconsistent. Twiggs, McQuillan, and Ferree (1999) offer an extended discussion of applying Guttman scaling to patterns of husbands' participation in household labor and conclude that husbands' household task performances "do not fit a strict pattern of performing all less sex-typed tasks before they move up to more sex-typed ones" (p. 720).

Semantic differential scales assume that respondents can locate their feelings or attitudes along a series of bipolar dimensions—that is, along several dimensions of extremes, such as valuable to worthless or appreciated to ignored. We might ask married persons how they feel about the housework that they do by indicating, as depicted in Table 7.2, the approximate number on the scale that corresponds to their feelings. A respondent who felt that her housework was appreciated by her family might circle 1 or 2, whereas one who felt that housework was ignored might circle 8 or 9.

Table 7.2	Semantic Differential Scale Measuring Attitude Toward Housework									
Interesting	1	2	3	4	5	6	7	8	9	Boring
Appreciated	1	2	3	4	5	6	7	8	9	Ignored
Valuable	1	2	3	4	5	6	7	8	9	Worthless
Important	1	2	3	4	5	6	7	8	9	Unimportant

One of the advantages of the semantic differential technique is that it allows the respondent's feelings about a concept—housework, in the preceding example—to exist along multiple dimensions simultaneously. Respondents can feel that their housework is appreciated but boring, for example. A full discussion of interpretation and use of semantic differential scales is beyond the scope of this text (the classic treatment is presented by Osgood, Suci, & Tannenbaum, 1957), but a variety of different analytic techniques may be applied to semantic differential data in the search for the underlying dimensions of feelings about the concept under study.

Likert scales are probably the most frequently used format for questionnaire items, especially those dealing with attitudes and opinions. When the response choices are similar to *strongly agree, agree somewhat, unsure, disagree somewhat,* and *strongly disagree,* the response categories are clearly ordinal in nature. Some researchers argue that individual Likert-style items can be treated as interval-level data, but this position is not universally held.

The response choices in Likert-style items are typically given arbitrary numerical values for analytic purposes. The *strongly agree* category might be coded as 5, *agree somewhat* as 4, through *strongly disagree* as 1. For example, to measure attitudes toward the employment of mothers of young children, we might present the items shown in Table 7.3.

The responses to a series of Likert-style items are often summed together to produce a scale score. To reduce the problems of acquiescence bias, some of the items in the scale are usually reversed. Notice that agreeing with item numbers 1 and 4 indicates a positive attitude toward employed mothers, but agreeing with item numbers 2 and 3 indicates a negative attitude toward employed mothers. When summing the scale scores, item Numbers 2 and 4 are reversed (*strongly agree* responses are coded 1, *agree-somewhat* responses are coded 2, and so forth) to produce a scale in which higher total scores means more favorable attitudes toward employed mothers. Greenstein (1996) used a Likert-style scale of gender ideology—that is, beliefs about men's and women's roles in families—in his study of inequalities in the division of household labor and marital quality.

	Response Choice				
Table 7.3 Likert Scale to Measure Attitudes Toward the Employment of Mothers					
Question	**Strongly disagree**	**Disagree**	**Unsure**	**Agree**	**Strongly agree**
1. Employed mothers can create as warm and loving a relationship with their children as mothers who stay at home.	1	2	3	4	5
2. Preschool children are harmed by having an employed mother.	1	2	3	4	5
3. Children cared for outside the home are at greater risk of becoming delinquent.	1	2	3	4	5
4. Having an employed mother provides a positive role model for children.	1	2	3	4	5

Using Existing Scales and Indices

Because so much research is being done that involves studying families and children, many scales, indices, and other measuring instruments have already been developed and tested by researchers. Most of these instruments are in the public domain, and many of the copyrighted instruments are available for use with permission of the original author. Why go to the trouble of creating your own scale when other researchers have already done so?

Where to Find Them

There are two outstanding sourcebooks of existing scales and indices for use in research on families and children. The *Handbook of Family Measurement Techniques* (Touliatos, Perlmutter, & Straus, 2001)—indexed by author, title, and subject—includes descriptions and source information for more than 1,000 instruments that measure marriage and family concepts. *Measures of Personality and Social Psychological Attitudes* (Robinson, Shaver, & Wrightsman, 1991) provides descriptions and source information on more general social-psychological measures. DeVellis's (1991) text is a very good general reference on constructing scales.

Permission, Copyrights, and So Forth

It's important to remember that many published scales, indices, and questionnaire items are copyrighted materials. Although a few scales are commercially produced and the owners require payment for their reproduction, many researchers will gladly give you permission to use their materials for research purposes at no charge, as long as you acknowledge the source of the materials. Write or e-mail the authors at their home institutions (as given in the published materials) to request permission, briefly outlining your proposed research. It's wise to keep a copy of the permission letter or e-mail in your files in case a question arises at some future date.

How Do We Evaluate Scales and Indices?

All the issues regarding validity and reliability discussed in Chapter 6 apply to scales and indices as well as to individual items. Clearly, we want our scales and indices to be both reliable (stable over time) and valid (actually measure what they are intended to measure). Besides these concerns, however, is a problem with multiple-item scales and indices: Many of the underlying constructs that family researchers measure with scales and indices are multidimensional.

Dimensionality

Earlier in this chapter, we discussed the concept of marital satisfaction and how it probably has multiple dimensions or aspects that are distinct yet almost certainly correlated with each other. Now, if marital satisfaction really is multidimensional, the scale or index measuring this concept should tap each of these multiple dimensions. But we have to respect this multidimensionality when we construct and use the scale; we can't simply add up a series of questionnaire items that tap multiple dimensions of marital satisfaction. This is the problem of **internal consistency** (or internal reliability).

Determining Internal
Consistency of Scales and Indices

To determine if a scale or index is multidimensional, two simple statistics often reported are the **split-half reliability** and **Cronbach's** (alpha) coefficient. Alpha is the more general measure, but both range from 0 to 1 and are interpreted in basically the same way: High values (that is, values close to one) indicate high levels of internal consistency and suggest that all or most of the items in the scale are measuring the same underlying concept. Low values, however, suggest that not all the items are measuring the same concept. Typically, alpha values greater than 0.70 or so are considered to indicate relatively good internal reliability, whereas values much less than 0.70 suggest that the scale is probably multidimensional and might better be treated as tapping more than one underlying concept. In a study of psychological distress and victimization among LGBTQ adolescents (Birkett, Newcomb, & Mustanski, 2015), a six-item scale of depression was used that had a Cronbach's alpha of .83.

Factor analysis is often used to study the dimensional nature of scales and indices. Factor analytic techniques (Gordon, 2015) can be used in an *exploratory* mode, to uncover the structure of concepts, or in a *confirmatory* mode, to study how well some predefined structure fits empirical data. Exploratory factor analysis can be used to examine which items in a scale seem to hang together in clusters or factors, suggesting underlying dimensions to the concept under study. For a good example of the use of factor analysis in human development research, see Basáñez et al. (2014).

How Do We Deal With
Missing Data in Scales and Indices?

A common problem encountered by researchers working with multiple-item scales and indices is that of missing data. Often, a respondent will answer some but not all the items in a scale. Construction of a scale score is usually dependent on the respondent having provided codable (that is, nonmissing) responses to all the items in the scale. How do researchers typically deal with this problem?

The first issue to consider when dealing with missing data is why the respondent failed to respond to a particular item or items. Some respondents find certain questions—for example, those dealing with income, sex, or drug use—too personal to answer in a questionnaire or interview. Other questions might not be answered because the respondent didn't understand the wording. A key issue in the treatment of missing data has to do with the respondent's motives and the relationship of nonresponse to other factors. In some cases, no other variables predict whether a respondent will provide a codable response to a particular item. This pattern is known as *missing completely at random:* The missing data do not represent any particular pattern, and every individual has the same likelihood of being a nonrespondent.

Often, however, the pattern of missing responses is related to some other variable or variables. Those with high-income levels seem to be less likely to respond to questions about earnings; those engaging in unlawful activities (e.g., drug use or domestic violence) seem to be less likely to respond to questions about those activities. In this pattern, known as *missing at random,* nonresponse is a function of some characteristic of the respondent.

If the data are truly missing completely at random, the missing data don't present much of a problem for analysis because the respondents who provided complete information are probably representative of the entire population. However, a systematic bias in the pattern of missing data can create serious problems for interpretation. Unfortunately, the pattern of missing data is often not random. Married persons who don't respond to an item about their spouse's income may not know the actual value because the couple is separated. Noncustodial parents who don't answer questions about their children may refuse to answer because of hostility surrounding the custody decision or because they are not involved with their children's lives. Persons undergoing marital conflict may not respond to questions about their family lives, and individuals who are cohabiting with an unmarried partner may indicate in an interview that they live alone. In each of these cases, failure to respond to the questionnaire item suggests a systematic bias in the response pattern.

Strategies for Dealing With Missing Data

One way of dealing with missing data is to simply eliminate from the working or analytic sample any respondent who doesn't provide codable responses to all the items in the analyses. This technique is known as **listwise deletion**, but it has at least two major drawbacks. First, if the data are not missing completely at random, the potential for bias in the working or analytic sample is enormous. It seems unreasonable to expect that those respondents who faithfully answered every single item in our questionnaire are exactly like those who failed to respond to at least one item. Researchers who use listwise deletion will generally perform auxiliary analyses to show that such bias, if present, does not change the substantive interpretation of the analyses.

Another, less common strategy of dealing with missing data is called **pairwise deletion**, in which a respondent is eliminated only from those analyses for which he or she provides a noncodable response. The problem here is that the size of the working or analytic sample can change from analysis to analysis, and it's never clear exactly which collection of respondents is being studied.

As a general rule of thumb, listwise deletion is the preferable technique, especially if the rate of missing data is relatively low (say, fewer than 10%). Missing data rates much higher than 10% require the researcher to consider whether the missing data present a problem for interpretation and generalization of findings. If the researcher goes ahead and submits a paper with relatively high missing data rates, it will be necessary to explain why this happened (e.g., respondents may have refused to answer certain sensitive questions) and why it is not a problem for interpreting the results (perhaps with additional analyses that demonstrate that those respondents who failed to respond to certain items did not differ substantially—say, in terms of age, race, gender, education, and income—from those who did respond). Most statistical analysis packages (R, Stata, SAS, etc.) have options to perform either type of deletion on relevant procedures.

High rates of missing data may suggest exploring other possible avenues, as well. **Means substitution** is one technique often seen in the literature. It assumes that the best estimate or guess for the value of the response that would have been made, had the respondent answered the question, is the overall mean value for that variable in the sample. For example, if a respondent didn't answer our question on number of years of education, we might substitute the mean value for years of education for that sample (based on those respondents who did answer the question). This is probably a reasonable strategy if the data for the education item are missing completely at random, but any systematic bias in the nonresponse patterns means substitution may produce misleading results.

Occasionally, researchers will use other statistical techniques to impute missing values. For example, a researcher may decide to impute a value for income, for those respondents who didn't answer the question, by basing a guess or imputation for income on the respondent's educational level. In some cases, several variables might be combined to produce such imputed values.

Questions about how to deal with missing data are among the most common we receive as professors teaching research methods and statistics. We suggest a simple solution: If there aren't many missing observations—say, less than 10%—use listwise deletion. If you are bothered by eliminating cases, do a comparison of the excluded cases to the included cases on key variables in your study. If there are a lot of missing observations, you have a more serious problem that probably can't be solved by statistical adjustment.

Despite the availability of these techniques, the fundamental question presented by missing data—especially when there are many missing observations—has to do with the underlying source of the problem. *Why* are respondents failing to answer particular questions? If the missing responses are not systematic—that is, if the failure to respond to a particular item is not associated with some other characteristic of the respondent, such as age, ethnicity, income, or education—then the missing data do not usually represent a major problem. However, high rates of nonresponse raise serious questions of questionnaire design and survey administration that probably can't be resolved purely by statistical means. Mailed questionnaires are likely to have the highest rates of missing data; with better questionnaire design and the use of follow-up questions and probes, telephone or personal interviews can usually keep the amount of missing data to an acceptable level. Little and Rubin (1989) give a thorough, but technical, presentation on the problems of missing data.

STUDY QUESTIONS

1. Locate an example of an original (i.e., one that hasn't appeared in previously published work) Guttman, Likert, or semantic differential scale or index in any of the major journals that publish research on families. Reproduce the scale items in your answer. What kinds of reliability and validity data do the authors report for the scale? Is the scale unidimensional or multidimensional? How do you know?

2. Find a published scale or index measuring some family-related concept in either of the two sourcebooks mentioned in this chapter. Then, find two articles in any of the major family journals that use that scale or index. For each article, report whether the authors use the scale or index as it was published or made modifications to the scale.

3. Think of two questions to which respondents might be likely to fail to respond in a mailed questionnaire. For each of the variables, discuss whether such nonresponse is likely to be random or systematic. If you think that the nonresponse is likely to be systematic, with what variable or variables would it be associated?

Studying Families and Children

Methods for Quantitative Data

After the variables of interest have been identified, the literature has been reviewed, and a research question or a hypothesis has been presented, the questions become, "How will the data necessary to study this problem be obtained?" "What technique of data collection should be used?"

One way to think about research methods is to imagine trying to listen to a distant radio station. Many factors make it hard to follow the broadcast: background noise, static, or maybe another station transmitting on the same frequency. You need to separate the signal from the noise. Just as a good radio receiver will allow you to pick out that weak radio station from the background noise, a good research design helps assess the true effect of some independent variable (or variables) on the dependent variable (or variables). Poorly executed research designs don't reduce the amount of background noise, making it difficult to draw any meaningful inferences from the data; the effect is lost in the noise created by extraneous factors. A good research design, however, will make it possible to separate the signal from the noise and determine any effect the independent variables are having on the dependent variable.

Researchers studying families and children have a wide assortment of research strategies from which to draw. It is essential to choose the right research strategy for the topic at hand. After we review the available research strategies in this chapter and in Chapters 9 and 10, we will return to the issue of how to select the best strategy for a particular research topic. Each of the strategies reviewed in this chapter—experiments, survey methods, observation, and nonreactive techniques—has both advantages and disadvantages to the researcher and to the topic being studied. This chapter is focused on methodologies that typically yield data which can be coded using numbers and can be analyzed using statistical procedures like those described in Chapter 12. While these research designs can also produce data that are textual, or more qualitative, we focus here on the methods and logic of collecting quantitative data.

Studying Families and Children Through Experiments

The idea of an experiment often conjures up images of a psychologist doing laboratory research. While experimental designs are relatively uncommon in research on families and children (with the notable exception of child development research, noted below), the basic logic of experimentation guides our decisions in other types of research strategies. Knowing something about the logic and design of experimentation can be useful even when using other research strategies.

In most experiments, the independent variable is manipulated—changed or modified by the researcher—to observe the effects on the dependent variable. In experimental design, the independent variable is often referred to as the **manipulation** or **treatment**. When we think of experiments, we're usually thinking of what are known as **laboratory**

experiments. This kind of experiment is usually conducted under highly controlled conditions. The ability to create precisely those conditions necessary to test a theory's predictions makes laboratory experiments especially valuable in testing formal theoretical models.

Bridges and Orza (1993) presented a good example of a laboratory experiment with their study of college students' evaluations of mothers differing in employment patterns following childbirth. Students received a written description of a hypothetical married mother and randomly were informed that the mother either (a) was continuously employed (resumed full-time employment following a 6-week maternity leave), (b) interrupted her employment (remained out of the labor force until her child was in the first grade), or (c) discontinued her employment at the time of the child's birth. The students were then asked to indicate how favorably they evaluated the mother. The independent variable here—the manipulation—is the employment status of the mother, whereas the evaluation of the mother is the dependent variable or outcome. The students reported a less favorable evaluation of the continuously employed mother than either the mother who interrupted her employment or the mother who discontinued her employment.

For obvious ethical reasons, laboratory experiments are usually impractical in family research. Imagine the outcry if a researcher wanted to conduct a laboratory experiment to study the effects of family structure (two-parent vs. single-parent) on child well-being and decided to randomly assign children to households! Social scientists do not usually have the freedom and flexibility to manipulate conditions the way physicists and biologists do. Exceptions arise when studying child development, as the field of developmental psychology has a strong tradition of using laboratory experiments to understand how the social environment shapes children's intellectual and psycho-social growth.

As an example, Chernyak and Sobel (2016) used laboratory experiments to better understand sharing behaviors among four- and five-year-olds. While most research on sharing behaviors among preschoolers suggests that they share equally and expect other children to do the same, their research looked at whether the value of the objects being shared makes a difference. It did, and they concluded that "value may be one way through which children resolve conflicts between fairness and favoritism" (pp. 348–349).

Another type of experiment is the **field experiment**, which is often conducted as part of a social or educational program. Field experimentation combines elements of laboratory experiments and observational research in natural settings. Three major advantages typify field experiments. First, they allow for the modification of the existing real-world environment suitable for testing a theory. Second, field experiments use the existing environment to disguise or conceal the nature or existence of the experiment.

Finally, field experiments may be used either to test a theory in a natural setting or to apply a technique suggested by a theory. Another common use of field experiments is to evaluate the effectiveness of an innovative program. Researchers studying the effectiveness of a domestic-violence deterrence program might design a field experiment to compare domestic-violence rates in areas using the new program to comparable rates in areas under the existing program.

One well-known example of a field experiment in the study of families is the Seattle and Denver Income Maintenance Experiment (Hannan & Tuma, 1975). In this project, approximately 5,000 low-income families were randomly assigned to one of four experimental conditions: three different levels of financial support plus one control condition in which no financial support was provided. Some of the literature suggests that such income-support programs should make single mothers more attractive as potential spouses and, consequently, should affect the rate at which single women in the program would marry, but no such effect was noted in the experiment. Another body of literature suggests that such income-maintenance programs might have negative effects on marital stability—that is, married couples who receive income subsidies will be more likely to dissolve their marriages. Overall, income maintenance did tend to increase the rate of marital dissolution.

A recent example of a field experiment studying child well-being is presented by the Moving to Opportunity experiment (Chetty, Hendren, & Katz, 2016). Randomly selected families received housing vouchers that allowed them to move from high-poverty housing projects to lower-poverty neighborhoods. They concluded that "moving to a lower-poverty neighborhood when young (before age 13) increases college attendance and earnings and reduces single parenthood rates" (p. 855).

Another interesting example of a field experiment is Ownbey, Ownbey, and Cullen's (2011) study of home visitation programs based on the Health Families America model (HFA). They compared a treatment group of 140 at-risk mothers to a comparison group of 241 at-risk mothers and found that mothers who participated in the HFA program were significantly less likely to have rapid repeat births or teen repeat births.

The design of experiments—whether conducted in the laboratory under highly controlled conditions or in natural settings—is guided by consideration of **threats to validity**. This concept was introduced by Campbell and Stanley (1963) and elaborated on by Cook and Campbell (1979) to describe the various ways in which uncontrolled or extraneous factors can present alternative explanations of research outcomes. These alternative explanations can rival or conceal the presumed true effect—the effect of the independent variable on the dependent variable. Consequently, the most scientifically credible research designs should rule out these alternative explanations or threats to our ability to make inferences.

Campbell and Stanley outlined the major types of experimental designs and how each deals with the various threats to validity, which can be grouped into two broad categories. Eight possible threats to internal validity directly compete with our evaluation of the effects of the independent variables. The four possible threats to external validity deal with the generalizability of the results to settings other than that which is directly studied.

Threats to Internal Validity

Attrition refers to the fact that not all respondents who are present at the beginning of the experiment will be present for subsequent testing or measurement. Some respondents may move away, die, have scheduling conflicts, or simply choose not to appear for the study. If the attrition or loss of respondents is random or nonsystematic, it typically does not present a problem for interpreting the study's results. However, if differential attrition occurs—for example, certain kinds of respondents (e.g., low-income persons) are more likely to leave the study than others—it can complicate interpreting the effects on the dependent variable.

History refers to naturally occurring events that may affect the outcome of the study. For example, if your study was on the effectiveness of a series of television public service announcements about family violence and during the study a celebrity was arrested for assaulting his wife, this naturally occurring event could affect the reactions of your television audience to the announcements.

Instrumentation deals with changes in the measurement instruments or operations. Changing observers or measuring instruments over the course of the experiment may produce unintended effects on the dependent variable.

Maturation refers to changes in the participants as a result of time passing. Getting older and growing tired or hungry are examples of maturation; one's behavior changes as one ages or becomes tired, with possible effects on the dependent variable of interest.

Selection has to do with how respondents are assigned to treatment groups for the experiment. Selection is a particularly important problem if respondents are not assigned randomly. Imagine that a researcher is trying to evaluate the effectiveness of an anger-management training program for spousal abusers. Individuals are invited to participate in the program, but they cannot be required to do so. The spousal abusers who decide to participate are probably different in important ways from those who do not, and these differences could affect the outcome of the study.

Statistical regression can be a problem when respondents are assigned to groups based on extreme scores on a scale. It is well known that individuals who score at the extremes on an instrument tend to exhibit change in their scores toward the mean or average value over time. For example, high scorers on a measure of aggression tend to have lower scores when retested, even though the individuals' aggressive tendencies may not have undergone any real change.

Sometimes, simply responding to a questionnaire or other measuring instrument can produce changes in the respondents. **Testing effects** occur when respondents change their responses as a consequence of encountering the measuring instrument. For example, if answering questions about abortion causes respondents to rethink their attitudes about the issue, they may change their responses to the interview.

Finally, two or more threats to internal validity may combine to form what is known as an **interaction** effect. One common interaction effect is between selection and history. If participant assignment to control and experimental groups is not done at random (but instead the selection is done on the basis of some specific criterion such as school enrollment or place of residence), then the participants may experience different histories that may appear to be effects of the manipulation but in fact are due to preexisting conditions.

Threats to External Validity

The **reactive effect of testing** refers to the possibility that responding to a pretest might affect the respondent's reaction to the experimental manipulation, making it difficult to generalize the results of the experiment to nonpretested populations. In the anger-management training program mentioned earlier, the study might begin by giving the respondents a pretest consisting of a number of scenarios describing arguments between spouses and asking them to indicate what they would do in that scenario. The pretests would be scored in terms of how often the respondents indicated that they might resort to violence. Then, the respondents receive the anger-management training. The pretest questionnaire could sensitize the respondents to react differently to the training from the way they would if they hadn't encountered the pretest. Because spouse abusers outside the experiment would probably not receive the pretest before undergoing the training program, those results might be different from those in the experiment.

Interaction of selection and treatment occurs especially when respondents are not randomly assigned to treatment conditions. Imagine that a community wishes to evaluate the effectiveness of a marriage-preparation course. Volunteers are solicited from the population of engaged couples in the community. It's likely that those couples who volunteer to participate in such a program are different in important ways from couples who do not: They are probably more highly motivated, have more free time, and may have a stronger commitment to their partners than those who do not volunteer. These differences may interact with the effects of the marriage-preparation course to produce misleading results. In this case, the program might look much more effective than it really is.

The **reactive effects of experimental arrangements** refer to the fact that people who are aware that they are in an experiment may behave differently than they would normally. Also known as the *Hawthorne effect* (Roethlisberger & Dickson, 1939), this phenomenon results when the observational process itself causes the respondents to change their behaviors.

Multiple-treatment interference occurs in experiments where there are multiple treatments provided to the same set of respondents. In such studies, the effects of one treatment may be contingent on respondents having received some other treatment.

Dealing With Threats to Validity

Two techniques are unique to experimental designs that can eliminate or at least reduce many threats to internal validity. Creation of a **control group** provides a basis of comparison to a group (typically known as the **experimental group** or treatment group) that receives the experimental treatment. Control group members are typically treated in exactly the same way as those in the experimental group except that they do not receive the experimental treatment. (In some studies, the control group receives a placebo treatment designed to create the impression that they are receiving some type of experimental treatment.) At the end of the experiment, scores on the dependent variable for the participants in the control group are compared to the scores of those in the experimental group. All things being equal, differences between the responses of the control and experimental groups may be evidence of a genuine effect of the experimental treatment.

One problem with conducting experiments is ensuring that the participants' characteristics in the experimental and control groups are the same. In other words, at the start of the experiment, the control and experimental groups must be as nearly equivalent as possible. Otherwise, it may be difficult to conclude that any differences observed at the end of the experiment were really due to the effects of the experimental treatment (as opposed to some preexisting differences between the two groups). **Random assignment** is the primary technique used to achieve this equivalence. Assigning participants to the control and experimental groups randomly—especially when the groups are not excessively small—tends to create groups that are similar with respect to both measured and unmeasured characteristics. Without the use of control groups and random assignment, the results of experiments can be difficult to interpret. Campbell and Stanley (1963) distinguished between what they call **quasi-experimental designs**—which have some kind of control or comparison group but do not use random assignment to create the groups—and true **experimental designs**, which use randomization. Schutt (2009) presented a good introductory treatment of these experimental design issues.

Studying Families and Children Through Survey Methods

Most of us have had some experience with survey methods. If you're like us, you probably get several e-mails, mailings, or phone calls a month asking questions about what products you buy or which candidates you support. The mailed (or e-mailed) questionnaire has become an unwelcome guest in our mailboxes and inboxes. Maybe you have even had an interviewer come to your home or place of work to ask you questions directly. It's hard to miss the barrage of survey results on all manner of current events that appear in our magazines, newspapers, and the broadcast media.

Most survey research—regardless of whether the data are gathered by mail, over the phone, on the Internet, or in person—has three basic elements in common. First, survey research usually involves a relatively large number of respondents chosen to represent the population of interest. For most social research and public opinion polls, these samples are derived through probability sampling, most often some type of stratified random sample (sampling issues are discussed in Chapter 5). Second, the questions themselves are usually (but not always) closed-ended questions: The respondent is asked a question and given a limited number of possible responses from which to choose. Third, the responses are usually numerically coded and analyzed using computer software.

In comparing the major formats of survey research—mailed questionnaires, telephone interviews, Internet surveys, and personal interviews—we want to focus consideration around four major concerns: **response rate** (what percentage of the sample will actually respond to our questions), potential for **interviewer bias** (where the interviewer's characteristics affect the respondents' responses to the survey instrument), opportunities for flexibility and quality control, and cost.

Mailed Questionnaires

We all receive questionnaires in the mail. Some are from legitimate researchers; some are from political organizations seeking to bolster their candidate's standing; most are from marketing-research organizations promoting a product or gathering information to aid them in their marketing strategies. Mailed questionnaires are by far the least expensive survey format because they don't incur telephone expenses or interviewer or travel costs.

Minton and Pasley (1996) compared parenting styles of nondivorced fathers to divorced, nonresidential fathers using mailed questionnaires to 270 fathers. Their results indicated that divorced fathers felt less competent and less satisfied in their parenting role than nondivorced fathers.

Although the presentation of the questionnaire is standardized (i.e., no interviewer variations bias the respondent), certain populations are less likely to respond to mailed questionnaires. Those with poor reading skills, those who don't know the language of the questionnaire, and members of disadvantaged groups are less likely to respond to mailed questionnaires, thus creating significant problems of under- or overrepresentation of various groups.

The response rate to mailed questionnaires tends to be relatively low; even with repeated follow-ups, it is difficult to attain a 75% response rate in surveys of the general public. Surveys of specialized populations—for example, members of a professional organization or graduates of a particular university—tend to have better rates of response. Adding to the nonresponses of those who fail to return the questionnaire at all are those who respond only to some items in the questionnaire, a behavior that is more common in mailed questionnaire research than in the other formats.

Mailed questionnaires may be the optimal choice (a) when the researcher must keep costs to a minimum and is willing to tolerate relatively low response rates and (b) when the topic of the questionnaire is relatively straightforward. One key drawback to mailed questionnaires is that the lack of interaction between the researcher and the respondent, which excludes the possibility of in-depth questioning and clarification of questions, makes it difficult to ask questions about complex behaviors and attitudes.

Telephone Interviews

Historically, conducting survey research by telephone offered several benefits. First, the costs are relatively low; although generally more expensive than mailed questionnaires, telephone surveys are significantly cheaper than face-to-face interviews. Second, the ability of the researcher to directly oversee the interviewing staff and answer questions in real time allows a high degree of quality control over the process. Telephone surveys at one time had relatively high response rates and were a favored approach to collecting survey data. In recent years, though, response rates to telephone surveys have been declining.

The proliferation of mobile phones poses a different dilemma. Household phone numbers, or landlines, allow for households to have one contact point. Mobile phones are connected to individuals, allowing for greater access to individuals, rather than households, as the unit of analysis. Although the use of random-digit dialing allows for contacting individuals with unlisted numbers, an obvious major disadvantage of telephone surveys is that the potential respondent must have a telephone to be interviewed. We tend to think of telephone ownership as a sort of universal constant, but less than 94% of American households have telephones. About 1 in 4 low-income households does not have telephone service, creating the potential for serious bias in the kinds of populations that can be meaningfully studied.

Aided by the development of computer-assisted interviewing, the technology for doing large-scale survey research in a cost-effective fashion emerged quickly over the last 50 years. The integration of computers and telephone systems enabled researchers to conduct nationwide surveys quickly and efficiently. If the potential bias created by variations in telephone ownership across populations is not a consideration, then telephone interviews may be the method of choice. Buchanan, Maccoby, and Dornbusch (1991) used telephone interviews with 522 adolescents approximately 4.5 years after their parents divorced to study whether the children felt *caught* between their parents. Not surprisingly, they found that children were most likely to feel caught when their parents were in high conflict and least likely to feel caught when their parents cooperated.

However, completion rates for telephone interviews have dropped dramatically in recent years. This decline has appeared both in terms of contact rates—that is, whether the interviewer can actually speak to the respondent identified by the sampling frame—and in response rates. As an example, the Pew Research Center (see, for example, Kohut, Keeter, Doherty, Dimock, & Christian, 2012) reported declines in response rates of 36% in 1997 to 9% in 2012. Why has this happened? Couper (2017, pp. 125–126) lists three factors that have made the use of telephone interviews problematic.

1. The ease of screening out unwanted calls and the use of caller ID and voicemail makes it easy for potential respondents to ignore the request for an interview, and the widespread use of cell phones (as opposed to landlines) has made it more difficult and more expensive to contact and interview potential respondents because it is so much easier to screen incoming calls.

2. There are substantial differences between cell phone and landline-only households: political attitudes and behavior, Internet use, social views (Christian, Keeter, Purcell, & Smith, 2010), and health and health-related behaviors (Blumberg & Luke, 2016).

3. The portability of wireless telephone numbers makes it more difficult to construct geographically based sampling frames; one can have essentially any telephone area code and live in any part of the country (landline phones, of course, always have the area code of the residence in which they are located).

As Couper (2017) points out, these issues are not insurmountable but they do make telephone interviewing less desirable (and more expensive) than it used to be. In his presidential address to the American Association for Public Opinion Research, Dillman (2002) noted that "The telephone, which seemed the heir apparent to face-to-face interviews, is no longer an obvious choice for conducting many surveys" (p. 473).

Personal Interviews

Personal, or face-to-face, interviews are by far the most expensive mode of survey research. Costs of training interviewers and getting them to the respondents' homes or workplaces, especially in national samples, can be extremely high. Balanced against this high cost, however, are several distinct advantages. First, response rates tend to be relatively high. Second, the presence of the interviewer allows for the use of open-ended questions. Third, the interviewer can easily apply skip patterns (when certain questions are skipped contingent on the response to prior questions). Fourth, the interviewer can clarify questions that the respondent does not understand and probe if the response is unclear or superficial. Finally, interviews that are too long to be practical using mailed questionnaires or telephone interviews can often be accomplished using personal interviews.

Two other issues complicate the use of personal interviews. First, interviewers may introduce bias into the interview process (see the discussion about nonreactive measures that follows for some examples of how to avoid such bias). Also, certain types of respondents may be difficult to locate; young minority males, for example, are especially difficult to find at home. If sufficient funds are available, however, personal interviews are clearly the survey method of choice. Secret and Peck-Heath (2004) conducted personal interviews with 97 mothers, drawn from a random sample of public assistance recipients, to study the relationship between maternal employment and child well-being. In general, children whose mothers were employed had better health than children whose mothers had been unemployed for at least 2 years. Interestingly, children had better school performance if their mothers had either long-term employment or long-term unemployment, suggesting that the stability of maternal employment (rather than work status) was the key factor.

Time Diary Methods

Time-use diaries are often used when researchers want to collect information about how people spend their time, especially with regard to paid employment hours, leisure time, household work, and child-care. The diaries can be completed during a personal or telephone interview or through a self-administered form mailed to or left with the respondent.

Bryant and Zick (1996, pp. 369–371) presented an interesting summary of time-use **diary studies** going back to the 1920s, when the U.S. Department of Agriculture did a series of studies asking women to keep time-use diaries for a week (Kneeland, 1929). The use of such methods has continued to the present day, for example in Robinson and Godbey's (1999) work on leisure time and Jacobs and Gerson's (2004) research on family time pressures.

There are actually a number of techniques used to gather estimates of time use. Beeper studies equip a respondent with a pager or *beeper* programmed to beep at random. The respondents are instructed to record what they were doing (and in some cases, what they were thinking) when the beeper goes off. Telephone surveys, such as the American Time Use Survey discussed in Chapter 11, ask respondents to detail their activities during the previous 24 hours, noting their primary and secondary activities, the duration of those activities, and the presence of others during those activities.

In this literature, there is some debate as to the relative validity of different types of methods of measuring time use. Jacobs and Gerson (2004) presented a discussion of these issues, noting that some researchers (Robinson & Godbey, 1999) feel that time diaries provide more valid information because the diary entries are more detailed than the results of the other techniques. Others (Schor, 1991) contended that estimates based on time diaries are biased because the busiest people may be less likely to complete them. It may be that combinations of time-use data collection methods are necessary to obtain a complete picture of how people spend their time.

Surveys Over the Internet

According to Dillman, Smyth, and Christian (2009), "the two most significant advances in survey methodology during the 20th century were the introduction of random sampling in the 1940s and interviewing by telephone in the 1970s" (p. 352). The use of the Internet to collect survey data—through e-mailed questionnaires or interactive sites on the World Wide Web—promises to be equally important, perhaps even transformational.

Although e-mailed surveys are relatively limited in their ability to present complex survey questions and branching options—they are really mailed questionnaires delivered electronically rather than on paper through the mail—interactive online surveys have a number of attractive features. First, they are inexpensive; other than the instrument development and data processing, for which costs are incurred in any type of survey, the only costs involved are those for the hosting of the website itself. Second, the questions can offer sophisticated interaction between the respondent and the questionnaire. Complex skips and branches in the flow of questions can be easily programmed into the questionnaire but remain invisible to the respondent. Drop-down boxes with large numbers of choices simplify responses; pop-up menus can offer clarification. Graphics and audio-video information can easily be incorporated into the questionnaire.

For all their advantages, online surveys have notable disadvantages, too. Some possible respondents may not have the computer hardware and software required to handle cutting-edge websites. Some websites may appear differently on different kinds of browser software. By far the most serious problem, however, is presented by inequalities in access to the World Wide Web. Research (National Telecommunications and Information Administration, 1999) suggested that large differences in web use and access may exist by social class, race, and gender. In 2009, about one third of U.S. households had no online access (National Telecommunications and Information Administration, 2010). Consequently, current online surveys are likely to draw responses disproportionately from white, male, upper-middle-class respondents, but this situation is likely to change as online access becomes more widely available.

A recent example of an online survey is provided by Lannutti's (2005) study of the meanings of same-sex marriage. In this study, respondents were directed to a web-based survey and were asked open-ended questions about how they thought legal recognition of same-sex marriage might affect the lesbian, gay, bisexual, and transgendered community.

Other Modes of Survey Research

Some survey research involves leaving with respondents the questionnaires that will be picked up later or mailed back to the researcher. Other techniques involve having groups of respondents (e.g., in a classroom or workplace) complete questionnaires with researcher supervision. Both techniques allow some face-to-face contact with the respondent to clarify questionnaire items.

There is a lot of survey data collection out there that is not used for research purposes as we've described here. So-called push polls, usually conducted by political polling organizations, are designed not so much to gather public opinion but to shape it. The questionnaire items are written to increase positive responses about the chosen candidate or issue; the survey results are then used to prop up the candidate or issue in the press. Customer satisfaction surveys can be used for the purpose of improving service or, alternatively, to craft an image of the organization. One example with which you may be familiar is the automobile service survey. One of us had our car serviced by a local dealer; along with the itemized statement, we received a sample of a service survey that customers might get in the mail from the car's manufacturer asking questions about the service quality. On the sample questionnaire, all of the *completely satisfied* or otherwise highly positive responses were checked (in red ink, no less!). One has to wonder whether such a procedure produces valid information about customer satisfaction or whether the real purpose is to merely produce glowing responses about the dealership's service department. Online review tools such as TripAdvisor and Yelp fuel the culture of "survey" as a tool for crafting an image of an organization, thus undermining the use of surveys as scientific data collection strategies.

The issue of questionnaire design has been the subject of many books and articles. Schutt (2004), Blair, Czaja, and Blair (2013), and Dillman, Smyth, and Christian (2009) presented detailed discussions of the major concerns in constructing questionnaires and other types of survey instruments.

Studying Families and Children Through Nonreactive Techniques

Experiments, surveys, and observational techniques all intrude on the respondent's world. Consequently, they may affect the responses in such a way that the validity of our findings is impaired. Nonreactive techniques (sometimes called unobtrusive techniques) are designed to avoid intruding on the respondent's world by removing the researcher from the setting or behavior being studied. The errors that reactive or obtrusive research designs create can be examined in terms of whether they are introduced by the respondent or by the researcher. The following discussion draws from Webb, Campbell, Schwartz, and Sechrest's (1999) classic treatment of the subject.

Four Kinds of Errors Introduced by the Respondent

1. *The Guinea Pig Effect.* When people know that they are participating in a research project, they may alter their behavior. When we know people are watching us, our behavior may be different from when we think we are alone and unobserved.

2. *Role Selection.* People who are participating in research projects sometimes role-play or act the way they think the researcher wants them to act. Knowing that they were selected because they were members of a dysfunctional family, participants in a study on dysfunctional families might respond in unusual and unpredictable ways to an interviewer's questions. If, instead, potential respondents had simply been told that they would be participating in a general study about families, they might have given more valid responses.

3. *Measurement as Change Agent.* Sometimes, the research instrument itself can create change in the people it is studying. Perhaps the respondent might be asked questions about the appropriateness of child day care for children younger than 3 years old. A particular respondent might not have thought about this problem before, but being confronted with these questions might lead the respondent to form opinions on the spot—opinions the respondent, if not asked the questions, might not have formulated.

4. *Response Sets.* Respondents in a research study don't always respond honestly to the interviewer's questions. Sometimes, respondents tend to agree with statements, no matter how the statements are worded; this is known as the **acquiescence response set**. This response set is sometimes avoided with pairs of items constructed so that a respondent's agreement with both items represents an apparent contradiction that is apparent to the researcher.

Some respondents feel the need to make a good impression to present a favorable image to others. Such respondents may give what they believe to be the correct or socially acceptable responses to the questions. This type of response set is known as **social desirability**. It is well known, for example, that respondents overreport such socially acceptable behaviors as voting and underreport unacceptable behaviors such as child abuse. Studies of family life are particularly susceptible to problems with social desirability because of strong social norms about what constitutes a good family or good parenting. Many respondents may be unwilling to admit to behaviors that contradict these social norms.

Ordinal biases (also called positional biases) represent a third type of response set. Here, the order in which the questions are asked may affect the responses obtained.

Three Kinds of Errors Introduced by the Researcher

1. *Interviewer Effects.* Subtle and not-so-subtle aspects of the interviewer's demeanor and appearance can affect responses to our research.

Imagine how the race of the interviewer might affect responses to questions about race relations or how the results of interviews about police brutality conducted by police officers might be influenced. Even such factors as style of dress and variations in speaking styles (accents, grammar) might affect responses to an interview. In studies of families, the race and gender are potential sources of bias. Ethnic respondents may not be forthcoming about their family practices with outsiders, and some white respondents might be less than candid with interviewers of other races. Both male and female respondents might be unwilling to share the details of their intimate relationships with opposite-sex interviewers.

2. *Changes in the Instrument.* It's difficult to keep social science instruments constant over time. Interviewers change inflections; questions may have to be reworded in light of current events; alternate questionnaire versions may be necessary to avoid the biases created by response sets. When such changes occur, it is always problematic to discern whether the effects on the dependent variable are caused by the independent variable under study or are artifacts created by changes in the instrument.

3. *Population Restrictions.* It's not always obvious how much the data collection technique can affect the composition of the sample under study. We tend to think of the telephone as present in every U.S. household, but 1 in 4 central-city households with incomes less than $5,000 doesn't have a telephone (National Telecommunications and Information Administration, 1999). Clearly, using phone interviews can bias the sample away from low-income households.

Mailed questionnaires are also problematic for some populations, because they require the respondent to be able to read and have good enough English-language skills to understand and respond to the questions (not to mention having a mailing address). If the researcher doesn't provide interviewers who are fluent in languages other than English or provide alternative versions of the questionnaire, a sizable percentage of U.S. households will be eliminated from the sample; the 1990 Census indicates that as many as 3.1% of all adults in the United States do not speak English well enough for a survey interview.

Types of Nonreactive Research

Physical Traces

Human beings often leave behind evidence of their behaviors, often unaware that they've done so. When this evidence takes the form of selective wear or degradation of artifacts, it is known as **erosion**. When the evidence takes the form of the selective deposit of materials, it is known as **accretion**.

Erosion measures refer to selective wear that yields data that may be used to test theories or hypotheses about behavior. Some examples of erosion measures include assessing the popularity of museum exhibits by measuring the amount of wear on the flooring, use of library materials by assessing deterioration of bindings, and use of particular sites on the Internet by assessing the degradation of response time for the website's server.

Accretion measures deal with a selective deposit of materials. Whenever anthropologists study pottery shards, they are studying the selective deposit of materials unknowingly left behind by the people who made them. Other examples of accretion measures include estimating radio audiences by noting the stations to which car radios are tuned when they come in for service, studying the social class of the clientele of entertainment establishments by noting the book value of cars parked outside, and measuring alcohol consumption in various portions of the city by counting the number of empty liquor bottles found in trash bins.

The Running Record

All large organizations keep records, many of which—government records in particular—are open to the public by law. Other kinds of records—in the mass media, in particular—are public by their very nature.

Actuarial records are kept by many government agencies. Nearly 90 years ago, Winston (1932) studied the preference for male offspring in upper class families. His research design could have involved interviewing pregnant women, interviewing prospective fathers in hospital waiting rooms, or perhaps paying obstetricians to ask expectant couples about their gender preference. Instead, he chose a nonreactive design that involved analyzing birth records to determine whether the last-born children in such families were males more often than is likely to occur by chance, thus, suggesting a preference for male children.

Political and judicial records provide many data for research in the social sciences. Criminal-court records have long been used to study racial bias in sentencing procedures. Divorce-court records might be used to study the effects of various factors on child custody decisions. Carmichael (1985) used court records from New Zealand to show that women have been more likely to be awarded formal custody in recent years.

The mass media are often used to study trends in the public's perception of marriage and family issues. Middleton (1960) compared actual family sizes (based on government statistics) to ideal family sizes (based on fictional stories about families that appeared in popular magazines) and found that shifts in ideal family sizes tended to parallel shifts in actual family sizes. Atkinson and Blackwelder (1993) studied images of fathers in popular magazines using a similar strategy.

Advantages of the Running Record

Using the running record offers three major advantages. First, such data exist in large quantities. Certain vital statistics in the United States, for example, have been collected for more than 200 years. Much of these data are collected annually, simplifying analyses of trends over time. The second major advantage of using the running record is cost. Most governmental and mass media records are available at no cost or simply for the cost of duplicating the material. And, third, these are nonreactive techniques: Using them for research purposes is relatively nonintrusive.

Using the running record also has some disadvantages. One is the problem of **selective deposit**. Some data may never get into the public record; the court, for example, may seal birth records of adoptees. Second, **selective survival** is a problem. Inevitably, some records get lost or destroyed. Others may be deliberately removed. As a favor to a friend, for example, a police officer might remove information about an act of domestic violence from the criminal record.

The Episodic and Private Record

Records kept by individuals and private organizations are not usually part of the public record and are not generally kept continuously or over long periods of time. However, they still may represent a valuable source of research materials for the researcher who can gain access to them.

Sales records are often a good unobtrusive indicator of public opinion. Airline passenger anxiety, for example, might be measured by alcohol sales at airports or by air-travel insurance policy sales. Sales of burglar alarm systems might indicate public fear of crime. Sales of various over-the-counter contraceptive techniques could represent their relative popularity.

Industrial and institutional records may be used to investigate a wide range of research topics. Here, the primary problem is one of entrée. Most businesses are not eager to share their internal records with outsiders, and when they do, they often limit the types or amount of access to internal documents.

Content analysis of personal written documents is among the most well-known nonreactive or unobtrusive methods. In their classic, *The Polish Peasant in Europe and America*, Thomas, Znaniecki, and Zaretsky (1996) content-analyzed letters written home by Polish immigrants to study the acculturation process at the turn of the century. Janowitz (1979) studied the effects of Allied propaganda during World War II by studying letters and diaries written by Axis prisoners of war.

"Big Data" in the Study of Families and Children

A more recent nonreactive method of data collection incorporates what is known as "big data." A useful definition of big data was introduced by Laney (2001) in terms the three Vs: volume, velocity, and variety. *Volume* refers to the often-mind-boggling amounts of data involved—hundreds of millions of postings on social networks, for example. *Velocity* refers to the incredibly high speed at which the data elements are generated; think about how quickly tens of thousands of people can access the Web for information when a major social or political event occurs. And the elements of big data can take on a wide *variety* of forms: postings to social media sites, structured data such as online databases, unstructured data like videos or still images, text documents and e-mails, retail transactions from online vendors, and so forth.

Lazer and Radford (2017) present an excellent introduction to big data if you're interested in pursuing this method. They suggest that "Researchers have used big data to answer old questions in new ways and new questions never before answerable" (p. 32). So far, researchers in human development and family studies have been slow to adopt big data techniques, but as an example of what might be done, consider P. Cohen's (2012a) study. He asked, What Google searches correlate with suicide? He compared state-level suicide rates with results from Google Correlate (an online method of correlating keyword searches with other searches or other sources of data) and found that "the searches that are most common where there are more suicides (age adjusted), and least common where there are fewer suicides, are almost all about guns" (2012a). The correlations between suicide rates and searches about guns range from .82 to .90, a very strong relationship.

Secondary Analysis of Sample Surveys

Perusing journals that publish research on families and children, you may notice that many researchers didn't collect their own data: They used data collected by other researchers or agencies, often for very different research purposes. Chapter 11 is devoted to a presentation of secondary analysis and discusses many of the most popular data sets used for such research.

Ethics and Quantitative Methods

Like any research, studies that use methods for quantitative data often present ethical challenges. To understand these challenges better it is helpful to group quantitative methods into two broad categories: "active" studies that involve some kind of intervention or manipulation (chiefly laboratory and field experiments) and "passive" studies that seek to acquire information about the respondent without any deliberate attempt at manipulation or intervention (sample surveys, nonreactive measures in general, and most big data techniques).

In nearly all quantitative studies, the biggest ethical concern is usually confidentiality. A very simple rule to go by is to never store data with any identifying information (social security numbers, student or employee identification numbers, driver's license numbers, etc.). Instead, assign an arbitrary case number to each respondent and, if absolutely necessary, keep a separate file linking the case number to the identifier. A linking file might be necessary if you are doing a longitudinal study or an experiment with follow-ups so that you can connect the data from one session to that from an earlier session.

Whenever possible store the data in encrypted format. Any data stored online can be hacked but without identifying information confidentiality can usually be maintained. Never, ever store identifying information online—no matter how secure you think your computer system might be. Consider, for example, the cautionary tale of cancer researcher Bonnie Yankaskas at the University of North Carolina. A computer server under Yankaskas's control containing medical records of 180,000 women, many of whom were participating in clinical trials, was hacked. Apparently the unencrypted datafile included the social security numbers of 114,000 patients (Kolowich, 2011). In a process that went on for nearly two years, the university initially planned to terminate Yankaskas but eventually reached a settlement in which the university paid her legal fees and Yankaskas agreed to retire without admitting responsibility for the breach (Outlaw, 2011). While guaranteeing that the online server was not hackable was probably impossible, the confidentiality of the patients could have been preserved if an arbitrary case number (instead of the patients' social security numbers) had been used.

While confidentiality issues are also important in "active" research (e.g., when providing survey data that reveals private attitudes or behaviors, such as in the National Longitudinal Study of Adolescent to Adult Health discussed in Chapter 15), institutional review boards are just as concerned about potential harm resulting from the intervention or manipulation. The case of child psychiatrist Mani Pavuluri (discussed in Chapter 2) is an example of what happens in one of the rare instances where the IRB system fails. IRBs are charged with protecting not only the confidentiality and other rights of research participants; they are also concerned with the safety of those participants. Individuals participating in sample surveys or experiments should not be placed at risk simply by virtue of their participation. A key risk is potential psychological harm due to participation. Researchers need to be mindful of the possible psychological ramifications that may result due to the questions asked on a survey. For example, asking about possible child sexual abuse, either current or in the past, may trigger a negative psychological response. Thus, IRBs work with researchers to guarantee that all sensitive questions are necessary for the project at hand and that resources are made available to participants should a negative reaction occur (typically in the informed consent process).

Some Limitations of Quantitative Methods

It should be apparent that the methods described in this chapter—experiments, surveys, observation, nonreactive techniques, and secondary analysis of sample surveys—are all relatively structured. The quantitative researcher begins the research process by phrasing one or more research questions or hypotheses, which structure the nature of both the sampling process and the data collection instruments and techniques. The sample, instruments, and techniques can have the effect of limiting the types of knowledge that can be gathered or can even affect the outcome of the study. For example, if a written questionnaire is used, only those with some fluency (and reading ability) in the language can be studied. For a mailed questionnaire, only those with valid addresses can be surveyed. Telephone surveys may eliminate lower income individuals and families from the study because they are least likely to have telephone service in their homes, and those who don't have conventional landline phones. Another problem created by this structure is a limitation on what can be learned from respondents. In a mailed questionnaire, once the questionnaires have been sent to potential respondents, it's too late to add a new question or follow up on an existing one.

A body of techniques referred to as **qualitative research** presents an alternative to traditional quantitative methods. In contrast to the relatively structured approaches of surveys, experiments, and structured interviews, qualitative methods emphasize the unfolding nature of the research process. Chapter 9 presents an introduction to qualitative methods of studying families. Chapter 10 discusses the possibilities of what are known as **mixed-methods studies**, the combination of quantitative and qualitative methods in the same study to improve our understanding of some social phenomenon.

STUDY QUESTIONS

1. Find one example of each of the following quantitative research strategies in any of the major family or human development journals: experiment, sample survey, and nonreactive methods. Briefly describe the research technique in each article.

2. Using one of the studies you located in the first question, critique the research method using whatever criteria you feel are appropriate.

3. Choose a family or human development related topic of interest to you and present brief (about one paragraph) descriptions of how you might study that topic using each of the following: (a) an experiment, (b) a sample survey using telephone interviews, (c) a survey over the Internet, and (d) a nonreactive method.

Studying Families and Children

Methods for Qualitative Data

I n Chapter 8, we pointed out that quantitative research strategies, such as surveys and experiments, tend to be highly structured. Traditional structured interviews or questionnaires often inadequately assess the underlying justifications or motives people have for their everyday behavior. For example, a typical survey question in studies of housework is to ask women whether they think that the division of household labor in their families is fair. From their responses, we can determine how many wives say that the division of household labor in their families is fair and how many say that it is unfair. However, from such survey responses, we get little insight into why a particular wife feels that the division of household labor in her family is fair or unfair. Is it because she feels she does too much housework or because her husband does too little? Is she comparing the amount of housework she does to the amount done by her husband or to other wives that she knows? What does she mean by fair? What activities does she consider housework?

These are the kinds of questions that **qualitative research** methods excel at answering, those perhaps only answerable through the kinds of in-depth observation and interviews discussed in this chapter. Qualitative strategies tend to be relatively unstructured, and many qualitative methodologies argue against researchers imposing their own structures on the data. Punch (2013) suggested that quantitative data may be defined as empirical information in the form of numbers, while qualitative data are information about the world in the form of words.

Daly (2007) suggested that qualitative methods are especially valuable for family researchers because "the focus is not on identifying structural or demographic trends in families, but rather on the processes by which families create, sustain, and discuss their own family realities" (pp. 71–72). In Chapter 1, we identified an important difference between social research in general and research on families: Families are groups or systems of individuals. This emphasis on holistic understanding makes qualitative methods especially well-suited to studying families.

Qualitative Research Compared to Quantitative Research

From even a casual reading of the literature on qualitative research methods, clearly the goals of research using qualitative methods are substantially different from those of the quantitative techniques discussed in Chapter 8. These goals are the result of radically different epistemological orientations about the relationship of theory and research. Epistemological orientations may be thought of as assumptions "about how to know the social and apprehend its meaning" (Fonow & Cook, 1991a, p. 4). The researcher's epistemological orientation affects the topics studied, the types of questions asked, and the methods employed to answer these questions.

Generally speaking, research designs using methods of collecting and analyzing quantitative data are deployed in the sequence described in Chapter 1: exploration, description, prediction, explanation, intervention, and evaluation. Knowledge concerning the phenomenon of interest develops gradually but systematically, and hypotheses are derived from extant theory or empirical generalizations. Theory and hypotheses, then, precede the research process. This perspective is often referred to as *postpositivism* (Popper, 1964, 1992). Theory determines the choice of concepts to be studied and the procedures employed to measure those concepts.

Many researchers focused on collecting and analyzing qualitative data pursue a much different course, however, following what might be called a *constructionist* or *phenomenological* approach. Daly (2007) suggested that qualitative methods in family studies follow Weber's (1947) *verstehen* ("to understand") tradition and that "qualitative methods are suited to understanding the meanings, interpretations, and subjective experiences of family members" (p. 73), as qualitative family research seeks to provide family members' descriptive accounts of their own lived experiences.

The *grounded theory* school of thought (Corbin & Strauss, 2008; Glaser & Strauss, 1967) argues that theory can *emerge* from the data. Although a comprehensive comparison of grounded theory to positivist approaches is beyond the scope of this text, Punch (2013) pointed out that although traditional quantitative methods have usually emphasized a theory-verification model—that is, using research to test theories—grounded theory advocates a theory-generation model. In the theory-generation model, research findings precede theory, and researchers typically don't approach their research with specific hypotheses in mind. The grounded-theory approach, therefore, is most advantageous when there is no well-developed theory about the phenomenon of interest. For more discussion of the application of grounded theory to research on families, see LaRossa (2005). Donnellan, Bennett, and Soulsby (2015) presented an interesting example of grounded theory applied to the study of resilience in older spousal dementia caregivers, while Austin's (2014) research is an example of grounded theory focusing on identity development of transgender or gender nonconforming adolescents.

As noted in Chapter 8, not all quantitative research is positivistic, nor does all qualitative research follow the constructivist or phenomenological approaches. Rather, the researcher's paradigmatic approach and the methods employed are a function of the research question at hand.

Types of Qualitative Strategies

Despite many different styles of qualitative methods, Punch (2013) argued that a hallmark of qualitative research is that it is naturalistic—it tends to study people and groups in their natural settings. Although the nonreactive quantitative research techniques used to gather data in natural settings are clearly naturalistic, most quantitative research designs (such as surveys and experiments) are not. Miles, Huberman, and Saldana (2013) suggested eight recurring elements in qualitative research:

1. Qualitative research is conducted through intense and prolonged contact with the context under study.

2. The goal of the researcher is to gain a holistic overview of the context under study.

3. The researcher attempts to understand the context from the standpoint of the participants themselves rather than from the researcher's own perspective.

4. Although the research may, over time, isolate certain themes that may be reviewed with the participants themselves, the field notes and observations should be maintained in their original forms throughout the study.

5. A primary goal of qualitative research is to understand the ways that people come to understand, account for, take action, and otherwise manage their day-to-day activities.

6. Whereas many interpretations of the field notes are possible, some are more compelling than others for theoretical reasons or for reasons of internal consistency.

7. Relatively little standardized instrumentation is used.

8. Most analysis is done with words (as opposed to numbers). (pp. 6–7)

Despite many different ways to organize the various types of naturalistic qualitative research strategies, thinking in terms of three broad groupings that typically use different approaches is useful: case studies, ethnographies, and focus groups.

Case Studies

A case study is typically an intensive, in-depth study of a few cases—often a single case—where the goal is "to develop as full an understanding of that case as possible" (Punch, 2005, p. 144). Miles et al. (2013) defined a case as "a phenomenon of some sort occurring in a bounded context" (p. 25). In family research, the case under study is typically a single family or group of families who share some common trait (e.g., families headed by Latinos, single-parent families, or families with employed mothers), but it can also be individuals, dyads (couples), or even communities, organizations, or social programs.

In an example of a case study where families were the unit of analysis, Risman and Johnson-Sumerford (1998) studied the families of 15 married couples who divided housework and child-care equitably and regardless of gender "to determine how they arrived at this arrangement and what consequences such a distribution of household labor has on their relationship" (p. 23). For each family, a team, consisting of an interviewer for each parent and one for each child older than age 4 years, interviewed the family members independently in their own home. The interviews lasted from one to more than three hours and were tape-recorded and transcribed verbatim. Each interviewer also contributed field notes and an analytic summary to the interview. One member of the team also observed the family in their home from the time the parents arrived home from work until the children were asleep.

An example of a case study where the unit of analysis is the organization is Hochschild's (1997) examination of family-friendly policies at AMERCO, a Fortune 500 corporation located in the Midwest. She interviewed 130 employees at all levels within the corporation and talked with psychologists, child-care workers, and spouses of employees. She also did day-long observations of six families of AMERCO employees.

The unit of analysis in Kwak, Kramer, Lang, and Ledger's (2012) case study is the social program. Their study of the Wisconsin Family Care Program investigated challenges in end-of-life care management for low-income frail elders. Data were collected through interviews with county administrators, lead supervisors, and two focus groups with care-management team members as key implementation stakeholders for this program as it affected the elderly clients and their extended family members.

The Risman and Johnson-Sumerford (1998) study is a **multiple-case study**; Hochschild's and Kwak et al.'s are **single-case studies**. With these examples in mind, and drawing on the discussions of Punch (2013) and Yin (2009), we can suggest two basic characteristics of case studies in general. First, the focus of a case study is an example of something that is studied in-depth and in its natural context: a particular type of individual, family, or organization. The specific case is usually selected because it is presumed to typify similar cases; examination of that particular case can help illuminate the nature of similar cases.

Second, the researcher is likely to use multiple sources of data and methods of data collection. Risman and Johnson-Sumerford's study, for example, used both personal interviews with the family members and unstructured observations of the family going about their everyday lives. Hochschild, in her effort to understand how AMERCO employees attempted to resolve conflicts between work and family, used observations in the workplace, at home, and at a child-care center; interviews with employees and their spouses; and corporate documents. Kwak and colleagues utilized both interviews and focus groups to gather information about the implementation of the social program being evaluated.

Drawing on Punch (2013), eight issues are important to consider when evaluating a case study:

1. What, exactly, is the case under study?

2. What are its boundaries?

3. What was the main purpose of the study?

4. What were the research questions in the study?

5. Did the study use single or multiple cases?

6. How were the data collected and from whom?

7. How were the data analyzed?

8. What were the findings or conclusions of the study?

Ethnographies

Hammersley and Atkinson's *Ethnography: Principles in Practice* (2007), a classic text updated to reflect research practice in contemporary times, argues that the primary goal of ethnography is the description of cultures. In ethnographic research, observers are encouraged to make their preconceptions about the culture being studied explicit so "the culture is turned into an object available for study" (p. 9). Ethnographic research attempts to understand a culture or way of life from the point of view of its participants. In most ethnographic studies, the observer participates, over an extended period of time, in the lives of the people being studied. Thus, participant observation is a primary method of ethnographic research. The observer attempts to understand the events and meanings attributed to those events by the people being studied.

Although many of the best-known ethnographies are studies of cultures other than Western industrialized societies—for example, Margaret Mead's (1935) studies of New Guinea tribes—social and behavioral scientists also employ ethnographic methods to study groups close to home. Because ethnographic methods encourage the observer to deal explicitly with any preconceptions about the culture being studied, it is especially useful for the study of marginalized groups (e.g., disadvantaged minorities, the homeless, abused wives) in our own society. For more information on the use of ethnography to study families, see Descartes (2007) and Roy, Zvonkovic, Goldberg, Sharp, and LaRossa (2015). Good examples of ethnographic research in human development and family studies are Carol Stack's (1974) study of kinship ties among African Americans, Annette Lareau's (2011) study of the influence of social class on parenting and children's transitions to young adulthood, and Desmond's (2016) examination of home as a central component of family and community.

Drawing again from Punch (2005), several distinguishing characteristics of ethnographic research can be identified:

- First, ethnography attempts to uncover the shared cultural meanings of the group, as those meanings are critical to understanding the group's behavior.

- Second, the observer must be sensitive to the meanings that events have for those being studied. A primary goal of the research is to uncover these meanings. To do this, the observer has to take the perspective (standpoint) of those being studied.

- Third, the group or phenomenon is studied in its natural setting. The observer must directly experience the physical and social world of those being studied.

- Fourth, the exact focus of the ethnography will often not be evident before beginning the study; consequently, structuring the data and developing instruments will often be done as the research proceeds, rather than before beginning the project.

- Although fieldwork and, especially, participant observation are central to most ethnographic research, other techniques (for example, structured interviews, questionnaires, content analyses) may be used as necessary and appropriate.

- Finally, ethnographic research is a long and repetitive process. This is partially because it can take a long time for the observer to gain access to, and acceptance by, the group being studied and because "the ethnographic record needs to be comprehensive and detailed and typically focuses on things that happen again and again." (Punch, 2005, pp. 152–153)

Focus Groups

Focus groups are small groups (usually seven to 10 members) of individuals brought together to discuss a specific topic of interest to the researcher. A moderator leads and directs the discussion, but the process is essentially unstructured. Focus groups are used extensively in a number of areas for at least three purposes. Probably the best-known use of focus groups is in marketing research, which uses focus groups to gauge consumers' reactions to new products or advertising. Political consultants use focus groups to assess voter reactions to positions on issues and the relative attractiveness of candidates.

Social researchers use focus groups in either of two ways. First, the use of groups can aid development of instrumentation for more structured research techniques (e.g., surveys or personal interviews). Second, the focus group's interactions may be used as qualitative data in their own right in the study of a particular topic (Morgan, 1997). Many times, focus group data are used in conjunction with questionnaire data for triangulation around the research question using mixed methods (see Chapter 10). Beaulaurier, Seff, Newman, and Dunlop's (2007) research examining the factors influencing older women's reluctance to seek help when they experience intimate partner violence and Conroy et al.'s (2015) research on adolescents with depression are examples of research using focus group responses as qualitative data.

Stewart and Shamdasani (2014) identified several key advantages offered by focus groups:

- collecting data faster and at a lower cost than if individuals were interviewed separately

- direct interaction leading to more complete data, including nonverbal responses

- high face validity

- synergistic effect of group setting possibly leading to data or ideas that individual interviews may not have

- flexibility

- allows for full participation by children

- accessible and user-friendly results compared to quantitative research

Yet Stewart and Shamdasani also pointed out some disadvantages of this technique:

- low generalizability

- possible difficulty of creating an environment that encourages open participation by all group members

- the "live" and immediate responses sometimes seen as more accurate when they may not be

- the open-ended nature of the responses often making analysis and interpretation difficult

- the moderator possibly generating biased results by providing cues about desirable responses or by working toward consensus

Studying Families Through Observation

One popular method of studying families and children is through observation. Particularly in the study of very young children, observation can be a useful tool. Observational techniques are often used during the early stages of research as an exploratory tool. Let's say that you wanted to understand how free-forming playgroups work among preschoolers. This is an ideal problem for observational techniques, because your potential respondents probably cannot communicate the kinds of information you'd like to obtain through interviews (some may not even talk yet) or questionnaires.

As an example of an observational study, Bai, Repetti, and Sperling (2016) observed the spontaneous expression of positive emotions among 8- to 12-year-olds in the context of their everyday family interactions. Bai and colleagues found through their naturalistic observations that children's positive emotional expressions lasted longer and were more robust when others in the family expressed positive emotions and/or were engaged in joint leisure activities, highlighting the importance of social connectedness to the development of children's socio-emotional identities.

Five Criteria

We all observe behavior; we're all people watchers. And, as we pointed out in the first chapter, we are all more or less motivated to answer the *why* question: Why do people behave the way they do? However, if we all observe human behavior, what makes observation a scientific data collection technique?

Observation becomes a scientific tool when five criteria are met:

1. *The observation must serve a specific research purpose.* Simply sitting and observing—even if you take careful notes—isn't scientific research. The observation must be designed to accomplish a particular goal. In the study of free-forming playgroups described earlier, the researcher probably begins with only a rudimentary knowledge of the behavior of preschoolers and their playgroups. Observing preschoolers at play over time might sensitize the researcher to the key variables that are implicated in the process.

2. *The observation must be planned systematically.* To be a useful scientific tool, the observation must be planned systematically. At what times and on what days will you observe? It probably makes a difference if you observe preschoolers early in the morning (when they're still sleepy or perhaps suffering from separation anxiety after their parents have dropped them off at a day care center) or late in the afternoon (when they're tired) or on Mondays (when they're trying to reacclimate to their day care environment after a weekend at home). Because the nature of the observational technique tends to limit the amount of observation to take place, the researcher must plan the timing of the observations carefully.

   The observational researcher also has to have some idea of what to look for. Although some writers suggest that observers should enter the situation de novo (that is, without preconceptions or expectations), it's impossible to begin the observation without some expectations. It's important to ensure that these preconceptions don't structure your observations to the point that you miss the critical events and processes taking place.

3. *The observation is recorded systematically.* It is a truism that if we are to understand anything, we must give up hope of understanding everything. Observational research is no exception to this rule. It is impossible to record every aspect of an event: every spoken word, every gesture, every raised eyebrow. The observational researcher must make conscious decisions about which aspects of the event to record and how to record them. Bakeman and Gottman (1997) argued that the first step in observational research is to develop a coding scheme, which serves as "the lens through which [the researcher] has chosen to view the world" (p. 15). The three primary technologies for these recordings are written notes, audio or video recordings, or memory.

   Some field researchers take what are known as *field jottings:* phrases, quotes, and important words jotted during the observation that can be used to jog the memory when writing *field notes* (Lofland, Snow, Anderson, & Lofland, 2005). Most field researchers also write up field notes as soon as possible following each observation period.

4. *The observation is related to general propositions rather than specific examples.* The sociological literature is filled with case studies. However interesting these case studies might be, however, they are not of great scientific value unless they are related to general propositions derived from theories or specific hypotheses about general processes. This is perhaps the most important distinction between sociological research and journalism. To the journalist, the subject of the case study is interesting in and of itself. For the sociologist, although the case study may be interesting, it is primarily a means to an end: evidence to be used to test the validity of a general proposition, theory, or hypothesis.

5. *The observation is subjected to checks on reliability and validity.* Sometimes, it is said that because the researcher is part of the setting, issues such as reliability and validity are not important in observational research. Or you might hear the argument that observational research is somehow more valid than other research strategies. Despite these claims, issues of reliability and validity are just as important in observational research as they are in other research strategies. The issue of consistency among different observers is of particular importance.

Imagine, for example, an observational study of aggressive behavior among 3-year-olds. Part of the project involves coding nonverbal aggressive behaviors on the part of the children. The observer may be asked to make subjective decisions about which nonverbal behaviors should be coded as aggressive and which ones should not. If this measurement is truly reliable (in the sense of consistency), different observers should agree on which nonverbal behaviors should be coded as aggressive and which ones should not. Bai et al.(2016) provide detailed explanations of training given to observers in their study in order to be confident of the reliability of their observations. See Daly (2007) for additional detail on using qualitative methods in family and human development research.

Ethics and Qualitative Research

As noted in Chapter 2, all research must adhere to certain ethical standards. Qualitative research in human development and family studies is no different. There are specific challenges that may be encountered in the performance of more naturalistic studies, such as ethnographies, on families as well as in studies where participants are interviewed either individually or in focus groups. Confidentiality becomes extremely important when individuals and their responses to interview questions are known to not only the researcher but also to other participants. Protecting the identity of participants is important, especially in research where individuals may be disclosing something private about their family lives or those of others around them. For example, Hochschild (1997) had to strike a balance between providing enough context about AMERCO for readers to understand how the organization worked and protecting the confidentiality of the employees whom she included in her ethnography. Providing details on the organization could have led to individuals in the project being identified, thus violating confidentiality of their participation. In focus group and interview-based studies where responses to interview questions are audiotaped and in observational studies where behavior is video recorded, protection of confidentiality extends to include the layers of protection for the research recordings. Therefore, Institutional Review Boards ask in advance how researchers will protect the research materials produced by researchers such as Kwak and colleagues (2012) in their focus groups and Bai et al. (2016) in their observational study.

Another ethical hallmark of research is the voluntary participation of participants in the study. In the research designs described in Chapter 8, securing informed consent is typically straightforward. However, in the case of an ethnography, where the researcher is integrated into the social fabric of the families they are studying, informed consent becomes more complex. Do all people who visit the home of the participant while the researcher is present have to complete an informed consent form? Researchers sometime ask for a waiver of signature of informed consent if the participation in the study poses minimal risk to the participant. However, even when participants complete informed consent, they may not fully understand the research project. Lareau (2011) documents this challenge in the second edition of her ethnography. As she sought to secure consent for follow-up interviews from the participants of her study, she found that one family had misunderstood what her purpose had been in the original study (likening her to a reality TV producer rather than a researcher who would interpret their behavior). The mother in the family was so appalled at what she felt was not only an embarrassment of her family through the publication of Lareau's book but a breach of trust based on her relationship with Lareau that she threatened legal action if Lareau contacted her family again.

As we noted in Chapter 2, all researchers working with human subjects are obligated to treat our participants fairly. We do not like to deceive our participants about the purpose of our research or if we need to, we provide a debriefing after the study is complete to explain the deception. The fine line of deception is even more difficult to walk among researchers performing ethnographic work as they must decide how much of their research questions to disclose to participants whose trust is needed to complete a long-term project, all the while cognizant that sharing too much information could lead to reactivity that undermines the reliability of the study itself. Ethical research is both about protecting research participants from undue risk but also protecting the process of research itself. Research in human development and family studies using qualitative materials that attends to the protection of both participants and the process has the opportunity to provide substantial insight in to how and why social processes operate as they do.

Evaluating Qualitative Research

Although the structure imposed by quantitative methods can sometimes limit the researcher's ability to fully understand families, that same structure also provides security in the sense of well-established standards regarding the quality or soundness of research. A consensus among quantitative researchers is that we must be attentive to a number of key indicators of good research. Are the measures valid and reliable? Are the sampling procedures appropriate? Does the research design reduce the impact of extraneous factors and consider possible alternative interpretations? The design of the research and its instrumentation are determined by the theory. The theory suggests the appropriate unit of analysis and how the various concepts are measured.

In contrast to the relative consensus among quantitative research methods, qualitative methods in family research are characterized by a greater diversity in techniques and perspectives. Furthermore, what constitutes good qualitative research is open to a fair amount of controversy. Miles et al. (2013) wrote that qualitative methodologists "have this unappealing double bind whereby qualitative studies can't be verified because researchers don't report on their methodology, and they don't report on their methodology because there are no established canons or conventions for doing so" (p. 244). Gilgun (1992) suggested, "The downside of moving toward diversity of research methods, methodologies, and theories is insecurity. Qualitative researchers are prone to asking: Am I doing it right?" (p. 27). This is a problem that we (and we suspect many quantitative researchers) have when reading qualitative research studies: It is difficult to ascertain what, exactly, constitutes *good* qualitative research.

Gilgun (1992) argued that "a guideline for the conduct of qualitative research . . . is whether we are successful in communicating our processes and findings" (p. 27). Does the research faithfully communicate what the informants are saying? Is the research method getting in the way of what the informants are saying? These, of course, are exceedingly different questions from the ones that quantitative researchers would ask about their research.

In Chapter 10, we explore a possible reconciliation between the divergent philosophies and approaches of quantitative and qualitative strategies: mixed methods.

STUDY QUESTIONS

1. Find examples of each of the following qualitative research strategies in any of the major family-related journals: single-case study, multiple-case study, ethnography, and focus group. Briefly describe the research technique in each article.

2. Choose any one of the studies you located in the previous question and describe the methods used to protect the research participants during the study. Critically evaluate whether there was enough information provided to explain the ethical decisions made and protections provided.

3. Choose a family-related topic of interest to you and present brief (about one paragraph) descriptions of how you might study that topic using (a) a case study, (b) an ethnography, and (c) a focus group.

Studying Families

Mixed Methods

C hapter 8 (on methods for quantitative data) and Chapter 9 (on methods for qualitative data) might give you the impression that these are two totally different and mutually exclusive approaches to studying marriages and families. Indeed, some texts imply conflict between so-called quants and quals, and to be honest, there is some animosity held by some members of each side.

Since the 1980s, **mixed methods** has emerged as an approach that combines elements of traditional quantitative techniques along with the qualitative. Compared to traditional quantitative approaches (which have their basis in postpositivism) and qualitative approaches (usually identified with constructivism or phenomenology), the mixed-method approach has its epistemological or philosophical roots in pragmatism (see Cherryhomes, 1992). Creswell and Plano Clark (2007) suggested that pragmatists focus on the consequences of their research, placing primary importance on the research question. Not surprisingly, researchers adopting the pragmatist position are likely to choose from a wide range of research strategies, from the highly quantitative to the most qualitative.

Tashakkori and Teddlie (1998) suggested a threefold taxonomy of research studies: monomethod, mixed methods, and mixed models. *Monomethod* studies use either quantitative or qualitative techniques (but not both) exclusively throughout the research process. Such studies may use multiple data sources, but only one methodological strategy is employed in a given study. Although Tashakkori and Teddlie suggest that social researchers have moved beyond monomethod approaches, a quick scan of any major family-related journal will show that most current research still uses either qualitative or quantitative approaches—but not both in the same study (see Plano Clark, Huddleston-Casas, Churchill, O'Neil Green, & Garrett, 2008, for research on this very question).

Mixed-Method Approaches to Family Research

Mixed-methods research as a design makes use of the best and most appropriate methods to address a research problem. People tend to problem solve in a variety of ways. Combining scientific approaches to answer a research question is simply an extension of what we do in our "nonscientific" lives (Creswell & Plano Clark, 2007). And by combining multiple methods, we can counterbalance not only the weaknesses of some methods with the strengths of others, but also we can "produce a comprehensive empirical record about a topic" (Axinn & Pearce, 2006, p. 24).

Mixed-method studies combine qualitative and quantitative approaches in a single study. Creswell and Plano Clark's (2007) four-design framework is a useful typology for describing how methods can be combined when studying families. The designs may collect qualitative and quantitative data concurrently (triangulation and embedded designs) or sequentially (explanatory and exploratory designs). These designs, summarized in Figure 10.1, are each described in more detail in the next section.

Explanatory Mixed-Methods Design

The **explanatory mixed-methods design**, a sequential design, begins with quantitative techniques (e.g., statistical analysis of census data) and proceeds to qualitative methods (e.g., case studies or ethnographies) to further explore the meanings of the phenomena identified in the quantitative phase. Pearce's (2002) study of the effects of religion on fertility preferences provides an excellent example of the explanatory design. She began with data from a probability sample of more than 5,000 residents of the Chitwan Valley in South-Central Nepal. After developing a multiple regression model predicting family size preferences, she focused her attention on the respondents who expressed a desire for substantially larger families than that predicted by her model. She drew a random sample of 28 respondents from this group and conducted 90-minute interviews with each. This is the point where "cases that have not been predicted correctly can speak back to the process and suggest improvements in theory, measures, and methods" (p. 114).

Figure 10.1 Four Major Mixed-Methods Designs

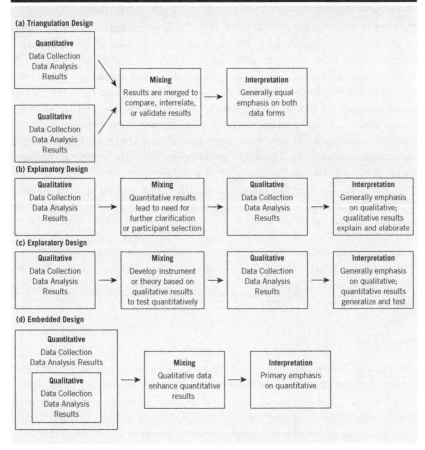

(a) Triangulation Design

Quantitative
Data Collection
Data Analysis
Results

Qualitative
Data Collection
Data Analysis
Results

Mixing
Results are merged to compare, interrelate, or validate results

Interpretation
Generally equal emphasis on both data forms

(b) Explanatory Design

Qualitative
Data Collection
Data Analysis
Results

Mixing
Quantitative results lead to need for further clarification or participant selection

Qualitative
Data Collection
Data Analysis
Results

Interpretation
Generally emphasis on qualitative; qualitative results explain and elaborate

(c) Exploratory Design

Qualitative
Data Collection
Data Analysis
Results

Mixing
Develop instrument or theory based on qualitative results to test quantitatively

Qualitative
Data Collection
Data Analysis
Results

Interpretation
Generally emphasis on qualitative; quantitative results generalize and test

(d) Embedded Design

Quantitative
Data Collection
Data Analysis Results

Qualitative
Data Collection
Data Analysis
Results

Mixing
Qualitative data enhance quantitative results

Interpretation
Primary emphasis on quantitative

Source: Mixed Methods Approaches in Family Science Research, Vicki L. Plano Clark, Catherine Huddleston-Casas, Susan Churchill, Denise O'Neill Green, Amanda Garrett, *Journal of Family Issues, 29*(11), 1543–1566, 2008. This figure is based on Creswell and Plano Clark's (2007) discussion of mixed methods designs.

As a result of the interviews, Pearce was able to refine the prediction model to more accurately predict fertility preferences. Equally important, the information gathered in the interviews allowed her to improve the measurement of key variables in the study. The interviews indicated that some of the respondents either had not understood key questions in the initial survey or had interpreted them in ways vastly different from what was intended. Not only did the exploratory mixed-methods design improve validity in measurement strategies for future studies (see Chapter 6 for more on validity), it produced a more ethically sound study overall by intentionally removing ambiguity around how items could be interpreted.

Exploratory Design

Exploratory designs are also sequential, although the research would begin with qualitative work (such as personal interviews with a small number of informants) and then use large-scale quantitative methods (such as mailed questionnaires) to test hypotheses developed in the qualitative phase. Mistry, Lowe, Benner, and Chien (2008) studied the ways in which low-income mothers (N = 32) negotiated financial hardship. Interviews uncovered not only the extent of economic stress in these households but also the decisions that women made to manage the stress. Balancing basic needs and symbolic purchases (such as graduation pictures or a day at the zoo), these women saw themselves as providers both in the traditional sense and symbolically. The interviews also detailed the financial management strategies that women employed to allow them to continue in their provider role. The insights gained about the stress around specific parenting practices and the importance of being considered a good provider were directly incorporated into a panel study of 516 families (800 children) that examined the influence not only of objective financial hardship but also of maternal responses to that hardship on child social outcomes. Knowing that mothers wanted to be good providers led to the inclusion of indicators of specific parenting practices and measures of psychological well-being into the survey questionnaire.

Triangulation

Triangulation designs bring together quantitative and qualitative approaches simultaneously in order to complement each design's strengths. To understand the variety of ways that social class could shape how men practice fatherhood, Shows and Gerstel (2009) used survey data from 55 physician and 41 emergency medical technician (EMT) fathers. They supplemented these survey data with observations "at nine work sites (representing four different types of organizations), including three hospitals (with two floors in two hospitals and the emergency room in the third), two EMT sites, two nursing homes, and two physician's private practices" (p. 168). Further, they included interview data from 13 EMTs and 18 physicians. All of these data in tandem allowed Shows and Gerstel to make claims about the distinct ways that social class, as it operates through the fathers' occupations, organized their fathering practices. For example, the physicians had trouble disengaging with their patients, often staying late and bringing work home. They emphasized the public aspects of fathering, such as presence at their children's sporting events, as a way to counterbalance their relative invisibility in the day-to-day tasks of child rearing. The EMT fathers, in contrast, had greater schedule flexibility and a set schedule that did not involve relationships with patients. As such, EMTs could work when their family was asleep or actively swap shifts with others in order to be available to do the private aspects of fathering.

Embedded Design

Embedded designs use one methodology (either qualitative or quantitative) to guide the study, but supplement with data from a different methodology collected concurrently. Unlike triangulation, the data are focused on different components of the research rather than comparing and contrasting understanding of the same phenomenon. For example, a researcher may implement a field experiment but also collect qualitative interviews about the research process itself. Embedded research has become a frequent research design in the health sciences, (e.g., Slade et al., 2008). However, the design has only recently begun to be incorporated into human development and family science disciplines (see also Plano Clark et al., 2008). For example, Bluth, Gaylord, Campo, Mullarkey, and Hobbs (2016) embedded qualitative data collection into the quantitative evaluation of a mindfulness-based self-compassion intervention program aimed at encouraging adolescents to develop self-kindness. In this pilot study, the qualitative data provided insight into the structure of the intervention program while the quantitative data evaluated the effectiveness of the program overall. However, this kind of research project is unusual, as embedded designs are uncommon as mixed-methods approaches used to study human development and families. Thus, this particular method of mixing research designs provides a clear opportunity for innovative human development and family researchers.

Mixed-Model Studies in Family Research

The third type of designs identified by Tashakkori and Teddlie (1998) are mixed-model studies, which "combine the qualitative and quantitative approaches within different phases of the research process" (p. 19) in a number of ways: for example, "a quantitative (experimental) design, followed by qualitative data collection, followed by quantitative analysis after the data are converted" (p. 19) using the quantitizing technique suggested by Miles and Huberman (1994). Simultaneous administration of both closed-ended (for example, Likert-style items) and open-ended questions in the same survey is also a mixed-model design.

In their comprehensive investigation into the covenant marriage phenomenon in Louisiana, Nock, Sanchez, and Wright (2008) implemented quantitative and qualitative techniques with a variety of primary and secondary data sources. To assess general attitudes, including attitudes toward the covenant marriage option, they utilized secondary data collected by the Gallop Organization (N = 527). Questions ranged from general thoughts on marriage, divorce, family, and gender to specific questions on family policy reforms, including knowledge and attitudes about covenant marriage. To understand attitudes from specific stakeholders in the debate around covenant marriage, they conducted focus groups with four different constituencies: (a) six married Protestant couples who had upgraded their marriages to covenant marriages; (b) nine feminist activists, several of whom had lobbied against the Louisiana covenant marriage bill; (c) 10 women from a large public housing project in New Orleans; and (d) 12 undergraduates. The general public knew very little about the covenant marriage option, unless they were members of a group such as Conservative Protestants who had been actively engaged in the issue from its inception. Many of the stakeholders expressed skepticism toward the intended outcomes of the covenant marriage legislation, for example, reduced divorce rates, a skepticism that was well founded given that the general public was ill informed about both the legislation and the distinctions between covenant marriage and a standard marriage.

Some Closing Thoughts on Choosing a Research Strategy

Conventional wisdom used to be that qualitative methods were useful only during the exploratory stage of research (to determine what concepts and processes were important to study). Having used qualitative methods to define the problem, social scientists would use quantitative methods to describe characteristics of the population and test hypotheses about the phenomenon of interest. Today, human development and family researchers recognize that the process can just as easily go in the opposite direction: Start with quantitative methods then proceed to qualitative techniques. More important, researchers are realizing that no single methodological strategy can answer all the questions we might have about children, adolescents, families, marriages, and aging adults.

Many methods texts instruct the student to choose the best research strategy for a particular problem, that is, to make the research strategy fit the problem. Although this is good advice, the reality is that no researcher excels in all the strategies mentioned in Chapters 8 and 9. Instead, most researchers specialize in one or perhaps two of these strategies. The researcher's methodological preference often dictates the choice of a research problem rather than the other way around. That is, a researcher trained in large-scale survey methods is unlikely to study problems requiring participant observation, those expert in experimental design are probably not going to choose research problems requiring content analysis, and so forth. Perhaps more important, relatively few researchers trained primarily in quantitative methods conduct qualitative research and vice versa. This is a strong argument for collaborative research by researchers with different types of methodological expertise.

Although we all need to be at least conversant in the major research strategies so we can critically read and evaluate any type of research, the mixed-method approach demands that we take this issue a step further. One barrier to this goal is that "scholars in the mainstream quantitative tradition (the positivists and postpositivists) and qualitative tradition (the constructivists) have not embraced mixed model studies" (Tashakkori & Teddlie, 1998, p. ix). This, too, is changing, although change is not uniform. For example, *The SAGE Handbook of Qualitative Research* (Denzin & Lincoln, 2011) has two chapters that explicitly deal with mixed methods, and there are now a plethora of texts that focus exclusively on mixed-methods research designs. However, texts that focus on classic quantitative methods mention mixed models in passing, if at all (e.g., Cook & Campbell, 1979; Kaplan, 2004).

We might argue that the mixed-method approach will come to dominate family research, and not only because no single methodology is likely to be able to answer all of our questions. Creswell and Plano Clark (2007) argued that "[m]ixed methods is, simply, best suited for addressing many of today's complex research questions, which require context and outcomes, meaning and trends, and narratives and numbers" (p. 184). The increasing diversification of family forms—single parenting, cohabiting couples, blended families, and gay, lesbian, bisexual, and transgender couples—suggests the need for alternative strategies of *knowing* about families, marriages, and other intimate relationships.

STUDY QUESTIONS

Develop a family-related research question that interests you.

1. How might you study this research question using a single *quantitative* technique from Chapter 8?

2. How might you study this research question using a single *qualitative* technique from Chapter 9?

3. Choose two of the four *mixed-methods* designs (exploratory, explanatory, triangulation, or embedded) and describe for each how might you study this research question.

4. How might you study this research question using a *mixed-model study* approach?

5. Finally, how would you evaluate the strengths and weaknesses of each approach for your particular research question?

CHAPTER 11

Using Other People's Data

M any people are surprised to learn that many published studies on families and children don't use data gathered by the authors themselves; they employ secondary data, or data that were initially gathered by some other organization or researcher. This chapter discusses the advantages and disadvantages of secondary analysis and describes many popular secondary data sets available for researchers studying families, children, and older adults. Finally, it describes sources of secondary data sets available for use.

Advantages and Disadvantages of Secondary Analysis

Secondary data are popular for various reasons. First and foremost is cost; even a small survey can be time consuming and expensive, and the cost of doing a limited statewide or national sample can easily run into six figures. Few researchers can afford large-scale primary data collection. Fortunately, the data produced by many large-scale surveys conducted by top-notch survey organizations are available to secondary analysts at little or no charge.

A second reason that secondary analysis is popular is data quality. Nationally known survey organizations, such as the National Opinion Research Center at the University of Chicago or the Institute for Survey Research at Temple University, can afford to invest large sums of money in training interviewers and employing supervisors to handle quality-control issues. They already have interviewers in place around the country to conduct personal interviews as well as computer-assisted laboratories to run telephone interviews. They have experts on staff to handle sampling issues and the design of instrumentation.

A third advantage of secondary analysis is the quantity of data. Most national survey interviewer teams interview more than 1,000 respondents in a matter of weeks or even days. Few researchers could ever interview 100 respondents within a reasonable time frame. Besides the benefits for generalizability, large samples make it feasible to study groups or individuals that are uncommon in the population. For example, a national survey of 1,500 households with children would probably include several hundred households where the parents are cohabiting but are not married.

Secondary analysis would seem to have it all: low cost, high quality, and large quantities of data. However, secondary analysis has at least three major drawbacks. First, the data have to already exist. For example, if you want to study Asian American single-parent households, you may be out of luck: A data set may not be available with sufficient information about this particular population. Second, even if you find a study that was used to gather data on the appropriate population, the interview may not have included questions on the key variables needed for the analyses. Alternatively, even if the appropriate questions were included in the original survey, they may not have been asked of the respondents you want to study. In many surveys, not all survey questions are asked of all respondents. The well-known National Survey of Families and Households, for instance, included extensive questions about performance of housework of all adult respondents in its first wave but interviewers gathered information about child-care only from parents of very young children.

In this chapter, we discuss the use of secondary data for studying families. Additional information can be found in one of the classic texts on secondary analysis (Hyman, 1987). Vartanian (2011) discusses working with secondary data, focusing on data that may be useful to scholars studying families. Andersen, Prause, and Silver (2011) provide a practical guide to using secondary data generally while Heaton (2004) focuses exclusively on how to perform secondary analysis with qualitative data.

If the appropriate data are available, the advantages to doing secondary analysis are tremendous. What kinds of secondary data sources are commonly used in research on families and children?

We provide summaries of sources of secondary data organized by the population being studied. Data are grouped together based upon how they may be used. We group some studies based upon the age of the individuals when the studies began (childhood, adolescence, or older adulthood). Studies on families and households are grouped together based upon whether the data were collected from the same families over time (panel data) or from different families (trend data).

Data on Children

Early Childhood Longitudinal Study

The Early Childhood Longitudinal Study (ECLS) examines three longitudinal studies: child development, school readiness, and early school experiences. The program provides national data on children at birth, and follows up at various points in their life, such as children's transitions to nonparental care, early education programs, and school. It also examines the children's experiences and growth until the eighth grade. ECLS provides data analyzing the relationships between the child and his or her family, school, and community. Their most recent cohort is a kindergarten class of 2010–2011, following the children from kindergarten through fifth grade. Their website is https://nces.ed.gov/ecls/.

National Survey of Children's Health

The National Survey of Children's Health has been conducted four times: 2003, 2007, 2011, and most recently in 2016 through the Census Bureau. Another round is scheduled for 2018. The 2016 version integrated two surveys: The National Survey for Children's Health and the National

Survey of Children with Special Health Care Needs (NS-CSHCN). This survey focuses on the physical and emotional health of over 91,000 U.S children ages 0 to 17 years of age. Data collection has focused on factors that may relate to the well-being of children, such as family interactions, parental health, school and after school experiences, neighborhood characteristics, and access to health insurance. The website for the National Survey of Children's Health is https://census.gov/programs-surveys/nsch.html.

Data on Adolescents

The National Longitudinal Study of Adolescent Health

The National Longitudinal Study of Adolescent Health is a nationally representative study that explores the causes of health-related behaviors of 90,118 adolescents in Grades 7 through 12 in 1994 and 1995 and their outcomes in young adulthood. The project examines how social contexts (families, friends, peers, schools, neighborhoods, and communities) influence adolescents' health and risk behaviors. Data were collected in four waves between 1994 and 2008 from adolescents, their parents and siblings, their fellow students, and school administrators, and, in later waves, romantic partners. The website is located at www.cpc.unc.edu/projects/addhealth.

National Longitudinal Surveys

The National Longitudinal Surveys (NLSs), sponsored and directed by the Bureau of Labor Statistics, U.S. Department of Labor, are used to gather detailed information about the labor market experiences and other aspects of the lives of six groups of men and women. Over the years, a variety of other government agencies—such as the National Institute of Child Health and Human Development (NICHD), the Department of Defense, the Department of Education, the Department of Justice, the National Institute on Drug Abuse, and the National School to Work Office—have funded parts of the surveys that provided data relevant to their missions. As a result, the surveys include data about a wide range of events such as schooling and career transitions, marriage and fertility, training investments, child-care use, and drug and alcohol use. The depth and breadth of each survey allow for analysis of an expansive variety of topics such as the transition from school to work, job mobility, youth unemployment, educational attainment and the returns to education, welfare recipiency, the impact of training, and retirement decisions.

The first set of surveys, started in 1966, consisted of four cohorts. These four groups are referred to as the older men, mature women, young men, and young women cohorts of the NLS and are known collectively as the original cohorts. In 1979, a longitudinal study of a cohort of young men and women ages 14 to 22 years commenced. This sample of youth was called the National Longitudinal Survey of Youth 1979 (NLSY79). In 1986, the NLSY79 was expanded to include surveys of the children born to women in that cohort and called the NLSY79 Children; and then, in 1994, the young adult children of these women began to be interviewed. In 1997, the NLS program was again expanded with a new cohort of young people ages 12 to 16 years as of December 31, 1996. This new cohort is the NLSY97.

The NLSY79 respondents were interviewed annually until 1994 and biennially since. Data collected during the surveys of the NLSY79 chronicle these changes and provide researchers with a unique opportunity to study in detail the life-course experiences of a large group of young adults representative of all American men and women born in the late 1950s and early 1960s.

The NLSY sampling design enables researchers to study the longitudinal experiences of this particular age group of young Americans as well as analyze the disparate life-course experiences of such groups as women, Hispanics, blacks, and the economically disadvantaged. The NLSY comprises three subsamples. The main sample is a cross-sectional sample of 6,111 youth designed to be representative of the noninstitutionalized civilian segment of young people living in the United States in 1979 and born between January 1, 1957, and December 31, 1964. Supplemental samples are designed to oversample civilian Hispanic, black, and economically disadvantaged white youth, as well as a sample of 1,280 youth who were enlisted in the four branches of the military as of September 30, 1978, for a total sample size of 12,686 in 1979.

Besides extensive information about education, training, employment, and earnings, the NLSY also contains a wealth of information of interest to researchers studying families and children. Information is also available about a respondent's marital status at each survey date, changes in marital status since last interview, and month and year that marital status was recorded, as well as information on a respondent's spouse, including birth and death dates, occupation, educational attainment, labor force status, religious affiliation, and (for select points in time) health limitations. Extensive fertility and child-care data have also been collected.

The NLSY Children data set provides information both on the experiences of NLSY women as they became mothers and on the birth and early childhood of their children. The availability of these child data, coupled with longitudinal information on the family background, education, employment histories, and economic well-being of each NLSY mother, provides researchers a unique opportunity to examine the linkages between maternal and family behaviors and attitudes and subsequent child development.

A battery of child cognitive, socio-emotional, and physiological assessments has been administered biennially since 1986 to the NLSY children. Beginning in 1988, those NLSY children ages 10 years and older answered a separate set of questions that gathered information on a variety of family-, school-, and job-related topics. In 1994, the young adult children began answering questions that mirror those their mothers have and continue to answer as part of the NLSY79. The NLSY has been the data source for thousands of published articles and dozens of research monographs. The NLS website is https://www.bls.gov/nls.

Data on Older Adults

Health and Retirement Study

The Health and Retirement Study (HRS) surveys approximately 20,000 people across America. Run by the University of Michigan, the study is supported by the National Institute on Aging (NIAU01AG009740) and the Social Security Administration. The goal of HRS is to provide data that can address important questions about the challenges and opportunities of aging. HRS includes the original study, in which data was collected in 1992, 1994, and 1996, and the AHEAD study, which data was collected in 1993 and 1995. These studies represent the U.S. population over the age of 50 in 1998. An additional five cohorts have been added into the study: children of the Depression (born between 1924–1930) and the War Babies (born between 1942–1947) (both added in 1998), the Early Baby Boomers (born between 1948–1953; added in 2004), the Mid Baby Boomers (born between 1954–1959; added in 2004), and the Late Baby Boomers (born between 1960–1965; added in 2016). Together, all the cohorts create a major national panel study of the lives of older Americans. The HRS website is https://hrs.isr.umich.edu/about?_ga=2.145101815.233038625.1510 695600772158201.1510695600.

Midlife in the United States (MIDUS)

MIDUS (Midlife in the U.S.) is a national sample of continental U.S. residents, ages 25 to 74, who were first interviewed in 1995–1996. In addition to a national probability sample (N = 3,487), the study included oversamples in select metropolitan areas (N = 757), a sample of siblings (N = 950) of the main respondents, and a national sample of twin pairs (N = 1,914). MIDUS focuses on patterns, predictors, and consequences of midlife development in the areas of physical health, psychological well-being, and social responsibility. The website for MIDUS is http://midus.wisc.edu/.

National Health and Aging Trends Study

The National Health and Aging Trends Study (NHATS) began in 2011 investigating the trends in late-life functioning; how these differ for various population subgroups; and the economic and social consequences of aging and disability for individuals, families, and society. NHATS gathers information on a nationally representative sample of Medicare beneficiaries ages 65 and older. The sample is refreshed periodically so that researchers may study national-level disability trends as well as individual trajectories. Annual, in-person interviews collect detailed information on the disablement process and its consequences. The website for NHATS is http://www.nhats.org/.

National Social Life, Health, and Aging Project

The National Social Life, Health, and Aging Project (NSHAP) is a longitudinal, population-based study that began in 2005 that examines the well-being of older Americans as a function of physical health and illness, medication use, cognitive function, emotional health, sensory function, health behaviors, social connectedness, sexuality, and relationship quality. More than 3,000 interviews with a nationally representative sample of adults born between 1920 and 1947 (aged 57 to 85 at time of interview) were initially conducted. In 2010 and 2011, nearly 3,400 interviews were completed for Wave 2 with these Wave 1 Respondents, Wave 1 Non-Interviewed Respondents, and their spouses or cohabiting romantic partners. Data in both waves include interview responses, responses to a self-administered questionnaire, and biomeasures. A third wave of data collection is anticipated in 2018. The website for NSHAP is http://www.norc.org/Research/Projects/Pages/national-social-life-health-and-aging-project.aspx.

The National Institute on Aging has compiled a list of publicly available databases for aging-related secondary analyses in the behavioral and social sciences. More information on the above data sources and others are available on their website: https://www.nia.nih.gov/research/dbsr/publicly-available-databases-aging-related-secondary-analyses-behavioral-and-social.

Data on Families and Households

Panel Studies of Families and Households

Each of these studies has longitudinal (panel) data on families, children, and households. The data sets can be complex and sometimes difficult to work with but they are a goldmine for researchers looking at change over time.

National Survey of Families and Households

The National Survey of Families and Households (NSFH) includes interviews with 13,007 respondents from a national sample. The sample includes a main cross-section of 9,637 households plus an oversampling of blacks, Puerto Ricans, Mexican Americans, single-parent families, families with stepchildren, cohabiting couples, and recently married persons. One adult per household was randomly selected as the primary respondent. Wave 1 of the National Survey of Families and Households was completed in 1987. Five years later, 10,007 surviving members of the original sample were reinterviewed for Wave 2, along with many current and former spouses, partners, children, and parents. A third wave was conducted in 2001 through 2002, where 9,230 main respondent, spouse, and focal child interviews were completed, along with 924 proxy interviews for respondents who were too ill to participate or were deceased.

A considerable amount of life-history information was collected, including the respondent's family living arrangements in childhood; the experience of leaving the parental home; marital and cohabitation experiences; and education, fertility, and employment histories. The design permits the detailed description of past and current living arrangements and other characteristics and experiences, as well as the analysis of the consequences of earlier patterns on current states, marital and parenting relationships, kin contact, and economic and psychological well-being.

This study has been undertaken explicitly to provide a data resource for the research community at large and has been designed in light of advice from many consultants and correspondents. To this end, the substantive coverage has remained broad, which permits the holistic analysis of family experience from an array of theoretical perspectives. Further information about the NSFH is available through its website at https://www.ssc.wisc.edu/nsfh/.

Marital Instability Over the Life Course

Booth, Johnson, Amato, and Rogers (2003) studied divorce proneness, marital problems, marital happiness, marital interaction, and marital disagreements. This study consisted of data drawn from a six-wave panel study. Initially, the investigators devoted considerable attention to female labor force participation as it related to marital dissolution and divorce proneness. For the last two waves, the investigators drew heavily on a life-course perspective to guide their investigation. Life-course theories emphasize the extent to which social behaviors are a product of individuals' relative positions along a developmental continuum. A total of 1,066 individuals completed all six waves. Topics addressed in the study include demographics (e.g., household characteristics, race, income, religion, education); history of marriage and divorce; premarital courtship history; marital behavior (e.g., division of labor, quarreling and/or violence); mental and physical health of husband and wife; employment (history, status, attitudes, aspirations); attitudes about children; satisfaction about various aspects of life (e.g., marriage, home, community); problem areas in marriage, divorce, and separation (including previous discussions and current behavior, attitudes about divorce); and involvement with friends, relatives, voluntary associations, and the community. More information on the Marital Instability Over the Life Course study can be found at https://www.icpsr.umich.edu/icpsrweb/NACDA/studies/3812.

Panel Study of Income Dynamics

The Panel Study of Income Dynamics (PSID), initiated in 1968, is a longitudinal study of a representative sample of U.S. individuals (men, women, and children) and the family units in which they reside. It emphasizes the dynamic aspects of economic and demographic behavior; but its content is broad, including sociological and psychological measures. Because of low attrition rates and the success of recontact efforts, the sample size has grown dramatically. The PSID began with information on 5,000 families in 1968, growing to more than 9,000 families and 22,000 individuals in 2010. As of 2010, the PSID had collected information about more than 70,000 individuals, spanning as many as 30 years of their lives. The study is conducted at the Institute for Social Research, University of Michigan.

The PSID has reinterviewed individuals from those households annually, whether or not they are living in the same dwelling or with the same people. Adults have been followed as they have grown older, and children have been observed as they advance through childhood and into adulthood, forming family units of their own.

Information about the original 1968 sample individuals and their current coresidents (spouses, cohabitants, children, and anyone else living with them) is collected annually. In 1990, a representative national sample of 2,000 Latino households, differentially sampled to provide adequate numbers of Puerto Rican, Mexican, and Cuban Americans, was added to the PSID database. In 1997 and 1999, a sample of 511 immigrant families was also added to the database. A Child Development Supplement is a collection of data from more than 2,300 families in 1997 when children were 0 to 12 years, in 2002 to 2003 when children were 5 to 18, and in 2007 to 2008 for children ages 10 to 18. Those turning 18 are now participating in the Transition to Adulthood study, which began collecting data in 2005.

The PSID provides a wide variety of information about both families and their individual members, plus some information about the areas where they live. The central focus of the data is economic and demographic, with substantial detail on income sources and amounts, employment, family composition changes, and residential location. Content of a more socio-logical or psychological nature is also included in some waves of the study. Information gathered in the survey applies to the circumstances of the family unit as a whole (e.g., type of housing) or to particular persons in the family unit (e.g., age, earnings). Although some information is collected about all individuals in the family unit, the greatest level of detail is ascertained for the primary adults heading the family unit. Access to the PSID website is at http://psidonline.isr.umich.edu.

Fragile Families & Child Wellbeing Study

The Fragile Families and Child Wellbeing Study collects data from a cohort of nearly 5,000 children born in large U.S. cities between 1998 and 2000. The majority of these children were born to unmarried parents, leading the authors of the study to label the families as "fragile families" due to their greater risk of economic and residential instability over time. The study includes interviews with mothers, fathers, and/or primary caregivers at birth and again when children are ages 1, 3, 5, 9, and 15. In-home assessments of the children were performed alongside the interviews. Six waves of data were available as of 2018. The website for the Fragile Families and Child Wellbeing Study is https://fragilefamilies.princeton.edu/about.

Studies With Trend Data
on Families and Households

In the United States, probably the best-known large-scale data sets available for research are those gathered by the U.S. Census Bureau, which conducts four series that are of particular interest to researchers interested in families and children.

Decennial Census

The Decennial Census is conducted every 10 years. In Census 2010, all U. S. households received the *short form* questionnaire that asks about only seven topics concerning members of the household: name, age, sex, Hispanic origin, race, relationship, and whether the home is owned or rented. The data from the Decennial Censuses are the closest information we have to population data about the entire United States. The 2010 Census website is https://www.census.gov/programs-surveys/decennial-census/decade.2010.html.

American Community Survey

In 2005, the Census Bureau launched the American Community Survey (ACS). Officially part of the Decennial Census, the ACS contains essentially the same questions that were once included on the Census long form. The ACS is sent to a rolling sample of addresses every month throughout the nation. Questions in ACS cover marital status and marital history, fertility, grandparents as caregivers, and other information family researchers may be interested in examining. The American Community Survey website is https://www.census.gov/programs-surveys/acs/.

Current Population Survey

For over 70 years, the Census Bureau and the Bureau of Labor Statistics have collected information about the population of the United States with the Current Population Survey (CPS). Although the collection of labor force information each month is the primary reason for the existence of the survey, over the years, other family-related items including educational enrollment and attainment, income and poverty information, fertility, and voting activity have been added to the CPS. In January 1994, the Census Bureau began collecting data on nativity, citizenship, year of entry, and parental nativity of respondents. The universe for the CPS is the civilian noninstitutional population of the United States.

The primary goal of the CPS is the development of statistical data about the civilian labor force, but it also obtains additional information about each member of the interviewed household, as well as labor-related data for the population age 15 years or older. The monthly survey captures information about characteristics such as age, race, sex, employment status, family characteristics, and marital status. Every March, the survey includes a set of special questions, called the *annual demographic supplement*. The March supplement captures additional information such as hours and weeks worked, monetary income received in the previous calendar year, and social program use. The CPS website is https://www.bls.gov/cps.

American Time Use Survey

The American Time Use Survey (ATUS) began in 2003. Individuals who have completed their eighth month of the CPS are eligible for the ATUS. From this eligible group, households are selected that allow for a demographically representative sample (estimated sample size is approximately 26,000 per year). One person age 15 or older is then asked to answer questions about their time use. Data are collected through telephone interviews, where individuals are then asked a series of questions corresponding to a time diary. Specifically, respondents are asked to provide a detailed account of their activities beginning at 4 a.m. the previous day and ending at 4 a.m.

the day of the interview. These data have been used to look at time spent in household tasks, child-care, leisure, and work. The American Time Use Survey website is https://www.bls.gov/tus.

In addition to these datasets available from the U.S. Census Bureau, there are a number of studies produced by other sources.

National Survey of Family Growth

The National Survey of Family Growth (NSFG) was initially designed to be the official fertility survey of the United States. Funded through the National Center for Health Statistics, the first five surveys of women, Cycles 1 to 5 (1973, 1976, 1982, 1988, and 1995), were based on personal in-home interviews of a national sample of civilian women ages 15 to 44. The goal of these surveys (where average sample size was approximately 9,000 women) was to provide reliable data on marriage, divorce, contraception, infertility, and health of U.S. women and infants.

The 2002 NSFG survey (Cycle 6) was designed to provide fertility and relationship data for both women and men. The survey was conducted through in-person interviews with 7,643 women and 4,928 men. Starting in 2006, the NSFG survey shifted to being conducted as a continuous survey. During the 2006–2010 time frame, 22,600 interviews were conducted, over 12,000 with women and over 10,000 with men. The 2011–2013 and 2013–2015 NSFG data files each include over 10,000 interviews. Beginning in September 2015, NSFG expanded its age range for both women and men from 15 to 44 to 15 to 49. The National Survey of Family Growth website is https://www.cdc.gov/nchs/nsfg/about_nsfg.htm.

National Study of the Changing Workforce

The Families and Work Institute administers a National Study of the Changing Workforce (NSCW) approximately every 5 years (1992, 1997, 2002, and 2008). While not a panel study, the NSCW is a collection of information on the intersection of work and family life alongside detailed information about work experiences from a representative sample of approximately 3,500 U.S. workers each wave. Information on work–life conflict, division of household and child-care tasks, and attitudes regarding maternal employment and shared household responsibilities among employed individuals are available for investigation, including for trend analysis. The Families and Work Institute website is www.familiesandwork.org.

General Social Survey

The General Social Survey (GSS) is a regular, ongoing, omnibus, personal interview survey of U.S. households conducted by the National

Opinion Research Center (NORC). The first survey took place in 1972, and since then, more than 55,000 respondents have answered more than 5,400 different questions.

From Americans' racial attitudes to the number of guns owned by women to musical preferences over a lifetime, the GSS measures trends in American attitudes, experiences, practices, and concerns. The various surveys include extensive information about family-size preferences, marital history, parenting issues, abortion, and divorce.

The mission of the GSS is to make timely, high-quality, scientifically relevant data available to the social science research community. Since 1972, the GSS has conducted 28 independent cross-sectional surveys of the adult household population of the United States. These surveys have been widely distributed and extensively analyzed by social scientists around the world. To date, the NORC has documented the publication of more than 14,000 scholarly publications and Ph.D. dissertations using the GSS data.

Since 1985, the GSS has had a part in the International Social Survey Program (ISSP), a consortium of social scientists from 48 countries around the world. The ISSP asks an identical battery of questions in all countries; the U.S. version of these questions is incorporated into the GSS. The ISSP regularly includes a supplement on family and gender issues, most recently in 2012.

The basic purposes of the GSS are to gather data on contemporary American society to monitor and explain trends and constants in attitudes, behaviors, and attributes; examine the structure and functioning of society in general as well as the role played by relevant subgroups; compare the United States to other societies, placing American society in comparative perspective and developing cross-national models of human society; and make high-quality data easily accessible to scholars, students, policymakers, and others at minimal cost. The GSS website is gss.norc.org/.

Sources of Secondary Data Sets

For most university students and faculty, the primary source of secondary data is the Inter-university Consortium for Political and Social Research (ICPSR). Established in 1962, ICPSR is a membership-based organization providing access to the world's largest archive of computer-based research and instructional data for the social sciences. ICPSR further serves social scientists around the world by offering training facilities in basic and advanced techniques of quantitative social analysis and other resources that facilitate secondary analysis. ICPSR provides facilities and services for an international community of scholars that no one college or university could offer independently.

The data holdings cover a broad range of disciplines, including political science, sociology, demography, economics, history, education, gerontology, criminal justice, public health, foreign policy, and law. ICPSR encourages social scientists in all fields to contribute to and use ICPSR's data resources. Many data sets are freely available with no restrictions, while others, particularly those with sensitive data, require special approval in order to obtain the data.

ICPSR includes among its members more than 700 academic institutions and research organizations worldwide. ICPSR member institutions pay annual dues that entitle their faculty, staff, and students to acquire the full range of services ICPSR provides. Individuals at nonmember schools can also order data for an access fee. Headquarters and central staff of ICPSR are located in the Institute for Social Research at the University of Michigan; the ICPSR home page is at https://www.icpsr.umich.edu/icpsrweb/.

Funded by the Office of Planning, Research and Evaluation, Administration for Children and Families (OPRE), U.S. Department of Health and Human Services, and organized by ICPSR and The National Center for Children in Poverty, The Child Care & Early Education Research Connections is a website that gives free access to thousands of publications and datasets. The goal of Research Connections is to promote high-quality research on families and children so that research can be used in policy decisions. The website provides compilations of data sets for use, research reports, and resources for constructing and evaluating research. Research Connections' website is https://www.researchconnections.org/childcare/welcome.

Another source of large-scale data sets on children, adolescents, and families and households across the life course (including data on adolescent pregnancy and prevention, aging, and maternal drug abuse) is Sociometrics, a private organization that provides research materials for behavioral and social scientists. These materials include data sets as well as implementation protocols for evidence-based programs designed to implement change. Research data on American families are available through searching the Sociometrics data archive. Researchers can choose to purchase one or several datasets or services from Sociometrics, depending on their research needs. Sociometrics' webpage is https://www.socio.com.

In 2018, Google launched Dataset Search, a search engine that allows users to find datasets wherever they are hosted. Datasets are searched based on such key information such as who created the dataset, when it was published, how the data was collected, and what the terms are for using the data. Dataset Search links to the information, analyzes where different versions of the same dataset might be, and finds publications that may be describing or discussing the dataset. See https://toolbox.google.com/datasetsearch.

Most secondary data tends to be quantitative, as survey data in particular lend themselves to broad distribution. However, there are sources of secondary qualitative data as well. The Murray Research Archive Original Collection Dataverse is the repository for quantitative and qualitative data at the Harvard University Institute for Quantitative Social Science. Data from almost 200 studies relating to family are archived there, many of them with qualitative data. The Murray Research Archive Original Collection Dataverse website is http://dvn.iq.harvard.edu/dvn. Researchers are also encouraged to do their own investigation to find other sources of qualitative data available for secondary analysis.

Future Trends in Secondary Data Analysis

Increasingly, major research project administrators are making their data available at no charge for download. Federally funded research is mandated to be made available to the public; any new data collected using federal funds must have a data repository and archiving plan for making the data available once the projected has been completed. Often, the data, codebooks, questionnaires, and supplemental materials from a project are available. The NLSY, the GSS, and the NSFH are among the projects that provide data in this fashion. Many universities are creating their own data-archiving system. Like the Harvard archive described above, these university-owned and maintained Web archives allow for access to data archived by university scholars as well as access to data that the university has purchased. The UNC-Odum Archive Dataverse is another example (https://dataverse.unc.edu/). Scholars based at a research institution should check to see whether their school has constructed one of these archives.

Further, research projects and data archiving sites have begun moving toward individually tailored data set construction and instant online analysis of data. Federally funded research projects, including the NLS studies and the Census Bureau, allow for immediate access to both data and analysis. For example, the NLS studies provide the means to construct a data set from their website, allowing users the ability to download only the variables needed for analysis—as well as filtering out cases that may not be relevant (e.g., filtering out men for analyses on pregnancy). The Census Bureau provides access to multiple Census data sources through their interactive applications allowing users to create tables and perform other data visualization procedures through their website. Similar to the NLS studies, the GSS has constructed an online tool for constructing a data set from the cumulative 1997 through 2016 files that includes only the variables and cases of interest, performing basic analysis, and preparing tabular and graphical results.

STUDY QUESTIONS

1. Use the Research Connections website (https://www.researchconnections .org/childcare/welcome) to locate a data set on a family-related topic of interest to you. Using the information contained in the abstract, answer the following questions about the project: (a) Who conducted the study? (b) When and where were the data collected? (c) What method was used to collect the data? (d) How many cases, observations, or respondents are included in the data set? (e) List three general areas or topics about the data collected in the study.

2. Find three family-related articles that each use a different data set discussed in this chapter (e.g., Current Population Survey, Health and Retirement Study, National Survey of Families and Households). Briefly describe each of the articles.

CHAPTER 12

Analyzing Data on Families and Children

A rticles and monographs studying families and children overwhelmingly report some type of statistical tests or measures, what are sometimes called quantitative analysis. Although the language of statistical analysis may seem a bit daunting at first, the good news is that you can develop a basic ability to interpret the results of common statistical techniques fairly easily.

Statistical techniques can be grouped into two general categories. **Descriptive statistics** are techniques used to summarize information about samples. **Inferential statistics** are used to make statements about population characteristics based on sample data.

Descriptive Statistics

Descriptive statistics allow us to summarize data gathered from large numbers of respondents. If you are studying only a few families, you could easily summarize the characteristics of those families in a paragraph or two. You could talk about their general neighborhoods, the parents' jobs, the number of children in each family, and so forth. This becomes impossible, however, if you're looking at more than a handful of respondents. Just listing the occupations of 400 sets of parents takes up several sheets of paper, which makes it difficult to get a grasp of the general patterns.

Descriptive statistics are designed to summarize the numerical distribution of sample data. We are generally concerned with three aspects of our sample distributions. **Central** tendency measures look at the location of our data: Where on the continuum are most respondents' scores located? Do they tend to have high-, low-, or middle-range scores? Second, we are concerned with the dispersion of the data. Measures of **variability** indicate how widespread or dispersed the data are across the continuum. Are most respondents' scores concentrated at one or two points along the continuum? Or are the scores somewhat evenly scattered? Finally, **measures of association** tell us how two or more variables are related to each other in the sample data.

Measures of Central Tendency

The most commonly reported measure of central tendency is the **mean** score, which is simply the numerical average of the scores. The mean is only appropriate for use with variables at the interval or ratio level of measurement.

Another common measure of central tendency is the **median** (also referred to as the 50th percentile), which is the score that divides the sample distribution in half. Half of the respondents' scores are above the median, and half of the respondents' scores are below the median. When government reports say that the median household income in the United States for 2016 is $59,039, this means that half of all households have incomes below $59,039 and half have incomes above that level. The median is appropriate for data measured at the ordinal, interval, or ratio levels.

Finally, the **mode** is the most frequently appearing score in the sample distribution. It is appropriate for variables at all levels of measurement.

When discussing central tendency of an interval- or ratio-level variable, family researchers will usually report only the mean for a variable unless the distribution of the variable is highly skewed one way or another. Family income is a good example of a variable with a highly skewed distribution; although most households are clustered in the lower end of the distribution, a few households are far out on the high end of the income range—which tends to pull the estimate of the mean value upward.

For example, in 2016, the U.S. Census Bureau reported that the mean, or average, income of American households was $83,143 (U.S. Census Bureau, 2017). This figure is misleading, however, because the distribution of household income is skewed or lopsided—there are far more households at the low end of the distribution than at the high end. However, a relatively small number of households with extremely high incomes can *pull* the mean upward. In fact, the median household income in 2016 was $59,039. In other words, even though the average, or mean, household income was $83,143, 50% of all American households reported less than $59,039 in income (in fact, approximately 20% reported less than $25,000 in income).

Measures of Variability

Probably the most frequently used measure of central tendency is the **standard deviation**, which measures the amount of variability in variables measured at the interval or ratio levels. Smaller values of the standard deviation indicate less variability in the scores, whereas larger values suggest more variability. A standard deviation of 0 means that all the scores are at the same point or value in the distribution; in other words, there is no variability in the distribution. The **variance** is the value of the standard deviation squared. Both the variance and standard deviation are appropriate only for data measured at the interval or ratio levels.

The **range** is simply the arithmetic difference between the lowest and highest scores in the distribution. For example, if the smallest household in a data set has only one member and the largest has 17 members, the range is $17 - 1$, or 16. The **interquartile range** is the difference between the first-quartile score (below which 25% of the scores fall) and the third-quartile score (below which 75% of the scores fall).

Let's illustrate these terms with a concrete example. Wave 1 of the National Survey of Families and Households surveyed 13,017 adults in the United States during 1987. The household incomes ranged from $0 to $988,672, yielding a range of $988,672. The first-quartile score was $6,000 (meaning that 25% of the households had total incomes of $6,000 or less), and the third-quartile score was $36,000, giving an interquartile range of $30,000. The mean, or average, total household income was $26,034, and the median household income was $18,000. The mode, or the most frequently reported income level, was $0. The standard deviation for the household-income data was $37,212, and the variance was $1,384,780,895.

Measures of Association

Family researchers often need to know how variables are related to (or associated with) each other. Is wives' income related to the probability of divorce? How are spouses' educational levels and frequency of marital violence associated? Are parental cognitive-ability levels related to the ability levels of children?

The choice of a specific **measure of association** is largely dependent on the level of measurement for the variables involved. When the variables are measured at the nominal level, commonly reported measures are lambda (λ_{yx}) and the **uncertainty coefficient** (U_{yx}). Each takes on values between 0 and 1, where 1 indicates a **perfect relationship**—that is, knowing the value of the independent variable allows you to perfectly predict the value of the dependent variable—and 0 indicates no relationship at all. Notice that these measures do not connote direction of the relationship because it doesn't make sense to speak of the direction of a relationship between two nominally scaled variables (i.e., we can't say that there is a positive or negative relationship between marital status and income; we can merely assert that some marital statuses have higher mean incomes than others).

For ordinal-level data, the measures of choice are usually **gamma** (γ) or **Somer's D_{yx}**. They range from −1 (indicating a perfect negative relationship) through zero (indicating no relationship) to +1 (indicating a perfect positive relationship). When working with ordinally scaled variables, the direction of the relationship is important and meaningful. That is, it makes sense to say that there is a positive association between mother's cognitive skills and those of her children.

The **correlation coefficient** (often referred to as Pearson's r) is the most commonly used measure of association for interval-level data. The correlation coefficient also ranges from −1 through 0 to +1. The **coefficient of determination** (often referred to as r^2) is the square of the correlation coefficient and ranges from 0 to +1.

When interpreting measures of association, it's important to remember that there are no perfect associations in real-world data. Correlation coefficient values of .1 or .2 are common in analyses of data on families, and the failure to attain values close to 1 (or even of .5) should not necessarily be taken as an indication that the relationship or association is not substantively important. As with most things in social research, we need to consider the values of the measures of association in the context of the research topic and especially in comparison to findings from similar studies.

Interpreting Cross-Classification Tables

Research findings involving categorical variables are often reported in the form of cross-classification tables. The construction of such tables is relatively straightforward. They consist of a series of rows (usually representing the categories of the dependent variable) and columns (usually representing the categories of the independent variable) that intersect to form a series of cells. The entries in the cells usually represent the number of observations in the sample that fall into that combination of values of the independent and dependent variables. Another value that might appear in the cells represents the percentage of respondents within a particular category of the independent variable who also possessed a particular category of the dependent variable.

Table 12.1 is an example of a cross-classification table. Notice that the table has a descriptive title ("Effects of Marital Status on General Happiness") that identifies the independent (marital status) and dependent (general happiness) variables. The source of the data, the General Social Survey (a national sample of 2,858 American adults interviewed in 2016), is given beneath the table. The rows of the table represent the categories of the dependent variable (happiness): *very happy, pretty happy,* and *not too happy*. The columns of the table represent the categories of the independent variable (marital status): *currently married, separated, divorced, widowed,* and *never married*.

Table 12.1 Effects of Marital Status on General Happiness

Happiness	Marital Status					Totals
	Currently Married	Separated	Divorced	Widowed	Never Married	
Very happy	465 (38.5%)	26 (25.7%)	100 (20.2%)	59 (23.5%)	156 (19.4%)	806
Pretty happy	657 (54.4%)	46 (45.5%)	281 (56.7%)	126 (50.1%)	490 (61.0%)	1,600
Not too happy	86 (7.1%)	29 (28.7%)	114 (23.0%)	66 (26.2%)	157 (19.5%)	452
Totals	1,208 (100%)	101 (100%)	495 (100%)	251 (100%)	803 (100%)	2,858 (100%)

Source: General Social Survey, 2016.

Note: Table entries are cell frequencies and, in parentheses, column percentages.

In each cell in the table are two numbers. Examine the cell for persons who are married and very happy (the upper left cell in the table). The cell entries inform us that there were 465 such people out of the 2,858 respondents. These 465 married people who said that they were "very happy" make up 38.5% of the 1,208 currently married people in the sample. Put another way, the table tells us that of the currently married people in our sample, in addition to the 38.5% very happy people, 54.4% said that they were "pretty happy," and only 7.1% said that they were "not too happy."

Now, while it may be interesting to know what percentage of married people say they are "very happy," our concern in constructing a cross-classification table is to learn something about the *relationship* between two variables. To do this, we need to compare the results for married people to respondents in the other categories of marital status. If we compare the figures with those of never-married individuals, an interesting picture emerges. Married people are twice as likely as those who have never been married to be very happy: Almost 40% of the married people said that they were very happy, whereas only 19.4% of the never marrieds felt this way. And whereas only about 7% of the married persons said that they were not too happy, nearly one fifth of the never marrieds fell into this category.

The general strategy for interpreting cross-classification tables, therefore, is fairly straightforward. If the table is set up properly (with the categories of the independent variable represented in the columns of the table and the categories of the dependent variable in the rows) and the percentages are calculated correctly (within categories of the independent variable), then we can compare percentages within categories of the dependent variable across categories of the independent variable.

Interpreting this table, we can conclude that married persons are more likely to say that they are very happy and less likely to say that they are not too happy than are persons of any other marital status. In other words, it looks as if marital status is associated with general happiness: Married people tend to be happier than those who are separated, divorced, widowed, or never married.

A logical next step is to calculate the appropriate measure of association (for this particular table, the uncertainty coefficient would be a good choice) to measure the strength of the association between marital status and general happiness. The uncertainty coefficient for these data is .037. Although this value is not particularly large (recall that the uncertainty coefficient ranges from 0 to 1), in the context of the research problem, a result of .037 is about in the range of what a researcher would expect to find for these two variables. Any conclusions about the existence of an association, however, require what is known as an inferential test.

Inferential Statistics

The purpose of descriptive statistics is to describe the characteristics of a sample. Typically, however, we are not primarily concerned with the characteristics of the respondents in the sample; we are more interested in knowing something about the characteristics of the population from which the sample data were drawn. For example, it's nice to know the value of the median family size in a particular sample of families, but the value of the median family size in the entire population from which the sample was drawn probably is more interesting.

Inferential statistics are designed to make inferences or estimates about the population values of measures of central tendency, variation, or association based on sample data. Inferential statistics use the characteristics of probability samples to make estimates about the likelihood, or probability, that a particular population parameter is equal to a particular value or within a particular range of values. Whenever authors write about significance levels or probability levels, they are almost certainly using inferential statistics to make estimates of population values.

There are at least two different uses of the term *significance* in the research literature. One has to do with **substantive significance**. Simply put, substantive significance asks, "Is this a difference that really matters?" If the median family size for one group is 3.32 persons and the median for another group is 3.14 persons, the two groups have *different* median family sizes. But is this a large enough difference to make a difference? That is, do any theoretical, social, or policy implications result from this difference of .18 persons? This type of question can be answered only in the context of the research question. In some areas of research, a difference of .18 might be important indeed; in others, it may be trivial.

Statistical significance, however, refers to the results of inferential tests. In their most general form, tests of statistical significance ask, "How likely is this (or a more extreme) result to have occurred by chance?" The conventional standard for statistical significance is the .05 (or 5%) level, suggesting that such a result would occur only 5% of the time by chance alone. Inferential tests with results at or beyond this level (that is, probability levels equal to or less than .05) generally indicate "real" effects or differences in the populations from which the data were drawn. An author might write that a particular difference is "statistically significant beyond the .05 level," meaning that the probability associated with the inferential test was .05 or less.

Another way of thinking about statistical significance is in terms of inferences about populations. Analyses of sample data are often used to make inferences about the populations from which the samples were drawn. When researchers perform significance tests on sample data, they are attempting to test hypotheses about the population based on the sample data. For example, we might want to compare income levels for husbands and wives from a national sample of 900 married persons. In the sample, the mean (average) income for husbands might be $6,000 more than the mean income for wives. In other words, the mean income levels for husbands and wives in this sample are, without question, different; the differential between the two groups is $6,000. However, we are less concerned about these particular 900 husbands and wives than we are with what these sample data can tell us about the total population of husbands and wives in the United States (about 61 million married couples at last count). Consequently, the sample data might be used to test the hypothesis that, in the population from which the sample data were drawn, husbands average $6,000 more in annual income than do wives. A statistically significant result on this hypothesis test might lead us to conclude that the sample data do indeed support the idea that husbands average $6,000 more in income than wives.

One important caveat: Statistical significance does not necessarily imply substantive significance. That a given difference or effect is statistically significant at or beyond the conventional .05 level does not, by itself, mean that the difference or effect is substantively important. Generally speaking, statistically significant results are easier to obtain as the size of the sample increases, so even fairly trivial effects can show up as statistically significant in large samples. For men in the 2016 General Social Survey, for example, the correlation coefficient between the size of one's family of origin (that is, one's number of siblings) and one's perception of the ideal family size (the number of children one wants) was .125, suggesting that men from larger families tend to prefer having more children. Primarily because of the large sample size (N = 836), this coefficient is statistically significant (with a probability level of less than .01); but substantively, this is a relatively weak association (recall that a correlation coefficient of zero means no association). Even though this association is statistically significant, it may not be substantively significant.

To put this into perspective, consider that the 2016 General Social Survey male respondents who had no siblings said that they preferred to have an average of 2.91 children. Those who had one sibling preferred (on average) 2.98 children, those who had two siblings favored 2.88 children, and those with three siblings preferred 3.23 children. So although the correlation between size of family of origin and ideal family size is statistically significant, the effect is not strong—only a difference of .32 children between those who had no siblings and those who had three siblings.

Commonly Reported
Tests of Statistical Significance

The Chi-Squared Test

One of the most frequently appearing tests of statistical significance is the **chi-squared** (χ^2) test. This test is often used to determine whether sample data—typically reported in a cross-classification table—are indicative of an association in the population from which the data were drawn.

Chi-squared has a minimum value of 0, but its upper limit depends on the sample size and the number of rows and columns in the table. To determine its statistical significance, we can consult tables that appear in most statistics texts. For Table 12.1, the calculated chi-squared value is 197.61 with an associated probability less than .0001. This statistically significant outcome can be interpreted in at least two ways. The outcome of this test suggests that (a) the arrangement of data in the table is unlikely to have occurred by chance and (b) an association probably exists between the independent and dependent variables in the populations from which the data were drawn. Substantively, this outcome leads us to conclude that a relationship between marital status and happiness exists—married people seem to be happier than those who have never married (or, at least, married people are more likely to say that they are "very happy" than are never-marrieds).

Tests of Significance for Measures of Association

Most measures of association have their own specific tests of significance. For data reported in cross-classification tables, we usually rely on the chi-squared test for information about statistical significance of the association. Generally speaking, these tests ask whether the sample data suggest that the association in the population from which the data were drawn is nonzero (i.e., that an association exists). A statistically significant result suggests that the association in the population is nonzero; that is, an association probably exists between the two variables in the population from which the data were drawn.

Tests for Means

Much of the research on families and children boils down to comparisons of mean scores. For example, do children cared for in group day care centers have higher average scores on measures of aggression than children cared for at home? Do husbands of women employed full-time do more housework, on average, than do husbands whose wives are not employed? Do white, African American, and Hispanic elderly individuals differ in the number of volunteer hours they perform?

When we are comparing means for exactly two groups—children cared for in group day care with children cared for at home, for example—we typically perform what is known as a **t-test for independent samples**, or t-test. The t-test compares the two sample means (and their variances) and produces a **t-statistic** and an associated probability value. Statistically significant t-statistics suggest that (a) the differences between the two groups are unlikely to be by chance and (b) a difference in means probably exists between the two groups in the populations from which the data were drawn.

If the independent variable has more than two categories—say, ethnicity coded as white, African American, Hispanic, or other—the usual test of significance for the differences in means is known as **analysis of variance** (ANOVA). The ANOVA yields an *F*-statistic that is interpreted in much the same way as *t*: Statistically significant *F*-values suggest that (a) the differences between the three or more means are unlikely to be by chance and (b) a difference in means probably exists between the groups in the population from which the data were drawn.

Multiple-Regression Analysis

Multiple-regression analysis allows the researcher to assess the simultaneous effects of multiple independent variables (both categorical and continuous) on a single continuous dependent variable. For example, we might wish to study the effects of father's education, mother's age at childbirth, family income, and race on child cognitive ability. We could do a series of separate tests, examining the relationship between each independent variable and child cognitive ability separately, but the effects of the independent variables likely overlap. For example, we know that father's education and family income are positively associated: Better educated fathers tend to have higher incomes. If we examine the separate correlations between each independent variable and child cognitive ability, then we'll probably find a statistically significant relationship. How much of each correlation is shared, however? By including all the theoretically relevant independent variables in a multiple-regression model predicting child cognitive ability, we can determine how much each variable accounts for variations in child cognitive ability, net of the effects of the other variable.

In such models, a regression (or slope) coefficient is reported for each independent variable in the model. In the most common form of multiple regression—unstandardized or metric regression—the regression coefficients are interpreted as the predicted amount of change in the dependent variable for a one-unit increase in the value of the independent variable. In a model predicting hours worked per week, a regression coefficient of .52 for the independent variable *years of education* indicates that the model predicts that hours worked per week increases by about .52 hours for each one-year increase in education.

A **test of statistical significance** is associated with each regression coefficient; a statistically significant result suggests that, net of the effects of all other variables in the model, the independent variable probably affects the dependent variable in the populations from which the data were drawn.

Another question that regression models can answer is how well we can predict the value of the dependent variable. The measure used here is known as the *multiple coefficient of determination,* or more commonly as R^2. R^2 ranges from 0, indicating no ability to predict the dependent variable, to 1, meaning that we can predict the value of the dependent variable perfectly without error. R^2 can also be interpreted as the proportion of variation in the dependent variable that is described by the independent variables collectively in the model. For example, a multiple regression model that yields an R^2 of .40 suggests that, taken together, the independent variables account for 40% of the variation in the dependent variable. Owing to relatively high levels of measurement error, the large number of variables that affect human behavior, and some degree of randomness in human behavior, social researchers rarely see R^2 values greater than .50.

Table 12.2 presents an example of a multiple regression table from Greenstein's research on the effects of early maternal employment on child cognitive ability. The first entry in the table—the Model R^2 of .37—indicates that the model fits the data relatively well. About 37% of the variation in the dependent variable (Peabody Picture Vocabulary Test-Revised [PPVT-R] score, a measure of cognitive ability) is accounted for by the 20 variables in the model.

Table 12.2 Regression Analysis Predicting PPVT-R Scores

Variable	Coefficient (b)
Model R^2	.37*
Child's characteristics	
Birth order	−4.21*
Low birthweight	−2.00
Age (in years)	1.77*
Region of residence	
Northeast	3.92
Midwest	3.88*
South	2.42
Mother's characteristics	
Mother's AFQT score	.15*
Age at child's birth	.08

(Continued)

(Continued)

Variable	Coefficient (b)
Mother's characteristics	
Never married at time of child's birth	−3.55
Married at time of child's birth	1.70
Education (in years)	−.05
Currently never married	3.34
Currently married	−3.25
Family environment	
Early family income ($1,000)	−.04
Cognitive-stimulation level	.40*
Emotional-support level	.11*
Maternal employment over first 4 years of life	
Continuously employed full time	−4.41
Continuously employed part time	7.50
Intermittently employed	4.05
Average weekly hours employed	.35
Constant	33.43*

Sample size = 511 non-Hispanic, non-black females. *Indicates $p < .05$.

Source: Based on information from Greenstein (1995). PPVT-R is Peabody Picture Vocabulary Test-Revised; AFQT is Armed Forces Qualifying Test.

The remainder of the table shows the estimated effects of each of the independent (or predictor) variables in the model. An asterisk next to a coefficient indicates that the effect is statistically significant beyond the conventional .05 level or that the sample data suggest an effect of that independent variable on the dependent variable in the population from which the sample data were drawn. For example, birth order has a statistically significant effect of −4.21 on PPVT-R score, meaning that any particular birth order (first born, second born, third born, and so on) is predicted to have a PPVT-R score 4.21 points lower than the score of the previous birth order. Low birthweight, however, does not have a statistically significant effect on PPVT-R score; that is to say, the effect of being a low-birthweight baby is not significantly different from 0 (in other words, no effect). The key finding from this table is that none of the various measures of early maternal employment have statistically significant effects on child cognitive ability.

Some Thoughts About Statistical Analysis

Benjamin Disraeli reportedly said that there are "liars, damned liars, and statisticians." Unfortunately, it's true that in the hands of a skilled (and perhaps unethical) researcher, statistics can be used to confirm almost any hypothesis. Perhaps more common is the uninformed or unintentional use of the wrong statistic or inappropriate technique that leads to a questionable conclusion. Nowhere is the adage "A little knowledge is dangerous" truer than in statistical analysis. Although it probably takes several courses in statistics to become really competent in this area, the material in this chapter provides a passing familiarity with the more common statistical techniques reported in the family and human development literatures.

Any good textbook on social or behavioral statistics will provide you with additional information on the techniques discussed in this chapter. Two particularly good texts are Agresti's *Statistical Methods for the Social Sciences* (2018) and Frankfort-Nachmias and Leon-Guerrero's *Social Statistics for a Diverse Society* (2009). For in-depth treatment of specific topics, consult the Sage Applied Statistics Series.

STUDY QUESTIONS

1. Almost every journal article about families or children that analyzes quantitative data will report some measures of central tendency and measures of variation. Find an example of a measure of central tendency and a measure of variation in a journal article and interpret their values.

2. Find an example of a cross-classification table in a journal article on a family- or human development-related topic. What are the independent and dependent variables in the table? Briefly interpret the findings reported in the table.

3. Find an example of a measure of association in a journal article on a family- or human development-related topic. What are the independent and dependent variables in the association? Briefly interpret the value of the measure of association reported in the table. Is it statistically significant?

4. Locate an article in a family- or human development-related journal that reports the results of a multiple-regression analysis. What is the dependent variable in the analysis (that is, what variable is the regression analysis predicting)? Interpret the R^2 value for the analysis and the regression coefficient for one variable that has a statistically significant effect.

13

Advanced Topics in Family Data Analysis

As we noted in Chapter 1, one of the key differences between research on families in particular and social and behavioral research more generally is that families are systems of individuals. When studying families, what precisely are we studying? Do we focus on individual family members to understand what family life is like, an approach more often taken in survey and other quantitative research designs (Chapter 7)? Do we focus on the process of creating everyday family life, oftentimes the approach employed in qualitative research design (Chapter 8)? Are we combining the two (Chapter 9)? As we discussed in Chapter 2, these are in part questions about the unit of analysis. Questions around the unit of analysis have greater implications for quantitative data analysis than for qualitative data analysis. In this chapter, we address more advanced issues around the analysis of quantitative data, beginning with one approach to analyzing quantitative panel data.

The Idea of Nested Entities

When we ask people to define *family*, they usually invoke some definition about groups of people who have some sort of relationship with one another. However, quantitative data on families tend to be collected from one person in each family. It is unclear whether, for example, information on a questionnaire given by one spouse about another spouses' housework time is accurate. So it would make sense, then, to collect data from both spouses, to get a better understanding of the actual division of housework tasks. Or, if we are interested in child development, we may want to collect data from parents on all of their children or on the same set of children over time. The problem with this approach is that analyzing data from both spouses, or from parents and children simultaneously, or from the same children over time violates one of the underlying assumptions of multiple regression (Chapter 11): All observations must be independent of one another. The results of tests of statistical significance would be misleading because of the inherent similarities of responses of spouses, siblings, or family members with one another. Fortunately, there are statistical analysis techniques that address this concern.

Analyzing Nested Data

When we study families and children, our data are often in hierarchical or **nested** form. For example, siblings are nested within families, students are nested within classrooms; families are nested within neighborhoods, and so forth. To address the similarities of siblings, students, or families in statistical models, the analysis technique must take into consideration that the responses of people in clusters (families, classrooms, or neighborhoods) or the same person over time (as in panel data) are related to one another. There are several analysis techniques that can statistically control for the fact that data on individuals over time (panel data) or members of the same family or some other cluster (like a school or neighborhood) would not be independent but may be similar.

Individual Change Over Time

Many research questions in family studies—say, questions about child development or marital stability—analyze panel data, where multiple responses from the same individuals are included in the statistical analysis. This kind of design (where, for example, you might include data on children each year from kindergarten through fifth grade to examine the factors influencing their academic achievement) must take into consideration the fact that many factors about kids do not change over time and may be correlated with academic achievement. Mother's educational attainment, for example, probably doesn't change very much after children are born and is what statisticians call a time-invariant covariate. Other factors that are correlated with academic achievement may change over time, such as the amount of interaction with their teachers at school (time-varying covariates). In their study of the factors influencing 10,666 children's academic achievement through fifth grade, Li-Grining, Votruba-Drzal, Maldonado-Carreño, and Haas's (2010) study of children's trajectories of academic achievement include information about the same children over time using **latent growth modeling**, a statistical approach that allows researchers to disentangle the influence of background characteristics from the influence of factors that may change over time on initial academic achievement. They found that children with more adaptive (as opposed to rigid) approaches to learning not only began kindergarten with higher achievement scores but also had a faster rate of improvement in achievement scores through fifth grade.

Carey Cooper and colleagues (2009) use a similar approach in their paper examining the factors associated with maternal parenting stress over time. Their analysis, using information from 1,844 mothers, disentangled the influence of time-invariant characteristics, such as race, immigrant status, and number of children, from time-varying characteristics, such as relationship status, socioeconomic resources, and social resources, on mothers' reports of parenting stress at four time points over a 5-year period. Specifically, they are able to show that regardless of relationship status at the beginning of the study, more transitions into and out of relationships (i.e., cohabitation, marriage, and/or breakup or divorce) led to increased parenting stress. Social resources, such as family support and religious service attendance, led to a small decrease in parenting stress after relationship transitions occurred but were more influential in limiting the amount of stress that occurred due to the relationship transition.

More information on latent growth modeling can be found in Jung and Wickrama (2008).

Information From Multiple Family Members

There is bound to be some similarity in responses to questions about family life across multiple family members. In a study where couples are the unit of observation and the unit of analysis, responses to questions about neighborhoods and extended kin relationships are likely to be similar, and due to *homogamy* (the pattern of individuals marrying someone like themselves), responses to attitude questions may be correlated. For example, Dew and Yorgason (2010) study the relationship between economic stress and marital conflict in 3,853 retirement-age couples. Using data from both spouses, they include measures of economic stress that would influence either (or both) spouses' reports of marital conflict, such as their overall income, assets, mortgage cost, and consumer debt. Using a statistical analysis technique called **structural equation modeling**, Dew and Yorgason are able to include independent measures of each spouse's background characteristics (e.g., education and reports of worry and depression), as well as their shared marital characteristics in order to predict marital conflict, all while taking into consideration that as part of a couple, there may be similarities in the spouse's responses.

More information on structural equation modeling can be found in Kaplan (2009) and general information on analysis of dyads can be found in Maguire (1999) and Sayer and Klute (2005).

In their paper on children's academic and behavioral outcomes, Levine, Emery, and Pollack (2007) used panel data on 2,908 children under age 15 and 1,736 young adults ages 15 or older to examine how maternal age at birth influenced children's early life outcomes. Previous research had found that children who were born when their mothers were young, say as teenagers, were more likely to have poor academic performance and to display problem behaviors. Levine and colleagues use data on multiple children from the same mothers to assess whether being a teen mother was a direct causal factor for children's subsequent academic and behavioral challenges or if there were other factors such as social class or birth order that could explain differences in kids' outcomes. Including siblings allowed the researchers to examine the outcomes of children born into the same household (albeit at different times) to the same mothers, although the mothers' ages would differ for each child. This kind of analysis (called a **fixed effects** approach) can take into consideration the similarities of siblings (such as mother's race or educational attainment) so that members of the same family can all be included in a research study without biasing the results.

Detailed information on using fixed effects models can be found in Allison (2009).

Individuals in Social Context

Another way in which family members can be clustered or nested is within social contexts. Families do not live in a vacuum. Social context influences the opportunities that family members have and in the case of political contexts, the legal frameworks within which people operate. Neighborhood characteristics likely influence the kinds of opportunities children and parents have to interact with others, school structure likely influences children's educational outcomes, and state laws or national culture likely influence the ways in which family members are able to form and maintain family relationships. We may intentionally sample within these clusters to see how family life is influenced not only by individual family characteristics but also simultaneously by the characteristics of the neighborhood, school, or country. We have to take into consideration that, within each cluster, people's responses may be similar to one another.

Roche and Leventhal (2009) asked whether neighborhood disorder (measured as neighborhood problems with drugs and drug dealing, gangs, assault and muggings, burglaries, unsafe streets, burglaries and thefts, abandoned houses, unsupervised children, and children with whom parents do not want their child to associate) directly or indirectly influences adolescents' sexual debut. Using a statistical technique called **multi-level modeling**, Roche and Leventhal found that there were no neighborhood-level influences on sexual debut once the adolescents' individual characteristics were taken into consideration. Their analysis also found that as neighborhood disorder increased, higher levels of family routines and parental knowledge (i.e., awareness of youths' friends, whereabouts, and activities) were more strongly associated with a lower probability of youth sexual debut.

Geist and Cohen (2011) also use multi-level modeling to look at the performance of housework by individuals in 13 countries. Comparing data from cross-sectional surveys performed in 1994 and 2002, they note that not only are there differences across countries in the amount of housework that women and men perform but also that national context affects the pace of social change in the division of housework. Specifically, Geist and Cohen found that while individuals living in countries with more egalitarian social policies (such as parental leave or the absence of discriminatory policies for women) reported a more egalitarian division of housework, there was greater change toward gender equality in the division of housework from 1994 to 2002 in countries that were less egalitarian. Not only does national context influence the amount of housework (and the division of that labor) performed, perhaps by setting national "standards" (p. 842) for housework, but, Geist and Cohen argue, national context shapes also the pace at which individuals within the country can work toward a more equal division of housework in their own homes.

Detailed information on multi-level modeling can be found in Raudenbush and Bryk (2002) and Snijders and Bosker (1999).

Final Thoughts on Nested Entities

The statistical procedures you choose to perform on your data should not be a deterrent nor a draw for constructing any particular research design. If you have a research question that is best answered by collecting data that explicitly acknowledges the inherent interrelationships of individuals, families, and other units of analysis, then collect the data that you need in order to answer your research question. Statistical procedures are simply tools for allowing you to answer your question. That statistical techniques now are able to handle nested data means that researchers no longer have to make hard choices about limiting our research design or making inferences from our data that may be biased due to our research design. Instead, see these tools as additional encouragement to be creative in your research design, much like the increased acceptance of mixing research methods (Chapter 9) can potentially lead to new and creative designs.

STUDY QUESTIONS

1. Find a journal article on a family-related topic that uses panel data to look at individual change over time. What is the dependent variable? Describe the time invariant and/or time varying independent variables.

2. Find a journal article on a family-related topic that analyzes data from multiple individuals in the same family. Determine the variables that had unique information from each individual and those that had information that was the same for all family members.

3. Find a journal article on a family-related topic that analyzes data on individuals nested in social contexts. What is the dependent variable? Describe the independent variables that are present for each level of the analysis (e.g., individual, household, country).

Evaluating Programs in Human Development and Family Science

M any authors divide social research into two broad categories. Basic social research is concerned with developing and testing theories about the social world, and its intended audience is scientists and academics. Applied social research, however, is designed to solve specific problems in society. The intended audience of applied social research is practitioners, agency workers, and government officials.

Before creating or implementing social programs or clinical interventions, it is important to gauge the need or demand for such programs. And once such programs are operating, it is reasonable to ask whether (or how well) they work. Do anger-management programs for abusive husbands reduce the rate of domestic violence? Do preschool enrichment programs enhance school performance among disadvantaged children? Do specific types of family therapy differ in their efficacy? **Evaluation research** is applied social research designed to develop, monitor, and measure the effectiveness of social programs and policies.

The methods and techniques of evaluation research are essentially the same as those used in other types of social research. Issues such as reliability, validity, and generalizability are just as important as they are in studies concerned with testing or developing theories. However, there are two major complications faced by evaluation researchers. First, unlike most basic social research, evaluation research studies the needs for and effects of programs on real individuals and families. Rather than asking theoretical questions such as, "How is social class related to the likelihood of domestic violence?" evaluation researchers ask applied and focused questions such as, "How can we reduce the rate of domestic violence in XXX county?" or "Does this particular program reduce the rate of domestic violence in the YYY metropolitan area?" In other words, the activities and findings of evaluation researchers usually have meaningful consequences for the lives of individuals and their families.

A second major complication faced by evaluation researchers has to do with political concerns. Most basic social research operates in something of a vacuum, and the results of basic social research rarely get much attention outside of the journals and monographs within a particular academic discipline. Evaluation research tends to operate in a public arena, however, because most social programs (and often their evaluations) are paid for with public dollars. Publicly funded social programs will typically please some people but infuriate others. Political ideology plays a major role in the implementation, funding, and maintenance of most social programs, with those on the political left generally advocating more public spending and those on the political right usually opposing it. Evaluation researchers must be constantly aware of the conflicting demands placed on them. Agency officials often want evaluation results that indicate that their programs are working because null results could threaten their funding. Critics of the programs typically want results that suggest that the programs don't work.

Project D.A.R.E. (Drug Abuse Resistance Education) is an excellent example of how social intervention programs can stir up controversy. D.A.R.E. is a program that uses law enforcement officers to speak in schools, promotes a zero-tolerance message, and attempts to increase peer pressure against drug use. In 1999, the D.A.R.E. program was offered in more than 80% of all U.S. school districts. Lynam and his colleagues (1999) tracked more than 1,000 students who participated in D.A.R.E. during the sixth grade. Although their research suggested some initial improvements in students' attitudes toward drug use, these changes did not persist over time. There were no changes in actual drug use initially or over a 10-year period. The authors of the study conclude that, in conjunction with the findings of many other evaluations, "the preponderance of evidence suggests that DARE has no long-term effect on drug use" (Lynam et al., 1999, p. 590).

Why, despite these and similar findings, does D.A.R.E. remain so popular with parents and school administrators? First, it is intuitively plausible that teaching children to resist the temptation to use drugs, cigarettes, and alcohol should reduce substance abuse among adolescents; consequently, the program draws a great deal of support from those who don't take the time to look at a scientific evaluation. Second, the program appears to work; most children who go through D.A.R.E. don't use drugs. What isn't so obvious to most laypersons is that, even without D.A.R.E. in operation, most adolescents don't use drugs anyway. This second point shows the necessity for rigorous evaluation of social programs and the careful use of comparison groups to determine whether a treatment program actually produces effects.

Evaluation research is directed at three major questions. First, we need to know whether a problem exists and, if so, its parameters. Is there a shortage of reasonably priced child-care in XXX county? If so, what are the needs for such child-care: How many children, what ages, and what rates can their families afford to pay? This first step in evaluation research is known as needs and social impact assessment.

Once a problem is identified, a program may be implemented to deal with it. At some point, the program's sponsors will want to know if the program is working. Outcome research can evaluate the results of the program to see if it is solving the problem defined during the needs assessment.

Having determined that the program is effective, process research asks, How does the program work? What mechanisms or processes does the program stimulate or implement that bring about the desired outcome? Each of these three steps is discussed in the following sections.

Needs and Social Impact Assessment: What Is the Problem?

Needs assessment is typically directed at one or more of four issues. First, needs assessment may be concerned with estimating the extent of a problem. If we implement a program aimed at reducing domestic violence, we first need concrete information concerning numbers of cases of domestic violence and their severity. It is important to know the scope of the problem and its distribution across such dimensions as social class, race, and geographical location. For example, Gillum's (2008) research reports the results of needs assessment of African American women who were domestic violence survivors.

Second, policymakers need to know something about potential use or how many individuals or families are likely to take advantage of the program. This information, combined with data on the extent of the problem, can indicate how comprehensive our intended program should be and help determine potential costs and needed resources.

Third, needs assessment might be used to prioritize problems within the communities under study. Policymakers need to know what problems the community feels are important to solve and which have the most serious implications for individuals and the community. Because financial resources are limited, the problems that require funding must be prioritized. Mutchler, Somerville, Khaniyan, and Evans's (2016) report investigating the specific needs, interests, and preferences of a locality's older population yielded specific recommendations for policymakers regarding how best to support the growing population of older residents.

Finally, research might study the long-term potential for problems that might require interventions. For example, a fast-growing area might have adequate low-income health care available today, but will additional facilities be available for the growing population? Such questions require information about population growth, projected economic conditions, and the supply of and demand for health care services.

Outcome Assessment: Does It Work?

In its most basic form, outcome assessment asks simple questions: Is the program successful? Does it work? One way of operationalizing success is to ask whether the program is achieving the goals set forth in its initial formulation. A program to reduce domestic violence might aim for a 20% reduction in domestic violence cases over an 18-month period. If there is at least a 20% reduction, then the program may be judged to have been successful.

Not surprisingly, there are intense political and financial pressures on agency heads to show that their programs work. About 20 years ago, a documentary film titled *Scared Straight* followed 17 male youths on a visit to Rahway State Prison in New Jersey. The fairly graphic film showed lifers haranguing teens to scare them away from a life of crime and violence. The film drew wide acclaim—it won an Oscar—and policymakers in 39 states adopted the idea for their local delinquency programs. The supporters of the Scared Straight program made wide-ranging claims about the success of the program at reducing delinquent behavior.

About the time that Scared Straight programs became popular, Greenstein served as a consultant to a local group concerned with reducing juvenile delinquency. The project used a classic experimental design—randomly assigning adolescent boys to either an experimental Scared Straight group that visited a local prison or a control group that did not—and followed up with multiple outcome measures over a year. The data clearly showed that there were essentially no differences between the boys in the experimental group and those in the control group in terms of arrests, disciplinary problems, truancy, or classroom performance. By all accounts, the program didn't seem to have made an impact on these boys; it certainly wasn't producing the results expected after sizable investments of public funds. However, the outcome assessment showed that there was a small (but statistically significant) difference in self-esteem scores: The boys who had made the prison visit had slightly higher self-esteem than the control group. In their pitch to the funding agency for continued support, the program director talked at great length about how the increases in self-esteem were just what the program had been aiming for all along.

The lesson here is that the goals of the program—that is, the outcomes that will indicate that the program has been successful—have to be explicitly laid out at the beginning of the program. No one involved in the Scared Straight program described earlier had any particular interest in self-esteem until the outcome assessment showed differences between the two groups of boys. Because the goals of the program had never been defined, almost any difference at the outcome assessment might have been presented as a successful outcome. Recently, Finckenauer, Gavin, Hovland, and Storvoll (1999) wrote about the general lack of evidence supporting the value of the Scared Straight program in reducing juvenile delinquency.

Process Research: How Does It Work?

Ideally, social programs aren't implemented without a strong theoretical or conceptual foundation. The theoretical foundation should describe why and how the process will work; the outcome assessment should demonstrate whether the particular implementation works or not. In the real world, however, social programs are often (some cynics would say usually) implemented without a theoretical basis. There is often pressure on agencies to quickly implement programs to meet some real or perceived need, or there may simply not be time in the funding cycle to conduct basic research concerning the theoretical processes underlying some behavior of interest.

Consequently, in many evaluation studies, one evaluation goal is to identify precisely how the program brings about change in its participants. If the intervention is theory driven, the instruments used to assess the process should include indicators of the variables theorized to bring about changes in the participants in the project. Bean, Forneris, and Halsall (2014) detail the mixed methods (see Chapter 10) used to evaluate the Girls Just Wanna Have Fun physical activity program, describing how both qualitative and quantitative assessments were used during the evaluation process to determine the effectiveness of the program.

The task of evaluating the process for an intervention that isn't based on an explicit theoretical or conceptual foundation is somewhat more difficult. For example, a program for battered women designed to provide them with temporary housing, clothing, food, and child-care while they look for and find employment probably doesn't have a theoretical basis; instead, the program has a pragmatic basis. We don't need a theory to tell us that mothers can't look for work if they have to stay home to care for their young children. As an indication of the process involved in the program, we probably want indicators of how many job interviews the women had while in the program and to compare these data to comparable women not participating in the program. Unlike interventions with theoretical underpinnings, the decision about which variables to measure is not straightforward. In theoretically based interventions, the theory indicates which variables are important to measure; in interventions without a theoretical basis, only our common sense and professional judgment can guide us in the design of our instrumentation.

Some Thoughts About Randomization in Evaluation Research

After you've read a few evaluation studies and compared them to the discussion in Chapter 8 and other sources, you may feel like you should discount any experimental evaluation study that doesn't randomly assign respondents to treatment conditions. You may recall that a primary purpose of random assignment is to equate the treatment groups in terms of both measured and unmeasured (and perhaps unmeasurable) characteristics. Ideally, the experimental and control groups in a randomized experiment will show no pretreatment differences between factors relevant to the outcome or processes under study. After all, one of randomization's great benefits is that it eliminates all sorts of threats to validity, right?

The issue of random assignment of participants to treatment conditions in evaluation studies has been the subject of much discussion in the methodology literature. Critics of randomized experiments have made four major arguments: (a) Random assignment is not practical in evaluation research, (b) randomizing respondents to treatment conditions ignores qualitative aspects of the process under study and of the respondents, (c) such experiments give us little information when there is no statistically significant effect of the treatment on the outcome variable, and, perhaps most seriously, (d) random assignment of respondents to treatment conditions is unethical because it deprives members of the control group of efficacious treatments.

There is widespread agreement on the difficulty of achieving random assignment in evaluation studies. Random assignment is most readily achieved in studies of respondents in institutions (e.g., patients committed to mental health facilities, prisoners, military personnel, students). Human development scholars may be interested in evaluations of intuitionally housed programs whose interventions used random assignment to assess their effectiveness within a subpopulation, such as the assessment of middle school sexual education programs (Markham et al., 2014). However, human development and family scholars study a wide variety of situations. It is more difficult to create equivalent groups, say, of families experiencing domestic violence or of families with preschool-age children.

The second argument—that randomized experiments ignore qualitative aspects of the respondents and the process under study—is simply wrongheaded. Such experiments can study qualitative outcomes as easily as quantitative outcomes; and the fact that respondents were randomly assigned to treatment conditions does not rule out the possibility of gathering qualitative data about the respondents.

The third argument suggests that a finding of *no difference* between control and experimental groups in a program evaluation is of little value in program design and assessment. Nothing could be further from the truth. To implement a successful policy, we need to know what does and what does not work. A *null finding* (that is, a finding of no statistically significant difference between the experimental and control groups on the outcome variable) in a program evaluation may not tell us precisely what does work, but it certainly tells us what doesn't work. Such a finding suggests the need to find alternative theories or implementations if practitioners are to bring about change and achieve program goals. Unfortunately, due to the process of peer review described in Chapter 4 that emphasizes published work making a particular kind of contribution to the literature, research that documents no effect of an intervention program is difficult to find.

The final criticism is perhaps the most important of the four. It holds that if the treatment is effective, it is unethical to withhold it from the members of the control group. Alternatively, if the treatment is ineffective, it is unethical to subject members of the experimental group to it, lest it raise false hopes or potentially harm the experimental respondents. Boruch (1975) responded to this criticism directly, suggesting that failure to experiment may itself be unethical because it deprives us of the knowledge of which treatments are likely to be effective in the long run.

One way to handle the problem of withholding an effective treatment is by providing remedial treatment to the control group as appropriate. The issue of false hopes can be mitigated by careful presentation of the goals and procedures of the study to potential respondents, and the issue of potential harm to experimental respondents should be handled through a conscientious review of the procedures involved. Of course, all research should pass through the appropriate Institutional Review Board (IRB) (discussed in Chapter 2) for consideration of ethical issues and possible harm to the project's participants.

So where does this leave us in terms of randomized program evaluation studies? Although such studies are preferable to those without random assignment, we must recognize that many of the problems under study by child and family researchers don't easily lend themselves to randomized experiments. In such cases, we are limited to quasi-experimental designs (Cook & Campbell, 1979) that may leave one or more of the threats to validity discussed in Chapter 6 open to question.

The Relationship Between Applied and Basic Research

At the beginning of this chapter, we pointed out a fundamental difference between basic and applied social research: Basic social research is primarily concerned with developing and testing social theories, whereas applied social research is designed to solve specific problems in society. The two types of research are far more similar than they are different, however.

Both basic and applied research draw from the same toolkit of research strategies: surveys, experiments, nonreactive measures, observation, and qualitative techniques. Both approaches are concerned with reliability and validity of measurement. Regardless of whether we're testing a theory or developing an intervention, it is essential that our indicators provide consistent and stable measurements and that they are measuring what we think they are measuring. Both approaches have the same concerns about sampling, representativeness, and generalizability of findings, as well as technical issues, such as scaling and questionnaire construction.

On another level, there is a reciprocal relationship between basic and applied social research. Applied research often draws on theories developed by basic social research to develop and implement social intervention programs. The direction of basic social research is often determined by social problems uncovered or highlighted by applied research. Workers in applied environments—social services organizations, government agencies, not-for-profit groups—must be familiar with evaluation techniques in general, but they must also be comfortable with basic research. A good general treatment of evaluation methods was presented by Rossi, Lipsey, and Henry (2018); you may also want to look at Owen (2006) or Berk and Rossi (1999). For a discussion about program evaluation specifically in marital and family therapy research, see Leber, St. Peters, and Markman (1996).

STUDY QUESTIONS

1. Locate a published example of a needs assessment, outcome assessment, or process research on a family-related topic of interest to you. Briefly describe the project and its findings.

2. Choose a family-related issue (e.g., school violence, teenage sexuality, elder care) of interest to you. Describe how you might go about assessing (a) the need for programs dealing with that issue in your community and (b) the effectiveness of such programs. How might you design an evaluation? What outcomes would you measure?

CHAPTER 15

The Politics of Research on Families and Children

Political Concerns in Research on Families and Children

Like any other public activity, research on families and children does not take place in a vacuum. Certain theories may seem to confer privileged status on some groups or imply that other groups are somehow inferior. Research findings may be in the interest of some but pejorative to others. Those who find the results of a particular study flattering or supportive of their own ideological position will want to disseminate those results as widely as possible. Those who are unhappy with the findings of a particular study or find it to be inconsistent with their own beliefs may wish to reinterpret, discredit, or even suppress those findings.

In recent years, the debate over so-called family values has produced many flash points across the family-research enterprise. One area that has received much attention is the role of fathers in families. At one end of the political spectrum are neoconservatives who argue that "fatherlessness is the most harmful demographic trend of this generation" (Blankenhorn, 1995, p. 1) and that responsible fathering is most likely to occur within traditional, two-parent heterosexual marriages. At the other end of the political range are liberals and feminists who suggest that "neither fathers nor mothers are essential to child development and that responsible fathering can occur within a variety of family structures" (Silverstein & Auerbach, 1999, p. 397).

What does this mean for researchers studying fathers (or any other politically sensitive issue)? It means that one can expect one's findings to be challenged. If one finds, for example, that children in fatherless households have more behavioral problems than those in households with fathers, then you may be criticized by those on the left; if you find that the presence of fathers makes little difference in child well-being, then you may be criticized by the right. Regardless of your design and your findings, someone, somewhere is going to find a reason to criticize your work. As a researcher, all you can do is produce sound research that can withstand scholarly scrutiny. Research contributes to knowledge, and (particularly in the information age) knowledge is power. The pressures on researchers to produce findings consistent with (or at least not critical of) the existing power structure may affect publication channels, research funding, and even employment opportunities.

Control of Publication Channels

Publication of research findings is an important part of science because one of the fundamental norms of science is that scientific knowledge should be public and shared. One might even argue that "Scientific knowledge in its pure form is a classic public good" (Dalrymple, 2003, p. 35), that is, something that is available to all members of a society without profit. However, political pressures can affect the research process by limiting or suppressing publication. An interesting example of this in the child and family studies area occurred in early 1999, when the American Medical Association (AMA) fired the *Journal of American Medical Association* editor George Lundberg for allegedly injecting the journal into presidential politics. As editor, Lundberg accepted and published a paper that was presented by the authors as a contribution to "the current public debate regarding whether oral sex constitutes having . . . sexual relations" (Sanders & Reinisch, 1999). It was reported that 59% of 599 students surveyed at a large midwestern university in 1991 did not regard oral-genital contact as having "had sex." The issue was politically sensitive at the time, because the Clinton impeachment trial was entering its second week and a major point of contention dealt with exactly how *having sex* was to be defined.

You may recall from Chapter 4 that major professional journals publish only 1 or 2 out of every 10 manuscripts submitted. Perhaps half of the rejected manuscripts either are inappropriate for publication in a particular journal—the subject matter is not within the journal's purview, for example—or are so poorly done that they do not merit serious consideration of publication. Most journal editors will freely admit, however, that they reject many competent manuscripts because of lack of publication space.

What determines which of the competent manuscripts are published and which are rejected? A study of authors of often-cited scientific papers suggested that the use of innovative methods and reinterpretations of secondary data were associated with difficulties in publishing (Campanario, 1993). In an interesting experiment, after altering the authors' names and institutions, Peters and Ceci (1980) submitted 11 articles for publication that had been previously published by mainstream journals of psychology. Only about 10% of the reviewers and editors recognized that the articles were previously published; at the same time, only about 14% of the reviewers recommended publication. Apparently, the stability of the review process over time is not very high.

All of this suggests that journal editors have a great deal of latitude in deciding what does and does not get published. Inevitably, editors' personal biases affect their decisions. Some of these biases are methodological, others theoretical, and some are political. Given the large number of competent manuscripts to fill a limited amount of journal pages, all three of these biases are going to affect editorial decisions. And because faculty reappointment and tenure decisions are often based in large part on quality and quantity of publication, journal editors have a great impact on the academic job market given that much of the scholarship published in academic journals is performed by faculty in colleges and universities.

Control of Research Funding

Funding agencies also have a great impact on the family research process. Agencies have to decide how much to spend and on what types of research, who will get funding to do the research, and how to make sure that the funds are used responsibly. Just as in the editorial process leading to publication, so too does a review process lead to decisions about which projects to fund. In recent years, this funding process has become highly politicized. No better example exists than the controversy surrounding the American Teenage Survey (ATS), an $18 million project intended to survey a nationally representative sample of 20,000 adolescents. The goal of the study was "to increase understanding of the patterns of adolescent sexual and contraceptive behavior and the causes of these patterns" (Udry, 1993).

In 1989, the National Institute of Child Health and Human Development (NICHD) approved a grant proposal for this project and funded the project in May 1991. In July 1991, Secretary of Health and Human Services Louis Sullivan, appearing on a talk show on the Christian Network, was asked why he was funding this study. Sullivan had apparently never heard of ATS, but shortly afterward, he announced its cancellation.

The Congressional Record (1991, September 12) reported that Senator Jesse Helms declared in the Senate,

> These sex surveys have not—have not—been concerned with legitimate scientific inquiry as much as they have been concerned with a blatant attempt to sway public attitudes in order to liberalize opinions and laws regarding homosexuality, pedophilia, anal and oral sex, sex education, teenage pregnancy, and all down the line. (pp. S12861, S12862)

Fortunately for science, the ATS eventually was transformed into the well-funded and very productive National Longitudinal Study of Adolescent Health ("Add Health" mentioned in Chapter 11). Now approaching its 25th year of data collection, the Add Health study was the most-downloaded file from the Inter-University Consortium for Political and Social Research (Top Downloads January 1—June 1, 2018, 2018) and has been identified as "a national treasure" by the National Institute of Child Health and Human Development (University of North Carolina at Chapel Hill, 2014).

Although criticism of the ATS came primarily from the political right, the political left can become equally involved in the scientific funding process. In 1992, the National Institutes of Health (NIH) cancelled a conference on the subject of "Genetic Factors in Crime" that had been funded after peer review. Critics charged that the conference was inherently racist because it was to explore the genetic rather than environmental origins of criminal behavior.

The two projects described earlier were both approved by federal agencies and then, after preliminary work had commenced, had funding withdrawn. Funding agencies can also have substantial effects on the topics and methods used by researchers through their choices of projects to fund. Although nearly all granting agencies use some form of peer review, final funding decisions rest with agency personnel whose budgets are often scrutinized by members of the executive and legislative branches of government, not to mention the media. Decisions by individual researchers about what topics to study and what methodological techniques to use are undoubtedly affected by the types of studies funded in the past as well as perceptions of future funding trends.

Control of Employment Opportunities

In its most extreme form, political pressure might affect a researcher's ability to find employment. Researchers studying unpopular topics or those known for producing research findings critical of the status quo might find their job possibilities limited. One reason for the tenure system at universities is to make it possible for faculty to choose research topics without fear of dismissal on political or ideological grounds. Without such protection, faculty would constantly look over their shoulders to make sure that their work wasn't offending those in the power structure. Nevertheless, until fairly recently, research on LGBTQ individuals and/or families was relatively unpopular, and researchers working in this area often found their employment possibilities restricted.

Some Closing Thoughts

In Chapter 1, we pointed out that this text focuses on how scientific research methods can help us to understand families and children. One point we want to emphasize is the conditional nature of science. It is impossible to prove a theory or hypothesis because theories are not about specific locations in space, time, or culture; they are abstract and therefore universal. To prove a theory would require that its predictions be shown to hold for all empirical instances of the theory—past, present, and future. Of course, this is physically impossible. So we acknowledge the conditional nature of theory confirmation, aware that next week, or next year, or in the next century some researcher may find that the theory doesn't always apply. This is the nature of science: Theories are created, tested, confirmed, and eventually rejected and replaced (Kuhn, 2012; Toulmin, 1972). Over time, *anomalies* (findings that are inconsistent with the theory's predictions) are found. As the number of anomalous findings increases, confidence in the theory starts to fall, until eventually a new theory emerges that accounts for all the phenomena correctly explained by the old theory and the anomalies that weren't accounted for.

Science's conditional nature reminds us that perfect theories, perfect hypotheses, and perfect research designs do not exist. In particular, research designs are the result of compromises and trade-offs. In Chapter 5, we discussed the trade-off between the cost of a sample and the amount of sampling error incurred. Generally, as the sample size increases, sampling error decreases, but costs increase. Consequently, the sample size drawn in most studies is a compromise between how much money is available for the project and how much sampling error the researchers are willing to tolerate. You will be unlikely to ever meet a survey researcher who wouldn't have liked to have a larger sample than the one actually gathered. Similarly, research instrumentation often involves a trade-off. Items or questions that might have been interesting to study often have to be omitted from the research protocol because of lack of time or space. Any study published anywhere in the literature can be improved, if only in some small way:

a slightly larger sample, additional questionnaire items, a better interview technique, or longer periods of observation.

Science works because we don't take our findings for granted: We are constantly questioning our methods, samples, and theories. Popper (2002) argued that "science is one of the very few human activities— perhaps the only one—in which errors are systematically criticized and fairly often, in time, corrected" (p. 293). Others (e.g., Ioannidis, 2012) are not so sure. One example of this self-correcting process is the retraction of the Wakefield et al. (1998) study that purported to find that the administration of the MMR (measles, mumps, rubella) vaccine was associated with the onset of autism spectrum disorders (ASD) in school-age children. As parents came to see the vaccine as unsafe, vaccination rates dropped to less than 80%; the incidence of mumps reached epidemic levels in Britain in 2005 (Smith, 2010). Twelve years after the original publication, the publishing journal (*The Lancet*) retracted the paper on methodological grounds, although the myth of a link between the MMR vaccine and autism persisted. A recent study (Jain et al., 2015) of nearly 100,000 children found that there was "no harmful association between MMR vaccine receipt and ASD even among children already at a higher risk of ASD" (p. 1534). The self-correcting process of science may work slowly but generally it works. We encourage you to read research reports with a critical eye. Whether you encounter them firsthand in scientific journals or monographs or secondhand in the popular press, you will probably begin to see flaws or shortcomings in the research that you read. You may read a journal article and wonder, "Why didn't they ask questions about such-and-such a topic? Why didn't they control for duration of marriage in their analysis? Couldn't they have interviewed the husbands as well as the wives in their study?" You may read a news article about a new survey and have questions about the sampling procedure. You may see a blog post about some research findings and wonder about appropriateness of the control group in the study. As you find flaws in published research, remember that these researchers work under time and cost constraints like everyone does in every line of work.

The fact that you're asking yourself these questions is a good sign: You're becoming a critical consumer of family research. Just because an article or book is in print—even in a major journal or by a well-known publisher—doesn't mean that it's the last word on the topic. But you can't tell the good research from the bad without some training, and that's what we hope this text has provided for you. Use your knowledge to be an active critical consumer of research to enhance your work, your life, and the lives of those around you.

Glossary

Abstract: A brief (100–150 word) summary that usually appears at the beginning of a journal article

Accretion: In nonreactive techniques, evidence left by accumulation or addition to some characteristic or quantity

Acquiescence response set: Tendency of some respondents to give responses that *agree* regardless of the respondent's true opinions or feelings

Analysis of variance (ANOVA): Statistical test of significance for comparing three or more sample means

Applied social research: Research primarily intended to solve specific problems in society

Attrition: A threat to internal validity that refers to the fact that not all respondents who are present at the beginning of the experiment will be present for subsequent testing or measurement

Basic social research: Research that is primarily concerned with developing and testing theories about the social world

Causal effect: A relationship in which some independent variable actually affects, causes, or produces change in some dependent variable. *See also* Spurious effect

Causal mechanism: Factor or process which is believed to produce some outcome

Central tendency: Statistical measures that summarize the location of the data along a continuum

Chi-squared (χ^2) test: A test of statistical significance often used to determine whether two categorical variables are independent

Cluster sampling: A sampling procedure in which the sampling elements are selected in at least two stages; the first stage involves the random selection of clusters, and the last stage involves the random sampling of elements within clusters

Coefficient of determination (r^2): A measure of association for interval-level data; it is the square of the correlation coefficient

Conceptualization: The process of specifying exactly what is meant by a term

Concurrent validity: Relating the results of a measurement procedure to other measurements taken at approximately the same time. *See also* Criterion validity; Predictive validity

Consistency: A form of reliability across items (internal reliability or internal consistency) or across observers (interobserver agreement)

Construct: A theoretical creation that is based on observation but cannot be directly observed (e.g., marital satisfaction)

Construct validity: How well a measurement correlates with measures of similar constructs

Content validity: How well a measure taps the full range of dimensions or meanings of some underlying construct

Control group: In an experimental or quasi-experimental design, a group of respondents who do not receive the treatment or manipulation and whose outcomes are used for comparison with the experimental group

Control variable: Variable that is included in an analysis either because (a) it is believed that it affects the relationship between the independent and dependent variables; or (b) it is believed to affect the dependent variable, and including it in the analysis will permit the calculation of the *net* effects of the independent variable of interest. *See also* Moderator variable

Convenience sampling: Sampling elements are not chosen according to any particular sampling plan or procedure but are included in the sample because they are available or accessible

Correlation coefficient: A measure of association for interval-level data (also known as Pearson's *r*)

Criterion validity: How well a measurement predicts or correlates with external criteria, especially behaviors or alternative measures of the same phenomenon. *See also* Predictive validity; Concurrent validity

Cronbach's α (alpha): A statistical measure of internal reliability; it is the average of all possible split-half reliability coefficients for a given set of data and items; higher scores indicate that the items in the scale or index are probably measuring the same underlying construct

Cross-classification table: Table reporting the numbers of cases for each combination of the values of two categorical variables

Cross-sectional research design: Design where the data are gathered at one point in time

Dependent variable: Variable that is believed to be caused, produced, or affected by another variable or variables

Description: One of the five stages in the scientific process; identifying the characteristics of a process or phenomenon

Descriptive statistics: Techniques used to summarize information about samples

Diary study: Respondents complete a diary, usually describing the types of activities in which they are engaged and the amount of time spent in those activities

Direct observable: A quantity that can be observed directly (e.g., the number of people in a room)

Directional hypothesis: Prediction about the direction of an association (positive or negative) or the direction of the difference in means (larger or smaller)

Disproportionate stratified random sampling: Stratified sample in which sample elements are selected from strata in proportions that are different from those found in the population (often used to oversample from strata)

Electronic journal: Scientific journal that is published exclusively in electronic form, usually on the World Wide Web

Element: The unit about which data are gathered. *See also* Unit of analysis

Embedded mixed-method design: Studies that use one methodology to guide the study but also use a different methodology to supplement the data

Erosion: In nonreactive techniques, evidence left by deterioration or reduction in some characteristic or quantity

Evaluation: One of the five stages in the scientific process; assessing social programs to determine their effectiveness

Evaluation research: Applied social research designed to develop, monitor, and measure the effectiveness of social programs and policies

Experimental design: Any of a number of research designs that use random assignment of participants to treatment conditions along with comparison groups to permit assessment of the effects of a treatment on some outcome variable

Experimental group: In an experimental or quasi-experimental design, the group of respondents who receive the treatment or manipulation and whose outcomes are compared to the control group's outcomes (sometimes referred to as a treatment group)

Explanation: The process of showing why some event, outcome, or state of affairs occurs

Explanatory mixed-methods design: Design that begins with quantitative data and moves toward qualitative data to develop an explanation of some outcome

Exploration: The first step in the research process; various possible explanations for the phenomenon under study are considered

Exploratory mixed-methods design: Design that begins with qualitative data and moves toward quantitative data to develop an explanation of some outcome

Face validity: The extent to which the content of the items in a measurement appear to be measuring what the measurement is intended to measure

Factor analysis: Statistical technique for identifying the underlying patterns or dimensions represented by a number of questionnaire items

Field experiment: Experimental or quasi-experimental design conducted in a natural setting (as opposed to a laboratory setting)

Fixed effects models: Statistical approach that uses multiple observations from the same observational unit to study causal factors in a selected outcome

F-statistic: The calculated value that is the result of an analysis of variance to test differences in sample means

Gamma (γ): A measure of association for ordinal data

Guttman scale: A composite indicator that combines multiple questionnaire items; assumes that items form a hierarchy

History: A threat to internal validity that refers to naturally occurring events that may affect the outcome of the study

Hypothesis: A statement about the relationship between two or more variables

Independent variable: Variable that is believed to cause, produce, or affect some other variable or variables

Index: The result of summing, averaging, or otherwise combining the responses to multiple items to produce an indicator of some construct

Indirect observable: Indirect representation of some quantity (e.g., a person's response to a questionnaire item about his or her opinion concerning abortion)

Inferential statistics: Techniques used to make inferences about population characteristics based on sample data (sometimes referred to as hypothesis testing)

Informed consent: The requirement that potential research participants must be informed of possible risks resulting from their participation in a research project

Institutional Review Board (IRB): Committee composed of professionals and laypersons that reviews research proposals to ensure safe and ethical treatment of research participants

Instrumentation: A threat to internal validity that deals with changes in the measurement instruments or operations

Interaction: A threat to internal validity created when two (or more) threats to internal validity combine (e.g., testing effects may interact with selection)

Interaction of selection and treatment: A threat to external validity that occurs especially when respondents are not randomly assigned to treatment conditions

Internal consistency (internal reliability): The extent to which multiple items in a scale or index are measuring the same concept

Interobserver reliability: The degree to which multiple observers agree on what they have seen

Interquartile range: The difference between the 1st (lower) and 3rd (upper) quartiles, or the width of the middle % of the distribution

Interval level of measurement: Measurement that assumes all the characteristics of the nominal and ordinal levels and that the distances between scale values are constant and equal across the range of scores

Intervening variable: Variable that is affected by one variable and in turn affects a third variable. *See also* Mediator variable

Intervention: An applied program or policy designed to bring about change in some specific outcome or state of affairs

Interviewer bias: The interviewer's characteristics affect responses to the survey instrument (e.g., interviewer's demeanor or body language during the interview)

Laboratory experiment: Use of an experimental or quasi-experimental design in an artificial setting created for the purposes of the research

Lambda (λ_{yx}): A measure of association for nominal-level data

Latent growth modeling: Statistical approach used to disentangle the effects of background characteristics from the influence of factors that change over time

Level of measurement: Characteristics or properties of the results of a measurement operation (e.g., mutually exclusive categories, ordinality, equal intervals between scale points, theoretically defined zero point)

Likert scale: A composite indicator that combines multiple questionnaire items;

response choices typically range from "Strongly Agree" to "Strongly Disagree"

Listwise deletion: A technique used to deal with missing data by eliminating from the analysis all cases that have missing data on any of the variables in an analysis

Longitudinal research design: Design where the data are collected over multiple points in time

Manipulation: In an experimental design, an independent variable that is changed or manipulated to observe its effects on the dependent variable. *See also* Treatment

Maturation: A threat to internal validity that refers to changes in the participants as a result of the passage of time

Mean: The numerical average of a set of scores

Means substitution: A technique used to deal with missing data by replacing missing responses with the mean value for all nonmissing cases

Measure of association: A descriptive statistic that indicates the extent or strength of the relationship between two variables

Measurement error: The difference between the actual value of some construct and the value yielded by an operation measuring that construct

Measures of association: Statistical techniques to indicate how strongly (and in what direction) two or more variables are associated

Median (50th percentile): The middle score in a distribution; half of the scores are below the median, and half of the scores are above the median

Mediator variable: A variable believed to be affected by some other variable and that, in turn, affects another variable; a variable that mediates or transmits the effects of one variable on another. *See also* Intervening variable

Missing data: Condition created when a respondent fails to give codable responses to one or more questionnaire items

Mixed-methods studies: Studies that combine both quantitative and qualitative approaches in the same study design, either simultaneously or sequentially

Mixed-model studies: Designs emanating from the pragmatist paradigm, combining both qualitative and quantitative approaches in the study design

Mode: The most frequently occurring score in a set of data

Moderator variable: A variable that affects the relationship between two other variables (but doesn't affect those variables themselves). *See also* Control variable

Multidimensional: When a scale or index is tapping or represents more than one underlying construct or aspect

Multi-level modeling: Statistical technique to examine nested or hierarchical data

Multiple-case study: In-depth examination of a number of similar cases

Multiple-regression analysis: A statistical procedure for assessing the strength and direction of the simultaneous effects of multiple independent variables on a single dependent variable

Multiple-treatment interference: A threat to external validity that occurs in experiments when there are multiple treatments provided to the same set of respondents

Needs and social impact assessment: Determining the extent of a social problem and the need for programs to deal with that problem

Nested data: Data that are in hierarchical form; siblings are nested within

families, families are nested within neighborhoods, etc.

Newsgroup: A group of individuals interested in a common topic (e.g., child abuse, teen pregnancy, custody rights) that communicates over an Internet-based distribution system

Nominal level of measurement: Measurement that only assumes a mutually exclusive and exhaustive category scheme (e.g., religious affiliation, state of residence)

Nondirectional hypothesis: Prediction that an association exists (without predicting the direction of the association) or that a difference between groups exists (without predicting which group will have the larger mean or other score)

Nonprobability sample: Any of a number of techniques (including quota sampling, convenience sampling, snowball sampling, etc.) for which the probability of any given member of the population being included in the sample is unknown

Nonreactive techniques: Data collection techniques that attempt to remove the researcher from the setting or behavior being studied and minimize effects such as interviewer bias (also known as unobtrusive measures)

Operationalization: The process of translating abstract concepts into measurement operations

Ordinal (positional) biases: Effects on responses because of placement or ordering of items in a survey instrument

Ordinal level of measurement: Measurement that assumes all the characteristics of the nominal level and that the scale scores can be ordered along some meaningful continuum or dimension

Outcome assessment: Research to determine if an applied program is achieving its goals

Pairwise deletion: A technique used to deal with missing data that eliminates from calculations only those pairs of variables that have missing responses

Panel research design: Multiple responses from the same observational units are analyzed to study change over time

Peer review: Process whereby manuscripts or proposals are read and critiqued by other professionals to determine suitability for publication or funding

Perfect relationship: Association between two variables in which knowing the value of the independent variable allows you to predict the value of the dependent variable without error

Population: The set of all elements that meet a specified definition of range (e.g., the set of all registered voters in the United States; the set of all single-parent households in North Carolina)

Population parameter: Statistic that refers to some characteristic of a population. *See also* Sample statistic

Prediction: Statement about some future state of affairs based on the propositions of a theory

Predictive validity: Type of validity that indicates a measure's ability to correlate with (*predict*) measures taken at some future point in time. *See also* Concurrent validity; Criterion validity

Probability sample: Any of a number of techniques (including simple random sampling and stratified random sampling) for which the probability of any given member of the population being included in the sample is known

Process research: Research intended to determine how an applied program works

Purposive sampling: Nonprobability sampling technique for which elements are selected on the basis of their characteristics (and through any random sampling process)

Qualitative research: Research in which the focus is on non-numerical (especially textual) analysis and interpretation. *See also* Mixed-methods research studies

Quantitative analysis: Use of statistical techniques to analyze data represented by numbers

Quantitative methods: Research in which the focus is on numerical analysis and interpretation, especially using statistical techniques

Quasi-experimental design: Any of a number of research designs that do not use random assignment to treatment conditions but allow some inferences about the effects of a treatment on some outcome variable through the use of comparison groups or other techniques

Quota sampling: Nonprobability sampling technique in which elements are selected in proportion to known distributions in the population

Random assignment: In experimental designs, a technique in which research participants are assigned to conditions through a random process to create equivalent groups at the start of the experiment

Random measurement error: Error in the measurement process that is unrelated to the concept being measured Random sampling

Range: The arithmetic difference between the lowest and highest scores in a distribution

Ratio level of measurement: Measurement that assumes all the characteristics of the nominal, ordinal, and interval levels and that there is a theoretically defined zero point

Reactive effect of testing: A threat to internal validity that refers to the possibility that responding to a pretest might affect the respondent's reaction to the experimental manipulation, making it difficult to generalize the results of the experiment to nonpretested populations

Reactive effects of experimental arrangements: A threat to external validity; people who are aware that they are in an experiment may behave differently than they would normally

Reliability: The extent to which a measurement yields consistent results. *See also* Stability; Consistency; Internal reliability; Interobserver reliability

Replicate: In social and behavioral research, to repeat a previously published study (often to determine if there have been changes in some underlying process over time or to correct some type of methodological flaw)

Response rate: In survey research, the percentage of eligible respondents who actually respond to the questionnaire or other survey instrument

Review article: Article in a professional journal that doesn't present new research but instead reviews, summarizes, and critiques existing research on a specific topic

Sample: Some subset of elements drawn from a population

Sample statistic: Statistic that refers to some characteristic of a sample. See also population parameter

Sampling error: The differences between the characteristics of a sample and those of the population from which that sample was drawn

Sampling frame: The set of all elements from which the members of the sample are drawn

Sampling procedure: The technique or method through which the researcher determines which units (e.g., persons, families, organizations) to include in the data collection process

Scale: Summing, averaging, or otherwise combining the responses to multiple items that have a logical structure, usually using some procedure to ensure unidimensionality or some other characteristic

Search engine: An application that searches for Web pages containing specific information

Secondary analysis: Analysis using data gathered by other researchers or agencies for research purposes

Secondary data: Data gathered by other researchers or agencies

Selection: A threat to internal validity dealing with how respondents are assigned to treatment groups for an experiment; a particularly important problem if respondents are not assigned randomly

Selective deposit: Systematic effects on which records or information are placed in the running record

Selective survival: Systematic effects on which records or information stay in the running record once they are placed there

Semantic differential: A type of scaling procedure that uses bipolar dimensions (e.g., valuable to worthless; strong to weak; easy to difficult) to measure respondents' feelings or attitudes about some subject

Simple random sampling: Sampling procedure in which each and every element in the population has a known and equal probability of being included in the sample; elements are selected through a random process

Single-case study: In-depth examination of one example of some phenomenon, group, or condition

Snowball sampling: A nonprobability sampling procedure in which the sample grows by adding individuals identified by respondents or informants

Social desirability: Tendency of some respondents to provide answers that are biased in the direction of socially acceptable attitudes or behaviors

Somer's *D*: A measure of association for ordinal-level data

Split-half reliability: A measure of internal reliability that computes the correlation between the summated scores of two halves of the same index or scale; higher values indicate that the items tend to measure the same underlying construct

Spurious effect: When two variables appear to be causally related but, in fact, the association between the two variables is actually the result of the effects of a third variable

Stability: A form of reliability that measures the consistency of responses over time

Standard deviation: A measure of variability for interval- and ratio-level data

Statistical regression: A threat to internal validity resulting from assignment of respondents to groups based on extreme scores on some scale

Statistical significance: An indication of the likelihood that an observed difference or association could have occurred by chance or that a difference or association noted in a sample exists in the populations from which the data were drawn

Strata (singular: stratum): Mutually exclusive segments based on some readily observable characteristic such as zip code, county, or gender used in stratified random sampling

Stratified random sampling: Sampling procedure in which elements are selected at random from within population strata

Structural equation modeling: Statistical technique used to evaluate causal models

Substantive significance: A subjective determination of whether an observed difference or association is large enough to be worth paying attention to

Systematic measurement error: Error in measurement that is not random but instead is associated with some characteristic of the respondent

Test of statistical significance: Statistical procedure whereby an observed difference or association is evaluated to determine whether the difference or association is likely to have occurred by chance

Testing effect: A threat to internal validity that can occur when respondents change their responses as a result of their exposure to the measuring instrument

Theoretical role: How a variable is conceptualized to fit into a model (e.g., independent, dependent, control, intervening)

Theory: A set of abstract propositions that purport to explain some phenomenon

Threats to validity: Any of a number of factors (e.g., history, maturation, testing, selection) that create possible alternative interpretations of research outcomes, thereby making it difficult to determine if effects on the outcome variable are caused by changes in the independent variable

Treatment: In an experimental design, an independent variable changed or manipulated to observe its effects on the dependent variable. *See also* Manipulation

Triangulation mixed-methods design: Studies that combine quantitative and qualitative approaches simultaneously

t-statistic: The calculated value that is the result of a t-test

t-test for independent samples: A test of significance for comparing two sample means

Uncertainty coefficient (U_{yx}): A measure of association for nominal-level data

Unidimensional: When a scale or index represents a single underlying construct or aspect

Unit of analysis: The level of social life on which the research is focused (e.g., individuals, dyads (couples), families, organizations, counties, etc.)

Validity: The extent to which a measurement operation measures what it is intended to measure. *See also* Construct validity; Content validity; Criterion validity; Face validity

Variability: Statistical measures of how widely dispersed the data are along a continuum

Variance: A measure of variability for interval- and ratio-level data

References

Agresti, A. (2018). *Statistical methods for the social sciences*. Boston, MA: Pearson.

Allison, P. D. (2009). *Fixed effects regression models*. Thousand Oaks, CA: Sage.

Amato, P. R. (1989). Who cares for children in public places? Naturalistic observation of male and female caretakers. *Journal of Marriage and the Family, 51*(4), 981–990.

American Psychological Association. (2009). *Publication manual of the American Psychological Association* (6th ed.). Washington, DC: Author.

American Sociological Association. (2007). *American Sociological Association style guide* (3rd ed.). Washington, DC: Author.

Andersen, J. P., Prause, J., & Silver, B. C. (2011). A step-by-step guide to using secondary data for psychological research. *Social and Personality Psychology Compass, 5*, 56–75.

Atkinson, M. P., & Blackwelder, S. P. (1993). Fathering in the 20th century. *Journal of Marriage and the Family, 55*(4), 975–986.

Austin, A. (2016). "There I am": A grounded theory study of young adults navigating a transgender or gender nonconforming identity within a context of oppression and invisibility. *Sex Roles, 75*(5/6), 215–230.

Axinn, W. G., & Pearce, L. D. (2006). *Mixed method data collection strategies*. New York, NY: Cambridge University Press.

Babbie, E. (2010). *The practice of social research* (12th ed.). Belmont, CA: Wadsworth.

Bai, S., Repetti, R. L., & Sperling, J. B. (2016). Children's expressions of positive emotion are sustained by smiling, touching, and playing with parents and siblings: A naturalistic observational study of family life. *Developmental Psychology, 52*(1), 88–101.

Bakeman, R., & Gottman, J. M. (1997). *Observing interaction: An introduction to sequential analysis* (2nd ed.). New York, NY: Cambridge University Press.

Baron, R. M., & Kenny, D. A. (1986). The moderator-mediator distinction in social psychological research: Conceptual, strategic, and statistical considerations. *Journal of Personality and Social Psychology, 51*, 1173–1182.

Barrett, D. (2012). Presentation, politics, and editing: The Marks/Regnerus articles. *Social Science Research, 41*, 1354–1356.

Basáñez, T., Dennis, J. M., Crano, W. D., Stacy, A. W., & Unger, J. B. (2014). Measuring acculturation gap conflicts among Hispanics: Implications for psychosocial and academic adjustment. *Journal of Family Issues, 35*(13), 1727–1753.

Bean, C. N., Forneris, T., & Halsall, T. (2014). Girls just wanna have fun: A process evaluation of a female youth-driven physical activity-based life skills program. *SpringerPlus, 3*(1), 401–415.

Beaulaurier, R. L., Seff, L. R., Newman, F. L., & Dunlop, B. (2007). External barriers to help seeking for older women who experience intimate partner violence. *Journal of Family Violence, 22*(4), 747–755.

Berk, R. A., & Rossi, P. H. (1999). *Thinking about program evaluation* (2nd ed.). Thousand Oaks, CA: Sage.

Bhattacharjee, Y. (2013, April 28). The mind of a con man. *The New York Times*, p. MM44.

Birkett, M., Newcomb, M. E., & Mustanski, B. (2015). Does it get better? A longitudinal analysis of psychological distress and victimization in lesbian, gay, bisexual, transgender, and questioning youth. *Journal of Adolescent Health, 56,* 280–285.

Blair, J., Czaja, R. F., & Blair, E. A. (2013). *Designing surveys: A guide to decisions and procedures* (3rd ed.). Thousand Oaks, CA: Sage.

Blankenhorn, D. (1995). *Fatherless America: Confronting our most urgent social problem.* New York, NY: Basic Books.

Blumberg, S. J., & Luke, J. V. (2016). *Wireless substitution: Early release estimates from the national health interview survey, July-December 2015.* Retrieved from http://www.cdc.gov/nchs/data/nhis/earlyrelease/wireless201605.pdf

Bluth, K., Gaylord, S. A., Campo, R. A., Mullarkey, M. C., & Hobbs, L. (2016). Making friends with yourself: A mixed methods pilot study of a mindful self-compassion program for adolescents. *Mindfulness, 7*(2), 479–492. doi:10.1007/s12671-015-0476-6

Booth, A., Johnson, D. R., Amato, P., & Rogers, S. J. (2003). *Marital instability over the life course: A six-wave panel study, 1980, 1983, 1988, 1992–1994, 1997, 2000* [computer file]. University Park: Pennsylvania State University.

Boruch, R. F. (1975). On common contentions about randomized field experiments. In R. F. Boruch & H. W. Riecken (Eds.), *Experimental testing of public policy: The proceedings of the 1974 Social Science Research Council conference on social experiments* (pp. 108–145). Boulder, CO: Westview Press.

Bramlett, M. D., & Mosher, W. D. (2002). *Cohabitation, marriage, divorce, and remarriage in the United States* (series 22, no. 2). Washington, DC: Government Printing Office.

Brick, J. M., Brick, P. D., Dipko, S., Presser, S., Tucker, C., & Yangyang, Y. (2007). Cell phone survey feasibility in the U.S.: Sampling and calling cell numbers versus landline numbers. *Public Opinion Quarterly, 71*(1), 23–39.

Bridges, J. S., & Orza, A. M. (1993). Effects of maternal employment-childrearing pattern on college students' perceptions of a mother and her child. *Psychology of Women Quarterly, 17*(1), 103–117.

Broockman, D., Kalla, J., & Aronow, P. (2015). *Irregularities in LaCour (2014).* Retrieved from http://stanford.edu/~dbroock/broockman_kalla_aronow_lg_irregularities.pdf

Brooks Gunn, J., Phelps, E., & Elder, G. H. (1991). Studying lives through time: Secondary data analyses in developmental psychology. *Developmental Psychology, 27*(6), 899–910.

Bryant, W. K., & Zick, C. D. (1996). An examination of parent-child shared time. *Journal of Marriage and the Family, 58*(1), 227–237.

Buchanan, C. M., Maccoby, E. E., & Dornbusch, S. M. (1991). Caught between parents: Adolescents' experience in divorced homes. *Child Development, 62*(5), 1008–1029.

Bumpass, L. L., Martin, T. C., & Sweet, J. A. (1991). The impact of family background and early marital factors on marital disruption. *Journal of Family Issues, 12*(1), 22–42.

Bumpass, L., Sweet, J., & Martin, T. C. (1990). Changing patterns of remarriage. *Journal of Marriage and the Family, 52*(3), 747–756.

Campanario, J. M. (1993). Consolation for the scientist: Sometimes it is hard to publish papers that are later highly-cited. *Social Studies of Science, 23*(2), 342–362.

Campbell, D. T., & Stanley, J. C. (1963). *Experimental and quasi-experimental designs for research.* Chicago, IL: Rand McNally.

Carmichael, G. A. (1985). Children and divorce in New Zealand. *Journal of Marriage and the Family, 47*(1), 221–231.

Carney, D. R. (2015). *My position on "power poses."* Retrieved from http://faculty.haas.berkeley.edu/dana_carney/pdf_My%20position%20on%20power%20poses.pdf

Carney, D. R., Cuddy, A. J. C., & Yap, A. J. (2010). Power posing: Brief nonverbal displays affect neuroendocrine levels and risk tolerance. *Psychological Science, 21*(10), 1363–1368.

Cauhapé, E. (1983). *Fresh starts: Men and women after divorce.* New York, NY: Basic Books.

Centers for Disease Control and Prevention. (2017). *Teen pregnancy in the United States.* Retrieved from https://www.cdc.gov/teen-pregnancy/about/index.htm

Chafetz, J. S. (1978). *A primer on the construction and testing of theories in sociology.* Itasca, IL: F. E. Peacock.

Chase Lansdale, P. L., Mott, F. L., Brooks Gunn, J., & Phillips, D. A. (1991). Children of the National Longitudinal Survey of Youth: A unique research opportunity. *Developmental Psychology, 27*(6), 918–931.

Cheng, S., & Powell, B. (2015). Measurement, methods, and divergent patterns: Reassessing the effects of same-sex parents. *Social Science Research, 52,* 615–626.

Cherlin, A. (1991). On analyzing other people's data. *Developmental Psychology, 27,* 946–948.

Chernyak, N., & Sobel, D. M. (2016). Equal but not always fair: Value-laden sharing in preschool-aged children. *Social Development, 25*(2), 340–351. doi:10.1111/sode.12136

Cherryhomes, C. H. (1992). Notes on pragmatism and scientific realism. *Educational Researcher, 14,* 13–17.

Chetty, R., Hendren, N., & Katz, L. F. (2016). The effects of exposure to better neighborhoods on children: New evidence from the moving to opportunity experiment. *American Economic Review, 106*(4), 855–902. doi:10.1257/aer.20150572

Christian, L., Keeter, S., Purcell, K., & Smith, A. (2010). *Assessing cell phone non-coverage bias across different topics and subgroups.* Paper presented at the Annual Conference of the American Association for Public Opinion Research, Chicago, IL.

Claycamp, R. D. (2017). *Adverse determination and demand for payment of funds from R01MH81019, Mani Pavuluri, M.D., Ph.D., affective neuroscience of pediatric bipolar disorder.* Retrieved from https://assets.documentcloud.org/documents/4438787/Nov-28-2017-NIMH-Decision.pdf

Cohen, J. (1988). *Statistical power analysis for the behavioral sciences* (2nd ed.). Hillsdale, NJ: Erlbaum.

Cohen, J. S. (2018). The $3-million research breakdown. *The Chronicle of Higher Education, 64*(33). Retrieved from https://www.chronicle.com/article/The-3-Million-Research/243231

Cohen, P. N. (2012a). *Gun Google searches and suicide.* Retrieved from https://familyinequality.wordpress.com/2012/10/24/gun-google-searches-and-suicide/

Cohen, P. N. (2012b). *Time travel: Regnerus study timeline suggests superhuman abilities.* Retrieved from https://familyinequality.wordpress.com/2012/06/18/regnerus-study-timeline/

Coltrane, S. (1996). *Family man: Fatherhood, housework, and gender equity.* New York, NY: Oxford University Press.

Congressional Record. (1991, September 12). Washington, DC: US Government Publishing Office.

Connidis, I. A., & Campbell, L. D. (1995). Closeness, confiding, and contact among siblings in middle and late adulthood. *Journal of Family Issues, 16*(6), 722–745.

Conroy, D. A., Czopp, A. M., Dore-Stites, D., Dopp, R. R., Armitage, R., Hoban, T. F., & Arnedt, J. T. (2017). A pilot study on adolescents with depression and insomnia: Qualitative findings from focus groups. *Behavioral Sleep Medicine, 15*(1), 22–38.

Cook, T. D., & Campbell, D. T. (1979). *Quasi-experimentation: Design & analysis issues for field settings.* Chicago, IL: Rand McNally.

Cooper, C., McLanahan, S., Meadows, S., & Brooks-Gunn, J. (2009). Family structure, transitions and maternal stress. *Journal of Marriage and Family, 71*(3), 558–574.

Corbin, J., & Strauss, A. (2008). *Basics of qualitative research.* Thousand Oaks, CA: Sage.

Couper, M. P. (2017). New developments in survey data collection. *Annual Review of Sociology, 43*, 121–145. doi:10.1146/annurev-soc-060116-053613

Creswell, J. W. (2009). *Research design: Qualitative, quantitative, and mixed methods approaches.* Thousand Oaks, CA: Sage.

Creswell, J. W., & Plano Clark, V. L. (2007). *Designing and conducting mixed methods research.* Thousand Oaks, CA: Sage.

Cuddy, A. J. C. (2012). *Your body language may shape who you are* [video file]. Retrieved from https://www.ted.com/talks/amy_cuddy_your_body_language_shapes_who_you_are/up-next

Cuddy, A. J. C. (2015). *Presence: Bringing your boldest self to your biggest challenges.* New York, NY: Little, Brown.

Cuddy, A. J. C., Schultz, S. J., & Fosse, N. E. (2018). P-curving a more comprehensive body of research on postural feedback reveals clear evidential value for power-posing effects: Reply to Simmons and Simonsohn (2017). *Psychological Science, 29*(4), 656–666.

Dalrymple, D. (2003). Scientific knowledge as a global public good: Contributions to innovation and the economy. In National Research Council (Ed.), *The role of scientific and technical data and information in the public domain* (pp. 35–51). Washington, DC: The National Academies Press.

Daly, K. J. (1992). The fit between qualitative research and characteristics of families. In J. F. Gilgun, K. Daly, & G. Handel (Eds.), *Qualitative methods in family research* (pp. 3–11). Newbury Park, CA: Sage.

Daly, K. J. (2007). *Qualitative methods for family studies and human development.* Thousand Oaks, CA: Sage.

Davis, S. N., Greenstein, T. N., & Gerteisen Marks, J. P. (2007). Effects of union type on division of household labor: Do cohabiting men really perform more housework? *Journal of Family Issues, 28*(9), 1246–1272.

deNavas-Walt, C., Proctor, B. D., & Mills, R. J. (2004). *Income, poverty, and health insurance coverage in the United States (Current population reports Consumer income P60)* (pp. v). Washington, DC: US Government Printing Office.

Denzin, N. K., & Lincoln, Y. S. (2011). *The Sage handbook of qualitative research* (3rd ed.). Thousand Oaks, CA: Sage.

Descartes, L. (2007). Rewards and challenges of using ethnography in family research. *Family and Consumer Sciences Research Journal, 36*(1), 22–39.

Desmond, M. (2016). *Evicted: Poverty and profit in the American city*. New York, NY: Penguin Random House.

DeVellis, R. F. (1991). *Scale development: Theory and applications*. Newbury Park, CA: Sage.

Dew, J., & Yorgason, J. (2010). Economic pressure and marital conflict in retirement-aged couples. *Journal of Family Issues, 31*(2), 164–188.

Dillman, D. A. (2002). Presidential address: Navigating the rapids of change: Some observations on survey methodology in the early twenty-first century. *Public Opinion Quarterly, 66*(3), 473–494.

Dillman, D. A., Smyth, J. D., & Christian, L. M. (2009). *Internet, mail, and mixed-mode surveys: The tailored design method* (3rd ed.). Hoboken, NJ: Wiley.

Donnellan, W. J., Bennett, K. M., & Soulsby, L. K. (2015). What are the factors that facilitate or hinder resilience in older spousal dementia carers? A qualitative study. *Aging and Mental Health, 19*(10), 932–939.

Edwards, J. R., & Lambert, L. S. (2007). Methods for integrating moderation and mediation: A general analytic framework using moderated path analysis. *Psychological Methods, 12*(1), 1–22.

England, P., & Folbre, N. (2005). Gender and economic sociology. In N. J. Smelser & R. Swedberg (Eds.), *The handbook of economic sociology* (2 ed., pp. 627–649). Princeton, NJ: Princeton University Press.

Fielding, N., Lee, R. M., & Blank, G. (Eds.). (2008). *The SAGE handbook of online research methods*. London, England: Sage.

Finckenauer, J. O., Gavin, P. W., Hovland, H., & Storvoll, E. (1999). *Scared straight! The panacea phenomenon revisited*. Prospect Heights, IL: Waveland Press.

Fonow, M. M., & Cook, J. A. (1991a). Back to the future: A look at the second wave of feminist scholarship. In M. M. Fonow & J. A. Cook (Eds.), *Beyond methodology: Feminist scholarship as lived research* (pp. 1–15). Bloomington: Indiana University Press.

Fonow, M. M., & Cook, J. A. (Eds.). (1991b). *Beyond methodology: Feminist scholarship as lived research*. Bloomington: Indiana University Press.

Fortune, D., & McKeown, J. (2015). Sharing the journey: Exploring a social leisure program for persons with dementia and their spouse. *Leisure Sciences, 38*(4), 373–387.

Frankfort-Nachmias, C., & Leon-Guerrero, A. (2009). *Social statistics for a diverse society* (5th ed.). Thousand Oaks, CA: Pine Forge Press.

Frees, E. W. (2004). *Longitudinal and panel data: Analysis and applications in the social sciences*. Cambridge, England: Cambridge University Press.

Geist, C., & Cohen, P. N. (2011). Headed toward equality? Housework change in comparative perspective. *Journal of Marriage and Family, 73*(4), 832–844.

Gelles, R. J. (1978). Methods for studying sensitive family topics. *American Journal of Orthopsychiatry, 48*(3), 408–424.

Gilgun, J. F. (1992). Definitions, methodologies, and methods in qualitative family research. In J. F. Gilgun, K. Daly, & G. Handel (Eds.), *Qualitative methods in family research* (pp. 22–40). Newbury Park, CA: Sage.

Gillum, T. L. (2008). Community response and needs of African American female survivors of domestic violence. *Journal of Interpersonal Violence, 23*(1), 39–57.

Glaser, B. G., & Strauss, A. L. (1967). *The discovery of grounded theory: Strategies for qualitative research*. Chicago, IL: Aldine.

Golder, S. A., & Macy, M. W. (2014). Digital footprints: Opportunities and challenges for online social research. *Annual Review of Sociology*, *40*, 129–152.

Gomel, J. N., Tinsley, B. J., Parke, R. D., & Clark, K. M. (1998). The effects of economic hardship on family relationships among African American, Latino, and Euro-American families. *Journal of Family Issues*, *19*(4), 436–467.

Gordon, R. A. (2015, February). Measuring constructs in family science: How can item response theory improve precision and validity. *Journal of Marriage and Family*, *77*(1), 147–176.

Greenstein, T. N. (1990). Marital disruption and the employment of married women. *Journal of Marriage and the Family*, *52*(3), 657–676.

Greenstein, T. N. (1995). Gender ideology, marital disruption, and the employment of married women. *Journal of Marriage and the Family*, *57*(1), 31–42.

Greenstein, T. N. (1996). Gender ideology and perceptions of the fairness of the division of household labor: Effects on marital quality. *Social Forces*, *74*(3), 1029–1042.

Gubrium, J. F., & Holstein, J. A. (1990). *What is family?* Mountain View, CA: Mayfield.

Guttman, L. (1950). The basis for scalogram analysis. In S. A. Stouffer, L. Guttman, E. A. Suchman, P. F. Lazarsfeld, S. A. Star, & J. A. Clausen (Eds.), *Measurement and prediction* (pp. 60–90). Princeton, NJ: Princeton University Press.

Hallinan, M. T. (1998). Sociology and the goal of generalization. *Contemporary Sociology*, *27*(1), 21–24.

Hammersley, M., & Atkinson, P. (2007). *Ethnography: Principles in practice* (3rd ed.). New York, NY: Routledge.

Hampe, G. D., & Ruppel, H. J. (1974). Measurement of premarital sexual permissiveness: Comparison of 2 Guttman scales. *Journal of Marriage and the Family*, *36*(3), 451–463.

Hampton, K. N. (2017). Studying the digital: Directions and challenges for digital methods. *Annual Review of Sociology*, *43*, 167–188.

Hannan, M. T., Tuma, N. B., & Groeneveld, L. P. (1978). Income and independence effects on marital dissolution: Results from the Seattle and Denver income-maintenance experiments. *American Journal of Sociology*, *84*, 611–633.

Harrington Meyer, M. (2014). *Grandmothers at work: Juggling families and jobs.* New York, NY: New York University Press.

Heaton, J. (2004). *Reworking qualitative data.* London, England: Sage.

Heubner, A. J., Mancini, J. A., Wilcox, R. M., Grass, S. R., & Grass, G. A. (2007). Parental deployment and youth in military families: Exploring uncertainty and ambiguous loss. *Family Relations*, *56*(2), 112–122.

Hochschild, A. R. (1997). *The time bind: When work becomes home and home becomes work* (1st ed.). New York, NY: Metropolitan Books.

Hochschild, A. R., & Machung, A. (1989). *The second shift.* New York, NY: Viking.

Hyman, H. H. (1987). *Secondary analysis of sample surveys: With a new introduction.* Middletown, CT: Wesleyan University Press.

Ioannidis, J. P. (2012). Why science is not necessarily self-correcting. *Perspectives in Psychological Science*, *7*(6), 645–654.

Jackson, D. J., & Borgatta, E. F. (1981). *Factor analysis and measurement in sociological research: A multi-dimensional perspective.* Beverly Hills, CA: Sage.

Jacobs, J. A., & Gerson, K. (2004). *The time divide: Work, family, and gender inequality*. Cambridge, MA: Harvard University Press.

Jain, A., Marshall, J., Buikema, A., Bancroft, T., Kelly, J., & Newschaffer, C. J. (2015). Autism occurrence by MMR vaccine status among US children with older siblings with and without autism. *Journal of the American Medical Association, 313*(15), 1534–1540.

Janowitz, M. (1979). Inferences about propaganda impact from textual and documentary analysis. In W. E. Daugherty (Ed.), *A psychological warfare casebook* (pp. 732–735). New York, NY: Arno Press.

Jones, S. (1999). *Doing internet research: Critical issues and methods for examining the net*. Thousand Oaks, CA: Sage.

Jung, T., & Wickrama, K. A. S. (2008). *Social and Personality Psychology Compass, 2*(1), 302–317.

Kaplan, A. (1964). *The conduct of inquiry: Methodology for behavioral science*. San Francisco, CA: Chandler.

Kaplan, D. (2009). *Structural equation modeling: Foundations and extensions* (2nd ed.). Thousand Oaks, CA: Sage.

Kluwer, E. S. (2011). Psychological perspectives on gender deviance neutralization. *Journal of Family Theory & Review, 3*(1), 14–17.

Kneeland, H. (1929). Women's economic contributions in the home. *Annals of the American Academy, 143*, 33–40.

Kohut, A., Keeter, S., Doherty, C., Dimock, M., & Christian, L. (2012). *Assessing the representativeness of public opinion surveys*. Retrieved from http://www.people-press.org/2012/05/15/assessing-therepresentativeness-of-public-opinion-surveys/

Kolowich, S. (2011). Security hacks. *Inside Higher Ed*. Retrieved from https://www.insidehighered.com/news/2011/01/27/unc_case_highlights_debate_about_data_security_and_accountability_for_hacks

Konnikova, M. (2015, May 22). How a gay-marriage study went wrong. *The New Yorker*. Retrieved from https://www.newyorker.com/science/maria-konnikova/how-a-gay-marriage-study-went-wrong

Krueger, R. A., & Casey, M. A. (2009). *Focus groups: A practical guide for applied research* (4th ed.). Thousand Oaks, CA: Sage.

Kuhn, T. S. (2012). *The structure of scientific revolutions* (4th ed.). Chicago, IL: University of Chicago Press.

Kwak, J., Kramer, B. J., Lang, J., & Ledger, M. (2012). Challenges in end-of-life management for low-income frail elders. *Research on Aging, 35*(4), 393–419.

LaCour, M. J., & Green, D. P. (2014). When contact changes minds: An experiment on transmission of support for gay equality. *Science, 346*(6215), 1366–1369.

Laney, D. (2001). *3d data management: Controlling data volume, velocity, and variety*. Application Delivery Strategies. META Group. Stamford, CT. Retrieved from https://blogs.gartner.com/doug-laney/files/2012/01/ad949-3D-Data-Management-Controlling-Data-Volume-Velocity-and-Variety.pdf

Lannutti, P. J. (2005). For better or worse: Exploring the meanings of same-sex marriage within the lesbian, gay, bisexual and transgendered community. *Journal of Social and Personal Relationships, 22*(1), 5–18. doi:10.1177/0265407505049319

Lareau, A. (2011). *Unequal childhoods: Class, race and family life*. Berkeley: University of California Press.

LaRossa, R. (2005). Grounded theory methods and qualitative family research. *Journal of Marriage and Family, 67*(4), 837–857.

Larzelere, R., & Klein, D. M. (1987). Methodology. In M. B. Sussman & S. K. Steinmetz (Eds.), *Handbook of marriage and the family* (pp. 126–156). New York, NY: Plenum.

Lavin, M. R. (1996). *Understanding the census: A guide for marketers, planners, grant writers, and other data users* (Library ed.). Phoenix, AZ: Epoch.

Lavrakas, P. J. (1993). *Telephone survey methods: Sampling, selection, and supervision* (2nd ed.). Newbury Park, CA: Sage.

Lazer, D., & Radford, J. (2017). Data ex machina: Introduction to big data. *Annual Review of Sociology, 43,* 19–39.

Leber, D., St. Peters, M., & Markman, H. J. (2005). Program evaluation research: Applications to marital and family therapy. In D. H. Sprenkle & F. P. Piercy (Eds.), *Research methods in family therapy* (2nd ed., pp. 485–506). New York, NY: Guilford Press.

Levelt, W. J. M., Drenth, P., & Noort, E. (2012). *Flawed science: The fraudulent research practices of social psychologist Diederik Stapel.* Tilburg, Netherlands: Commissioned by the Tilburg University, University of Amsterdam and the University of Groningen.

Levine, J. A., Emery, C. R., & Pollack, H. (2007). The well-being of children born to teen mothers. *Journal of Marriage and Family, 69*(1), 105–122.

Levine, J. A., Weisell, R., Chevassus, S., Martinez, C. D., Burlingame, B., & Coward, W. A. (2001). The work burden of women. *Science, 294*(5543), 812–812.

Levinger, G., & Raush, H. L. (1977). *Close relationships: Perspectives on the meaning of intimacy.* Amherst: University of Massachusetts Press.

Lewin, K. (1951). *Field theory in social science: Selected theoretical papers* (1st ed.). New York, NY: Harper.

Li-Grining, C. P., Votruba-Drzal, E., Maldonado-Carreño, C., Haas, K. (2010). Children's early approaches to learning and academic trajectories through fifth grade. *Developmental Psychology, 46*(5), 1062–1077.

Little, R. J. A., & Rubin, D. B. (1989). The analysis of social science data with missing values. *Sociological Methods and Research, 18,* 292–326.

Loether, H. J., & McTavish, D. G. (1993). *Descriptive and inferential statistics: An introduction* (4th ed.). Boston, MA: Allyn & Bacon.

Lofland, J., Snow, D., Anderson, L., & Lofland, L. H. (2005). *Analyzing social settings: A guide to qualitative observation and analysis* (4th ed.). Belmont, CA: Wadsworth/Thomson Learning.

Long, J. S. (1983). *Confirmatory factor analysis: A preface to Lisrel.* Beverly Hills, CA: Sage.

Lynam, D. R., Milich, R., Zimmerman, R., Novak, S. P., Logan, T. K., Martin, C., . . . & Clayton, R. (1999). Project Dare: No effects at 10-year follow-up. *Journal of Consulting and Clinical Psychology, 67*(4), 590–593.

Maguire, M. C. (1999). Treating the dyad as the unit of analysis: A primer on three analytic approaches. *Journal of Marriage and the Family, 61*(1), 213–223.

Mann, C., & Stewart, F. (2000). *Internet communication and qualitative research: A handbook for researching online.* Thousand Oaks, CA: Sage.

Manyika, J., Chui, M., Brown, B., Bughin, J., Dobbs, R., Roxburgh, C., & Byers, A. H. (2011). *Big data: The next frontier for innovation, competition, and productivity.* Retrieved from https://www.mckinsey .com/~/media/McKinsey/Business%20 Functions/McKinsey%20Digital/Our% 20Insights/Big%20data%20The%20 next%20frontier%20for%20innovation/ MGI_big_data_full_report.ashx

Markham, C. M., Peskin, M. F., Shegog, R., Baumler, E. R., Addy, R. C., Thiel, M., . . . & Tortolero, S. R. (2014). Behavioral and psychosocial effects of two middle school sexual health education programs at tenth-grade follow-up. *Journal of Adolescent Health, 54*(2), 151–159.

Marshall, M. N. (1996). Sampling for qualitative research. *Family Practice, 13*(6), 522–525.

Marsiglio, W., Hutchinson, S., & Cohan, M. (2001). Young men's procreative identity: Becoming aware, being aware, and being responsible. *Journal of Marriage and Family, 63*(1), 123–135.

McCall, R. B., & Appelbaum, M. I. (1991). Some issues of conducting secondary analyses. *Developmental Psychology, 27*, 911–917.

Mead, M. (1935). *Sex and temperament in three primitive societies.* New York, NY: W. Morrow.

Menard, S. (1991). *Longitudinal research.* Newbury Park, CA: Sage.

Messer, B. L., & Dillman, D. A. (2011). Surveying the general public over the internet using address-based sampling and mail contact procedures. *Public Opinion Quarterly, 75*(3), 429–457.

Middleton, R. (1960). Fertility values in American magazine fiction, 1916–1956. *Public Opinion Quarterly, 24*(1), 137–143.

Miles, M. B., Huberman, A. M., & Saldana, J. (2013). *Qualitative data analysis: An expanded sourcebook* (3rd ed.). Thousand Oaks, CA: Sage.

Milgram, S. (1974). *Obedience to authority: An experimental view.* New York, NY: HarperCollins.

Minton, C., & Pasley, K. (1996). Fathers' parenting role identity and father involvement: A comparison of nondivorced and divorced, nonresident fathers. *Journal of Family Issues, 17*(1), 26–45.

Misson, S., & Sipthorp, M. (2007). *Wave 2 weighting and non-response* (ISAC technical paper, no. 5). Melbourne: Australian Institute of Family Studies.

Mistry, R. S., Lowe, E. D., Benner, A., & Chien, N. (2008). Expanding the family economic stress model: Insights from a mixed-methods approach. *Journal of Marriage and the Family, 70*(1), 196–209.

Molotsky, I. (1999, August 31). Study links teenage substance abuse and paternal ties. *New York Times,* p. A16.

Morgan, D. L. (1997). *Focus groups as qualitative research.* Thousand Oaks, CA: Sage.

Muller, C. M., Hormann, V., Fleischli, J., & Studer, F. (2015). Effects of classroom composition on the development of antisocial behavior in lower secondary school. *Research on Adolescence, 26*(2), 345–359.

Musick, M. A. (2014). *A review of methodological and ethical issues surrounding the New Family Structures study.* Retrieved from https://www.interpretationlgbt.com/ uploads/2/3/7/2/23720524/260747196-musick-s-report.pdf

Mutchler, J. E., Somerville, C., Khaniyan, M., & Evans, M. (2016). *The future of aging in the town of Chatham: Chatham Council on Aging needs assessment study.* Boston, MA: Center for Social and Demographic Research on Aging. Retrieved from http://scholar-works.umb.edu/demographyofaging/8

National Council on Family Relations. (2017). *2016 NCFR journal statistics.* Retrieved from https://www.ncfr.org/sites/ default/files/2017-09/NCFR%20Journal%20 Statistics%202016.pdf

National Research Council. (2003). *The role of scientific and technical data and information in the public domain: Proceedings of a symposium*. Washington, DC: The National Academies Press.

National Telecommunications and Information Administration. (1999). *Falling through the net: Defining the digital divide*. Washington, DC: Author.

National Telecommunications and Information Administration. (2010). *Digital nation: 21st century America's progress towards universal broadband access*. Washington, DC: Author.

Nock, S. L., Sanchez, L. A., & Wright, D. A. (2008). *Covenant marriage: The movement to reclaim tradition in America*. New Brunswick, NJ: Rutgers University Press.

Osgood, C. E., Suci, C. J., & Tannenbaum, P. H. (1957). *The measurement of meaning*. Urbana: University of Illinois Press.

Outlaw, J. (2011). *UNC-Chapel Hill, professor Yankaskas reach settlement*. Retrieved from https://uncnewsarchive.unc.edu/2011/04/15/unc-chapel-hill-professor-yankaskas-reach-settlement-2/

Owen, J. M. (2006). *Program evaluation: Forms and approaches* (3rd ed.). New York, NY: Guilford Press.

Ownbey, M., Ownbey, J., & Cullen, J. (2011). The effects of a health families home visitation program on rapid and teen repeat births. *Child and Adolescent Social Work Journal, 28*(6), 439–458.

Pearce, L. D. (2002). Integrating survey and ethnographic methods for systematic anomalous case analysis. *Sociological Methodology, 32*, 102–132.

Peters, D. P., & Ceci, S. J. (1980). A manuscript masquerade. *The Sciences, 20*, 16–20, 35.

Plano Clark, V. L., Huddleston-Casas, C. A., Churchill, S. L., O'Neill Green, D., &

Garrett, A. L. (2008). Mixed methods approaches in family science research. *Journal of Family Issues, 29*, 1543–1566.

Popper, K. R. (1964). *The poverty of historicism*. New York, NY: Harper & Row.

Popper, K. R. (1992). *The logic of scientific discovery*. New York, NY: Routledge.

Popper, K. R. (2002). *Conjectures and refutations: The growth of scientific knowledge*. New York, NY: Routledge.

Powell, B., Bolzendahl, C., & Steelman, L. C. (2010). *Counted out: Same sex relations and Americans' definition of family*. New York, NY: Russell Sage Foundation.

Punch, K. F. (2005). *Introduction to social research: Quantitative and qualitative approaches* (2nd ed.). London, England: Sage.

Punch, K. F. (2013). *Introduction to social research: Quantitative and qualitative approaches* (3rd ed.). London, England: Sage.

Raley, R. K., Sweeney, M. M., & Wondra, D. (2015). The growing racial and ethnic divide in U.S. marriage patterns. *Future Child, 25*(2), 89–109.

Ranehill, E., Dreber, A., Johannesen, M., Leiberg, S., Sul, S., & Weber, R. A. (2015). Assessing the robustness of power posing: No effect on hormones and risk tolerance in a large sample of men and women. *Psychological Science, 26*(5), 653–656.

Rapoza, K. A., Cook, K., Zaveri, T., & Malley-Morrison, K. (2010). Ethnic perspectives on sibling abuse in the United States. *Journal of Family Issues, 31*(6), 808–829. doi:10.1177/0192513x09359158

Raudenbush, S. W., & Bryk, A. S. (2002). *Hierarchical linear models*. Thousand Oaks, CA: Sage.

Regnerus, M. (2012). How different are the adult children of parents who have same-sex relationships? Findings from the New Family Structures study. *Social Science Research, 41*(4), 752–770.

Reynolds, P. D. (1971). *A primer in theory construction.* Indianapolis, IN: Bobbs-Merrill.

Risman, B. J., & Johnson-Sumerford, D. (1998). Doing it fairly: A study of postgender marriages. *Journal of Marriage and the Family, 60*(1), 23–40.

Robinson, J. P., & Godbey, G. (1999). *Time for life: The surprising ways Americans use their time.* University Park: Pennsylvania State University Press.

Robinson, J. P., Shaver, P. R., & Wrightsman, L. S. (1991). *Measures of personality and social psychological attitudes.* San Diego, CA: Academic Press.

Roche, K. M., & Leventhal, T. (2009). Beyond neighborhood poverty: Family management, neighborhood disorder, and adolescents' early sexual onset. *Journal of Family Psychology, 23,* 819–827.

Rocheleau, C. M., Romitti, P. A., Hockett Sherlock, S., Sanderson, W. T., Bell, E. M., & Druschel, C. (2012). Effect of survey instrument on participation in a follow-up study: A randomization study of a mailed questionnaire versus a computer-assisted telephone interview. *BMC Public Health, 12,* 579.

Roethlisberger, F. J., & Dickson, W. I. (1939). *Management and the worker: An account of a research program conducted by the Western Electric Co. Hawthorne works, Chicago.* Cambridge, MA: Harvard University Press.

Roskos, K. A., & Christie, J. F. (2017). *Play and literacy in early childhood: Research from multiple perspectives* (2nd ed.). New York, NY: Routledge.

Rossi, P. H., Lipsey, M. W., & Henry, G. T. (2018). *Evaluation: A systematic approach* (8th ed.). Thousand Oaks, CA: Sage.

Roy, K., Zvonkovic, A., Goldberg, A., Sharp, E., & LaRossa, R. (2015). Sampling richness and qualitative integrity: Challenges for research with families. *Journal of Marriage and Family, 77*(1), 243–260. doi:10.1111/jomf.12147

Sanders, S. A., & Reinisch, J. M. (1999). Would you say you "had sex" if . . . ? *Journal of the American Medical Association, 281,* 275–277.

Sayer, A. G., & Klute, M. M. (2005). Analyzing couples and families: Multilevel methods. In V. L. Bengston, A. C. Acock, K. R. Allen, P. Dilworth-Anderson, & D. M. Klein (Eds.), *Sourcebook of family theory & research* (pp. 289–313). Thousand Oaks, CA: Sage.

Schor, J. (1991). *The overworked American.* New York, NY: Basic Books.

Schutt, R. K. (2004). *Investigating the social world.* Thousand Oaks, CA: Pine Forge Press.

Secret, M., & Peck-Heath, C. (2004). Maternal labor force participation and child well-being in public assistance families. *Journal of Family Issues, 25*(4), 520–541.

Sherkat, D. E. (2012). The editorial process and politicized scholarship: Monday morning editorial quarterbacking and a call for scientific vigilance. *Social Science Review, 41,* 1346–1349.

Shows, C., & Gerstel, N. (2009). Fathering, class, and gender: A comparison of physicians and emergency medical technicians. *Gender & Society, 23,* 161–187.

Silverstein, L. B., & Auerbach, C. (1999). Deconstructing the essentialist father. *American Psychologist, 54*(6), 397–407.

Simmons, C., Steinberg, L., Frick, P. J., & Cauffman, E. (2017). The differential influence of absent and harsh fathers on juvenile delinquency. *Journal of Adolescence, 62,* 9–17.

Simmons, J. P., & Simonsohn, U. (2015). Power posing: Reassessing the evidence behind the most popular TED talk. Retrieved from http://datacolada.org/37

Simmons, J. P., & Simonsohn, U. (2017). Power posing: P-curving the evidence. *Psychological Science*, 28(5), 687–693.

Singal, J. (2015). The case of the amazing gay-marriage data: How a graduate student reluctantly uncovered a huge scientific fraud. *The Cut*. 29 May 2015. Retrieved from https://www.thecut.com/2015/05/how-a-grad-student-uncovered-a-huge-fraud.html

Singleton, R., & Straits, B. C. (2017). *Approaches to social research* (6th ed.). New York, NY: Oxford University Press.

Sjoberg, G., & Nett, R. (1968). *A methodology for social research*. New York, NY: Harper & Row.

Slade, M., Gask, L., Leese, M., McCrone, P., Montana, C., Powell, R., & Chew-Graham, C. (2008). Failure to improve appropriateness of referrals to adult community mental health services: Lessons from a multi-site cluster randomized controlled trial. *Family Practice*, 25, 181–190.

Smith, R. (2010, January 29). Andrew Wakefield: The man behind the MMR controversy. *The Telegraph*. Retrieved from https://www.telegraph.co.uk/news/health/news/7091767/Andrew-Wakefield-the-man-behind-the-MMR-controversy.html

Soloff, C., Lawrence, D., Misson, S., & Johnstone, R. (2006). *Wave 1 weighting and non-response* (LSAC Technical paper No. 3). Melbourne: Australian Institute of Family Studies.

Stack, C. B. (1974). *All our kin: Strategies for survival in a black community* (1st ed.). New York, NY: Harper & Row.

Stewart, D. W., & Shamdasani, P. N. (2014). *Focus groups: Theory and practice*. Thousand Oaks, CA: Sage.

Szinovacz, M. E. (1983). Using couple data as a methodological tool: The case of marital violence. *Journal of Marriage and the Family*, 45(3), 633–644.

Tashakkori, A. M., & Teddlie, C. B. (1998). *Mixed methodology: Combining qualitative and quantitative approaches*. Thousand Oaks, CA: Sage.

Thomas, W. I., Znaniecki, F., & Zaretsky, E. (1996). *The Polish peasant in Europe and America*. Urbana: University of Illinois Press.

Thomson, E., & Williams, R. (1982). Beyond wives' family sociology: A method for analyzing couple data. *Journal of Marriage and the Family*, 44(4), 999–1008.

Tichenor, V. J. (2005). Maintaining men's dominance: Negotiating identity and power when she earns more. *Sex Roles*, 53(3/4),191–205.

Top Downloads January 1–June 1, 2018. (2018). *ICPSR Bulletin*, 38(2), 20.

Touliatos, J., Perlmutter, B. F., & Straus, M. A. (1990). *Handbook of family measurement techniques*. Newbury Park, CA: Sage.

Toulmin, S. (1972). *Human understanding: The collective use and evolution of concepts*. Oxford, England: Clarendon Press.

Treas, J., & Drobnič, S. (Eds.). (2010). *Dividing the domestic: Men, women, and household work in cross-national perspective*. Stanford, CA: Stanford University Press.

Twiggs, J. E., McQuillan, J., & Ferree, M. M. (1999). Meaning and measurement: Reconceptualizing measures of the division of household labor. *Journal of Marriage and the Family*, 61(3), 712–724.

U.S. Census Bureau. (2010). *Statistical abstract of the United States*. Retrieved from http://www.census.gov/prod/2009pubs/10statab/law.pdf

U.S. Bureau of the Census. (2017). *Historical income tables: Households*. Retrieved from https://www.census.gov/data/tables/time-series/demo/income-poverty/historical-income-households.html

U.S. Department of Health & Human Services, Administration for Children and Families, Administration, & Children, Youth and Families, Children's Bureau. (2017). *Child maltreatment 2015*. Retrieved from http://www.acf.hhs.gov/programs/cb/research-data-technology/statistics-research/child-maltreatment

University of North Carolina at Chapel Hill. (2014). *Largest national study on adolescent health receives $28 million from NIH* [Press release]. Retrieved from https://uncnews.unc.edu/2014/09/25/largest-national-study-adolescent-health-receives-28-million-nih/

Udry, J. R. (1993). The politics of sex-research. *Journal of Sex Research, 30,* 103–110.

Vartanian, T. P. (2011). *Secondary data analysis.* Oxford, England: Oxford University Press.

Ventura, S. J., & Hamilton, B. E. (2011). *U.S. Teenage birth rate resumes decline.* Hyattsville, MD: National Center for Health Statistics.

Wakefield, A. J., Murch, S. H., Anthony, A., Linnell, J., Casson, D. M., Malik, M., . . . & Walker-Smith, J. A. (1998). Illeal-lymphoid-nodular hyperplasia, non-specific colitis, and pervasive developmental disorder in children. *The Lancet, 351,* 637–641.

Webb, E. J., Campbell, D. T., Schwartz, R. D., & Sechrest, L. (1999). *Unobtrusive measures.* Thousand Oaks, CA: Sage.

Weber, M. (1947). *The theory of social and economic organization* (M. Henderson & T. Parsons, Trans.). New York, NY: Free Press.

Winston, S. (1932). Birth control and the sex-ratio at birth. *American Journal of Sociology, 38,* 225–231.

Wood, P. (2013). The campaign to discredit Regnerus and the assault on peer review. *Academic Questions, 26*(2).

Yin, R. K. (2009). *Case study research: Design and methods* (4th ed.). Thousand Oaks, CA: Sage.

Zimbardo, P. (2007). *The Lucifer effect: Understanding how good people turn bad.* New York, NY: Random House.

Index

Page numbers followed by f indicate figure
Page numbers followed by t indicate table

Questionnaires
  item, 103
  mailed, 98–99, 106, 111
  single or multiple, 81–82
  techniques of, 103
Quota sampling, 65, 190

Race, influence on family life, 39f
Random assignment, 97, 190
Randomization, in evaluation research, 176–177
Random measurement error, 190
Random sampling, 61
Ranehill, Eva, 20
Range, 153, 190
Ratio level of measurement, 73–74, 190
Ratio variables, 73–74
Raush, H. L., 31
Reactive effect of testing, 96, 191
Reactive effects of experimental arrangements, 97, 191
References, in journal article, 48–49
Regnerus, Mark, 21–23
Regression coefficients, 160
Reliability, 74, 75
  defined, 191
  interobserver reliability, 76, 188
  remedial services, 16
  split-half, 87, 192
  thoughts on, 78–79
Religion system, 2
Religious affiliation, age at marriage and, 28
Remedial services, right to, 16
Replicate, 45, 191
Research Connections, 148
Researcher, errors introduced by, 105–106
Research findings, sharing with research participants, 16
Research funding, control of, 181–182
Research monographs, 52–53
Research on families and children
  control of employment opportunities, 182–183
  control of publication channels, 180–181
  control of research funding, 181–182
  differences between, 6–10
  ethics of, 13–24

fraud, 18–23
reason for doing, 1–11
rights of participants in, 13–16
role of Institutional Review Board, 16–18
sound, value of, 23–24
well-conducted, benefits of, 10–11
Research participants, risk or harm to, 14
Research strategy, choosing, 132–133
Respondent, errors introduced by, 104–105
Response rate, 98, 99, 100, 101, 191
  response sets, 105
  survey instrument, 98
Response sets, 105
Review article
  defined, 43, 191
Reviewers
  of journal article, 51
  of research monographs, 52–53
Rights of participants, in research, 13–16
Risk of harm, to research participants, 14
Risman, B. J., 38, 65, 116, 117
Robert Wood Johnson Foundation, 55
Robinson, J. P., 86, 102
Rogers, S., 142
Role selection, 105
Rossi, P. H., 178
Rubin, D. B., 90
Running record, 107–108
Russell Sage Foundation, 55

Scared Straight (film), 174
SAGE Handbook of Qualitative Research, The (Denzin & Lincoln, 2011, 133
Saldana, J., 115, 116, 125
Sales records, 108
Sample(s). See also Missing data; Sampling
  convenience, 64, 186
  defined, 57–58, 191
  error measurement, 74
  in journal article, 46
  nonprobability samples, 63–65, 189
  probability, 61–63, 190
  sample statistic, 61, 191
  size of, 65–66
  statistical significance, 18, 19
Sample statistic, 61, 191. See also Population parameter

Uncertainty coefficient (U_{yx}), 154, 193
UNC-Odum Archive Dataverse, 149
Undimensional, 82, 193
Unit of analysis
  defined, 193
  elements and, 57
  organization as, 116–117
  in social and behavioral research, 30–32
  social program as, 117
Unobtrusive techniques. *See* Nonreactive
  techniques
Unpublished documents, 54
US Census Bureau, 3, 7, 8, 11, 54, 137,
  145, 149, 152
US Department of Agriculture, 102
US Department of Agriculture,
  Cooperative State Research,
  Education and Extension Service, 55
US Department of Defense, 138
US Department of Health & Human
  Services, 2017, 3, 148
US Department of Labor, 138

Validity, 74, 76–77
  concurrent, 78
  construct, 78
  content, 78
  criterion, 77–78
  defined, 193
  face, 77
  predictive, 77, 190
  thoughts on, 78–79
  threats to, 94, 95–98
Variability. *See also* Research strategy;
  Statistical analysis
  causal effect, 32, 185
  defined, 193
  measurement procedure, 70–71
  measures of (*See* Measures of
    variability)

Variables
  in analysis, 25
  dependent, 26, 186
  independent, 26, 92, 187
  intervening (mediator or mediating),
    27–28, 188–189
  moderating (Control or moderator), 28
  simple causal model, 26–27
  theoretical roles in, 25
Variance, 153, 193
Vingerhoets, Ad, 19

Wall Street Journal, 18, 20
Washington Post, 18
Web content, 55
Web of Science, 42, 50, 52
Webb, E. J., 104
Weber, M., 114
"When contact changes minds: An
  experiment on transmission of
  support for gay equality" (LaCour &
  Green), 18
"White papers," 54
Winston, S., 107
Wisconsin Family Care Program, 117
Witherspoon Institute, 21
World Wide Web, 54
Wrightsman, L. S., 86

Yankaskas, Bonnie, 110
Yap, A. J., 20
Yelp, 104
Yin, R. K., 207

Zaretsky, E., 108
ZERO TO THREE, 55
Zick, C. D., 102
Zimbardo, P., 23
Zimmerman, R., 172
Znaniecki, F., 108

Made in United States
North Haven, CT
16 August 2024

56197679R00137